BUILDING AN IMPORT/EXPORT BUSINESS

Revised and Expanded

BUILDING AN IMPORT/EXPORT BUSINESS

Revised and Expanded

Kenneth D. Weiss

John Wiley & Sons, Inc.

New York • Chichester • Brisbane • Toronto • Singapore

Library of Congress Cataloging-in-Publication Data

Weiss, Kenneth D. (Kenneth Duane), 1940–
    Building an import/export business / by Kenneth D. Weiss.—Rev.
  & expanded.
       p.   cm.
    Includes index.
    ISBN 0-471-53626-1 — ISBN 0-471-53627-X (pbk.)
    1. Trading companies. 2. Export marketing. 3. International
  trade. I. Title.
  HF1416.W43   1991
  658.8—dc20   90-29113

Printed in the United States of America

10 9 8 7 6 5 4 3 2 1

This revision of Building an Import/Export Business *is dedicated to my parents, Byron and Delene Weiss, in the high desert near Palm Springs, California. After the 30 years that we have lived apart, they still have a deep understanding of my dreams, my strengths, and my weaknesses. They can still counsel me, better and faster, than anyone else on earth. Mother and Dad, thanks for being my parents, from my beginnings to the present and beyond.*

Contents

Acknowledgments

In this second edition of *Building an Import Export Business* I would like to, once again, acknowledge some people who helped with the first edition: George Haber of Information Services in Jericho, New York; Bill Laraque of the Standard Chartered Bank in Melville, New York; Bill Maron of Maron International Shipping Corporation in New York City; Arnold Ceglia of Sky-Sea Forwarding Corporation in Valley Stream, New York; Sherry Singer of Soller, Singer & Horn (attorneys at law) in New York City; and Charles Cardile of C & S Laboratory Consultants in New York City.

Thanks is due also the many readers who have written in response to the first edition, telling me of their import-export ambitions, plans, and activities.

Finally, acknowledgment is due to our dynamic world, which keeps the theatre of trade interesting by continually changing the scenery, the script, and the actors. Events have outdated the first edition of this book and set the stage for this expanded revision.

Introduction

What is the import/export business? Essentially, it is buying a product in one country and selling it in another. Or, it can be arranging for other people to buy and sell; such "matchmaking" can earn you commissions.

Who can go into this business? You'd be surprised. People who seemed to have little business potential have been very successful. This isn't to say that this business is easy; few are, and this message is repeated often in this book.

What does it take to succeed in the import/export business? Basically, a good idea, a little money, hard work, and some luck are all you need. A key element in success is to be able to sell or to have someone who **wants to buy from you**.

Two-way U.S. trade (imports and exports) is more than **$7 billion** dollars a year. Americans trade with nearly every country and every product on earth. Somewhere in this gigantic business, there is a place for you.

In this book, you will learn more about international trade, how to begin, and what it takes to be successful. Chapter 1 summarizes many aspects of the import/export business, and Chapter 2 gives the questions to be answered before you start. Chapter 3 will tell you how to set up an import/export business. Chapters 4 through 6 are all about buying and selling, while Chapters 7 through 10 describe the procedures in international trade. Chapter 11 tells where to get information and help as your business develops, and Chapter 12 discusses trade with the "new" Europe—both the European Economic Community and the hungry-for-trade nations of Eastern Europe.

Appendix A is the outline of a business plan for a small importer. Use this as a guide for writing your own business plan. Appendix B lists contacts in all 50 states, and Appendix C lists the offices of the U.S. and foreign commercial service.

Now, let's jump in, and see how you like the temperature of the water.

1

Jumping into the Water: Simple Scenarios

Greetings, and welcome to Guatemala City. You have just discovered some beautiful hand-woven wool jackets and are *sure* you can sell them in Toronto and Montreal. You have found what seems to be a reliable supplier and have gotten information on import regulations from the Canadian consulate. Now you are looking for a Guatemalan firm that can make bilingual labels for you, French and English. You wonder what else you will have to do to get your business started.

Greetings, and welcome to Washington, DC. You are a recently retired diplomat with excellent contacts in West Africa. One of your contacts is setting up a cable TV business and would like you to supply all the equipment, including the cable to "wire up" hundreds of homes. This sounds like a fabulous business opportunity. Is it as good as it sounds, or do the pitfalls exceed the potential?

Let's think about these business ideas.

IMPORTING THE WOOL JACKETS

The product may look lovely to you, but remember, you cannot make money unless you can get the jackets out of Guatemala and into Canada and sell them for a profit. The supplier may seem reliable but quality often tends to decrease gradually, especially with hand-made products.

You will be moving the jackets in small quantities, which will give you high costs per unit for transportation and insurance. Also, there will be marking regulations and customs duties and the cost of getting the goods out of Canadian customs.

Next you will have to get the product into retail distribution channels in order to move a significant quantity. The designs may not look good to buyers who have never traveled in Guatemala. And the prices . . . you will probably find that the jackets must retail for at least 4 *times* your cost in Central America.

When you evaluate these problems and think how many jackets you will have to sell to earn a living, you will probably see the venture as a way of passing time but not as a business.

EXPORTING THE CABLE TV EQUIPMENT

As a retired diplomat, you may not be inclined to get involved in all the details of an export business. Yet, your experience will make it easier for you than for most other people.

The *Thomas Register of American Manufacturers* in any library will give you suppliers of cable TV equipment, and they will probably be pleased to hear from you. Their prices will be reasonable by world standards, and because of your background they may agree to sell to you on credit.

Since the equipment involved is not considered "sensitive," there should be no difficulty with U.S. export control regulations, and the quantities will be sufficient to let you ship in full container loads. Best of all, there will be no marketing problems because you already have the customer.

Your major challenge will be (1) making sure you send exactly what the customer wants, (2) making sure you get paid, and (3) keeping the business going after the needs of your one customer have been satisfied. If you can meet these challenges, dive in!

Now let's look at two more examples.

THE "WORLD CLOCK"

Suppose you are looking through an export promotion magazine from Taiwan and see a small clock that tells the time in major world cities. You write for a catalog and price list and receive them immediately. You show the catalog to several people, being careful to not reveal the supplier's name and address to potential competitors.

Everyone thinks you have a good product so you buy an international money order from your bank and send it with a letter, asking for samples. You might have been able to get them for free, but didn't want to risk having the supplier delay shipment while he asked for and received your money.

While you are waiting for the samples, you phone the nearest U.S. Customs office and speak with a product specialist. He or she gives you the applicable tariff numbers, rates of duty, and marking requirements. Each battery, clock movement, and case should be marked indelibly, "Made in Taiwan," and the country of origin should be on the packages as well.

Also while waiting, you think about who might want to buy your product—a world time clock. You finally decide that the best "market segment" will be business executives who travel internationally. They will probably not buy clocks for themselves, but will receive them as gifts from relatives or from firms they do business with. You tentatively decide to sell the clocks through giftware channels.

Soon the samples arrive, by air mail. They come to your house marked, "Samples. No commercial value," and no customs duty is charged on them. You like their appearance, but not the packaging or the instructions. You plan, tentatively, to sell for about double your cost of $6.50 per unit.

From the yellow pages telephone directory, you identify gift shops in what appear to be "good" sections of the nearest major city. You phone them, ask who does the buying, and try to make appointments to "show them a new product that (you) may be adding to (your) line of imported merchandise." After 15 calls to 8 gift shops, you have 5 appointments.

The buyers generally like your merchandise but aren't thrilled with it. They have no criticisms of the clocks, but point out that the country-of-origin marking isn't legally correct and the packaging isn't very attractive. They think the item is "a $20 retail," which is quite far from 4 times your $6.50 purchase price.

With this doubtful outcome in mind, you decide to try a different marketing channel and approach buyers of "advertising specialty houses," which you also identify from the telephone directory. They tell you that the product is interesting but the price will have to be lower and should include imprinting with the name and address of the company that will be giving the clocks to its customers. No one makes a promise to buy from you.

Not easily discouraged, you decide to place a sample order to sell through giftware channels. You write the supplier and say you would like to purchase 2 cartons of 60 clocks each at a unit price of $5.50, shipped to you by air, "freight collect." That way you don't have to worry about terms of shipment, such as "f.o.b." (see Chapter 8) or about who will pay the shipping cost. You offer to pay 50 percent of the money in advance and 50 percent more 30 days after the shipment arrives. Thus, you and the exporter will each be trusting the other for half the money. You explain the U.S. marking requirements and ask for the order to be shipped immediately.

A few days later the supplier calls you by phone in the late afternoon, when it is early morning in Asia. He agrees to all your terms, except the price, saying that he cannot sell for less than $6.50 on such a small order. You give in and tell him to pack the clocks and wait for your order and payment. You consider asking the supplier for his bank and trade references but are afraid that, if you do, he might ask for yours!

Then you buy an international money order for $390 ($6.50 × 120/2) and send it by air mail, with an order form that you have bought at a stationery store and filled out. In the meanwhile, you register your business and order stationery and cards, as described in Chapter 3. You also contact other potential buyers.

Just 10 days later you receive a call from Jumping Air Freight. You decide to pick up the shipment yourself to save the cost of a customs broker, which you can do because (1) the value is low, (2) shipment was by air, and (3) the goods are not under quota. You have to pay only $272 for air freight (34 kilograms at $8.00), $26 for airline collect charges, and $79 for "estimated" customs duties. (The word "estimated" will be explained in Chapter 10.) The shipment came uninsured; forgot about insurance, didn't you?

Your total cost is $780 for the clocks, $298 for shipping, and $79 for duties, or $1,097. Adding in the approximate cost of your money orders, trip to the airport, and so forth, you reach a total cost of about $1,200. There are 120 clocks, so you paid $10 each. You note that the supplier did not improve the packaging, marking, or instructions.

Now you go back to the gift stores and offer the clocks for $156 a dozen ($13 per clock), with a 5 percent discount if they pay on delivery. You are successful! You sell some clocks. You deliver from stock (the trunk of your car) and offer to set up a small display in each store, unboxing a clock of each color and setting it to the correct time. Then you go back periodically to see how they are priced and whether they are selling.

If you sell the 120 clocks in a month and net $12 each ($13 minus discounts, your selling costs, and maybe a bad debt), your profit will be $240 (120 × $2). This won't make you rich, but may encourage you to try to expand the business.

You can't spend all your time visiting small stores, so you'll have to sell through wholesalers or "manufacturer's representatives." You choose the manufacturer's representative's route (see Chapter 6), finding them by advertising in *Gifts and Decorative Accessories* magazine. Also you cannot make a living just on world time clocks, so you keep watching publications for other products to add to your line of merchandise.

Suppose you can move from 120 to 1,200 items a month, and get the cost down so your gross profit is $3.00 a unit or $3,600. This should let you pay office and other expenses and have a nice part-time income.

ROLLS OF PAPER

Now you have started importing. You read a newspaper from Holland called *Export Channel* and find that a firm in Nigeria wants to import rolls of paper for bank accounting machines. You write (or phone, fax, telex, or cable) the buyer to ask exactly what he wants, how many, by when, and by which means of transportation. You also ask how he plans to pay and request bank and trade references.

The buyer gets back to you immediately with the information you requested. He also sends a piece from a roll of paper so you can see exactly what he is asking for. What he doesn't say is how much he expects to pay or how many other potential suppliers he is in contact with. He asks that you provide samples and prices immediately.

You decide to contact the Nigerian consulate about regulations on shipping paper rolls to that country and are given what appears to be reliable information. You also call the Nigeria desk officer of the U.S. Department of Commerce in Washington, DC, and you go to a library and read the applicable pages of the Dun & Bradstreet *Exporter's Encyclopedia.* A foreign freight forwarder would have been able to save you some of this work, but because you are just starting, you do it yourself. You send fax messages to the importer's trade references and ask your bank to check his bank reference. So far, it all sounds good.

Then you consult directories of manufacturers and find several that supply rolls of paper. You phone them and are happy to learn that most are pleased to sell to you for shipment to Nigeria. Some are willing to give you credit, if your rating is good, but they definitely want to collect *from you.* This means you can't work as an agent on this deal; you have to buy and resell. Three firms agree to send you sample rolls and price quotations.

Since the samples and information that arrive from the three manufacturers are almost identical, you select a supplier that seems pleasant to deal with and is located not far from a U.S. east coast seaport. You take that company's sample and contact a foreign freight forwarder, who helps you put together a quotation for 40 cartons of paper rolls. Each carton will cost you $86.90 at the factory, weighs 48 pounds, and measures 1.6 cubic feet.

Your cost calculation is as follows:

40 cartons of paper @ $86.90	$3476
Inland freight	140
Forwarding and related charges	199
Ocean freight on 1,920 pounds	975
Marine insurance	294
Banking and miscellaneous charges	180
TOTAL	$5264

There's one more important detail—profit. You doubt that big companies are interested in this small order, but there are probably other small suppliers in the United States, England, or Canada. You decide to add just 15 percent for profit. Maybe later you can negotiate a lower price from your supplier.

You prepare a quotation, "c.i.f. Lagos" (see Chapter 8), for $6053.60 ($5264 + 15 percent) and suggest sea freight and letter of credit terms (see Chapter 7). The same day you fax this quotation to Lagos you receive a fax in return. It asks for a "pro-forma invoice" (see Chapter 9) for 28 cartons by air freight, showing f.o.b. and c.i.f. prices (see Chapter 8). The customer needs this to obtain an import permit and to open a letter of credit.

You call the supplier to ask for the same carton price on just 28 cartons, and he agrees. He also agrees to 5/30 terms, which means you can take a 5 percent discount if you pay within 30 days of the date of the invoice. Your forwarder gives you an air freight quotation, which is much higher than the ocean freight, but forwarding and insurance charges are somewhat less. You prepare an invoice, write "Pro-Forma" across the top, and fax it to Nigeria.

The customer immediately faxes back that the air freight charge is too high and suggests that you contact a firm called "Pandair." With a lovely British accent, a representative of this company quotes $2610, plus $48 for insurance and processing charges. You send a new pro-forma and again, by return fax, receive the order.

You start to dial your freight forwarder's number to ask him to reserve space on a plane but, wait, there is something missing—the letter of credit. You call the firm in Nigeria and are assured that this has been taken care of. About a week later you receive a call from a bank in New York to advise you that a letter of credit has been opened in your favor by the ICON Merchant Bank in Lagos. A copy comes in the mail. You check it and find that all its terms are consistent with your agreement to supply the rolls of paper. You consider having it confirmed (guaranteed) by an American bank, but are told that this should not be necessary.

At this point, you order the paper from the supplier, to be addressed to the Nigerian customer and shipped to Pandair at John F. Kennedy International Airport in New York. You also have to buy special forms from the Nigerian consulate and have one of them, the *Certificate of Origin*, notarized by the New York City Chamber of Commerce. You send these documents and a letter of instructions to the freight forwarder who prepares a *Shipper's Export Declaration*, makes sure the 28 boxes get on the plane, and gets you a copy of the *Airway Bill*. With that, you can go to the advising bank and start the process of collecting on the Letter of Credit.

You could have made this shipment without using a freight forwarder, but his advice might have saved you from making some mistake that would invalidate the Letter of Credit. Also, you may need him in the future. You fax the Airway Bill number to the customer, take the discount and pay your supplier, and have dinner at a Nigerian restaurant to celebrate.

As in the import example, your task now is to turn an initial success into an ongoing business. Look for other items you can sell to the same supplier or for other suppliers who will buy rolls of paper. Build slowly and steadily, and always be careful of how you do business and who you do it with. That first valid Letter of Credit may be followed by a couple of others, but the fourth one might be counterfeit.

Now, let's look at some personal characteristics that can make the difference between success and failure, some questions you should find answers to before you go into business, and some financial examples.

2

Deciding Whether This Business Is for You

Although *anyone* has a chance of being successful in an import/export business, let's look at the characteristics that can *increase* your chances of success.

BUSINESS SKILLS

Importing and exporting can be fun and can let you travel abroad tax free, but you probably want to start a *business*, not a hobby. The more you know about starting and running a small business, the better chance you'll have of succeeding.

SALESMANSHIP

Selling is the name of the game. When working in Korea as a marketing advisor, I met a fellow consultant who had been in the plumbing supply business. He couldn't write like a PhD and he didn't have half their technical knowledge, but the Korean managers *loved* his work. Why?

Because he had practical experience and he could *sell.* He could sell his services, sell his ideas, and help his clients sell their products.

If you import you have to sell; if you export you have to sell. Nothing good will happen if you don't sell anything.

PERSISTENCE

Have you tried three times to start businesses and failed with all three? Then you're perfect for import/export. The person who makes it is the kind of person who has *the persistence to keep trying* until he or she succeeds.

You may be lucky and turn a quick profit, but it usually takes at least six months to start this kind of business and at least a year to begin making money. Large exporters can take a year just to identify, select, and negotiate with one foreign distributor. If you start, you should be prepared to make a long-term commitment.

INTEREST IN AND KNOWLEDGE OF INTERNATIONAL ECONOMICS AND POLITICS

How much do you know about the world in which you plan to do business? Suppose you are buying apples from Argentina and the government there installs a *multiple exchange rate* or an *export currency.* This means that, when you send dollars to Argentina, the central bank will change them to australs at a special rate. The exporter will be getting either more or fewer australs per dollar (usually more) than he did before. Will he then reduce the price to you? Probably not, unless you negotiate with him before doing business.

Suppose you are still buying apples, President Menem has a fight with his wife, the Argentine business community loses what little confidence in the future it had and stops spending its foreign currencies, and the country has to stop importing ingredients for fertilizer and insecticide. What will happen to your apples? What will happen to the customers who were waiting for your apples?

Still worse, suppose you were exporting the ingredients for fertilizer and insecticide to Argentina. Your customer might cancel an order when the shipment is already in Buenos Aires, or receive the order but say he doesn't know when he can pay you for it. This isn't likely, but it *has* occurred.

If you're not up to snuff on international economics and politics, particularly as they effect the countries you'll be dealing with, start reading the daily *New York Times* and look for a good, current, book on the subject.

LANGUAGE ABILITY

Most of the companies that import and export can communicate in English, but not all of them. Also, some of their key personnel may not speak English at all. You may find yourself speaking with a young Chinese associate because the boss knows only Mandarin.

The more languages you know the better, and the better you know languages, the more likely you are to avoid misunderstandings. In Spanish, for example, the word "acostar" means both *to put someone to bed* and *to accost someone.* Use it wrong, and your listeners might think you're selling pajamas instead of items for personal defense.

CULTURAL EMPATHY

Language is a part of culture, a broad term that also includes customs, religion, art, literature, and many other aspects of life. International businesspeople may *sound* like they're all the same, but inside, they're not.

AIDS has infected 20 to 30 percent of the population in some countries, partly because different *customs* have facilitated its diffusion. American firms have lost customers and suppliers.

Government approvals for foreign trade transactions took longer in the Cameroon in June and July, 1990, than they normally did. Why? because every morning radios and televisions in offices were tuned to the World Cup soccer games. If you have cultural empathy, you will *understand* this kind of occurrence, and your schedule will allow for it. If you do not have or want to acquire cultural empathy, international trade may not be the business for you!

WRITING AND SPEAKING

Your communications in importing and exporting should be clear and precise. Avoid idioms, although this is hard because we are so used to them, and try to say exactly what you mean. Don't tell your Japanese customer that you are "just tickled pink" to meet her or that you haven't seen her "in a coon's age."

There's a well-known case in which an American company got into trouble exporting pork livers to West Germany. The Germans wanted just the livers of *male* animals, which are firmer and fetch higher prices, but didn't say so. They assumed the Americans would know. The American exporter did not practice sex discrimination in its selection of pork livers, and ended up having to take a price reduction.

ATTENTION TO DETAIL

Importing and exporting involve many details, and some can be very important. I once received an order from Haiti for rolls of paper for calculators and adding machines. Like most products, paper rolls have numerous specifications, including the roll diameter, the roll width, the core diameter, the length of paper on the roll, the type of paper, the color, the number of plies, and so on. We were an exporting company and did not make paper rolls, so they had to be ordered from a manufacturer. The goods were shipped to the pier and then on to Port-au-Prince. All would have been fine except that someone had typed ³/₈ in. instead of ⁵/₈ in. for the core diameter, and the rolls were useless to the importer.

In Chapter 10, you will learn that many goods from most developing countries can enter the United States free of duty *if* they are accompanied by a Form A, Certificate of Origin. If you order the goods and forget to ask for a Form A, you'll be setting yourself up for unnecessary trouble.

MONEY

I know, and perhaps you do as well, of people who have started importing and exporting with just a few hundred dollars. Don't be fooled, though, by anyone who says you'll go from rags to riches by just buying his book or service.

The more money you have, the faster you can move. You can set up a real office, buy on credit, and travel to find foreign suppliers and customers. If you have just a few thousand dollars and risk it on one transaction and lose, you are out of business. A woman I know in Massachusetts started with just a small amount of money and went broke precisely when it looked as if she was going to be successful.

You can start this business as a *broker* or *agent*, with very little money, but I'll explain later why this is a very hard way to begin. To start as a merchant (buy and resell), part-time, you should have $10,000 or $20,000 to invest. To quit your job and start full time, $100,000 is probably a minimum.

Some Financial Examples

Let's look at two financial examples to see how money can be made in international trade. I've created two small businesses, an import merchant and an export agent.

The *import merchant* buys merchandise overseas, takes title to and possession of it, and resells to stores in the United States. She sells through manufacturer's representatives and pays them 15 percent on their sales. She works from her home or in a small rented office and keeps costs to a minimum. Summarized operating results, after several months in business, are as follows:

Import Merchant

Planned sales for month	$20,000	
Less cost of merchandise	− 12,000	(60%)
	8,000	
Less sales commissions	− 3,000	(15%)
	5,000	
Less operating expenses	− 2,000	(10%)
Profit before tax and owner's salary	$3,000	(15%)

Note that all figures are given as a percent of sales. Note also that monthly sales of $20,000 have produced a nice part-time, but not a full-time, income.

The *export agent* books orders from foreign buyers for products of American manufacturing firms. He probably has 5 or 6 "principals" who produce related goods so as to be able to offer a wide range of, for example, industrial lighting fixtures. This agent receives commissions from his principals that average 14 percent, but pays 6 percent to his own agents in foreign markets. He is working from a small, rented office and trying to hold down expenses. The financial summaries are as follows:

Export Agent

Planned sales for month	$100,000	
Times average commission earned	× .14	(14%)
	14,000	
Less foreign agents' commissions	− 6,000	(6%)
	8,000	
Less operating expenses	− 3,000	(3%)
Profit before tax and owner's salary	$5,000	(5%)

Note that the agent must sell *much* more than the merchant to make as much profit. This is because he is performing fewer functions and taking very little risk. He may be able to get orders without having his own agents abroad, but would then have to spend quite a bit more on communications and travel.

20 ESSENTIAL QUESTIONS

Before you go on with this book, read the following questions and think about some possible answers. Several of the questions and answers are important parts of an import/export business plan.

1. Why are you thinking of starting a business? What are your objectives?

If you are unemployed and think starting a business will be easier than finding a job, please reconsider. If you think you'll like the excitement of doing business internationally, read on and learn more about what the work may consist of. If you have found a great product, start only when you're sure there's a great market for it. If you have a large, stable customer, *start moving;* what are you waiting for?

2. What makes you think you will be successful?

Do you have business experience? International experience? Foreign language ability? A great business idea? Good contacts? Enough money? Remember that most new businesses fail rather quickly. You'll need a unique advantage in order to be a big success.

3. Do you plan to import, export, or both?

In general, it's not a good idea to start importing and exporting at the same time. Either one will give you enough to think about. I believe importing is the easier one for most people to start with because when you import, the *selling*, the hardest part of the business, is done in the United States where you know the turf and can more easily communicate with the customers.

4. Do you plan to work as a merchant, agent, broker, or some combination of the three?

An international broker can make money by arranging sales between unrelated parties, but it is very hard for a newcomer to establish contacts and confidence and to make deals. In terms of the amount of capital needed, the cheapest way is to start as an import agent for a foreign firm. The next cheapest is to be an export agent, then an import merchant, and finally an export merchant. Higher investment usually goes with higher profit potential.

5. When you start, will you be working full time or part time?

Full time is better, *if* you plan to start a business rather than a hobby and *if* you have enough cash to last until the profit is adequate. One person I know got laid off by his company (a bank) with a "golden parachute"—a year at full pay. He could afford to give full time to his new business. Another friend decided to give his all to a new import business but soon found that both he and his wife had to get part-time jobs to keep their bills paid.

6. Who, if anyone, can help you with the work in the beginning?

Working alone gets tiresome, and most people aren't good at everything. For example, do you like both selling and accounting? They are both essential but very different in nature.

One acquaintance had a simple plan—he would import children's clothing from the Caribbean and open a small store in which his wife would sell the products. Unfortunately, the wife very quickly tired of waiting on customers, dusting shelves, keeping records, and so on, and the business failed. I never heard what happened to the marriage.

7. Which type(s) of product(s) do you plan to trade?

This is one of the most important questions. Look for a product that you like and know something about, that can be obtained in sufficient quantity and consistent quality, that can be transported to and entered into market countries, and *that people will buy.* The exciting item that turns you on in a foreign country may be a total dud in the market. It may be that people who go to the country will buy it there, while people who don't go to the country will have no interest in it.

8. What will be your sources of supply—countries and/or companies?

Normally, your supplier should be a competent, reliable firm in a stable country. If you get that big order, and your goods arrive too late or are not of good quality, you will lose your profit, your time and expenses, and your reputation.

9. What is your target market?

Of the millions of people in the United States—or overseas if you are exporting—what are the characteristics of the people who will buy your product? Is there a *market segment* that you know well enough to pick as your target market? I once wasted several hours trying to sell natural bath salts from Jordan to cosmetics manufacturers before learning that these firms make their bath salts chemically. They leave the natural products to the health food industry.

10. How do you plan to sell to customers in the target market?

If you can't answer this question, you shouldn't start a business. If you have a monopoly on one of life's essentials, the buyers will beat a path to your door. Almost any other product will have to be *sold*, by you or by people whom you identify, hire or contract with, supervise, and pay.

11. What means of international transportation do you plan to use?

In general, you'll want to use air mail or courier for small shipments, air cargo for larger shipments, sea freight for still larger shipments, and road or rail for trade with Canada and Mexico. Chapter 8 will give you much more information about these shipping options.

12. What will be the shipping terms?

There are several standard shipping terms, such as f.o.b. (free on board) and c.i.f. (cost, insurance, freight), that you must know about and understand thoroughly. Small importers often begin buying c.i.f. by air freight while small exporters often begin shipping f.o.b./vessel or f.o.b./airport. Chapter 8 will give you additional information about these terms.

13. Which method of international payment do you plan to use?

What you would like and what you can get are often quite different. As an importer you would like easy credit terms, while as an exporter you would like to be paid before you ship. The people or firms on the other side of the transaction will also be looking out for themselves.

I once heard of a small businessman in Taiwan who received an order from the United States for live birds. The Taiwanese invested all his capital in purchasing and shipping the feathery creatures, did not get paid, and was out of business almost before he started. Do not let this happen to you.

14. Which U.S. and/or foreign government regulations will concern you?

Both importers and exporters are subject to the laws of all the jurisdictions they deal with. These include national, state, and local governments of both the importing and exporting countries.

For example, nearly all products are now free of duty in the U.S.-Canada trade, but only if they meet the applicable *rules of origin*. This book will help you learn how to find out which rules your business is subject to.

15. What will be your company's name and form of organization?

Should your business bear your name or a trade name you create? Should you incorporate? If so, which kind of corporation should you organize? If not, which legal form should your business take? Your answers to these questions have important implications, especially for liability and taxation.

16. What will you do for an office, office equipment, and supplies?

The biggest advantage of working in your own home is saving money, but there are several disadvantages. For example, during working house, you may not want to be that close to your spouse and kids, the refrigerator, or the garden tools.

Acquiring equipment for the home office has become more complicated than it used to be. This book will give you useful guidance about what you must have, what you might acquire, and what you really don't need to begin with.

17. How will you communicate with the outside world?

This is related to Question 16, but involves the various ways you can get a postal address, cable and telex addresses, and phone and fax numbers. You may not need all of these when you begin.

When the first edition of this book was written, the word "fax" was not even mentioned—a good example of how much change has already occurred and why this revision is needed.

18. Which service companies will you need, and how will you select them?

You'll certainly need a long distance telephone company and a bank, and perhaps a customs broker, freight forwarder, attorney, accountant, insurance company, courier, and others. This book will tell you how each can help you and how you can locate them.

Did you know, for example, that there are numerous low-cost courier services that operate between the United States, and just one specify foreign country. You may be able to get a small package brought, or delivered, for half what a major courier such as DHL would charge.

19. Where will you get information and help as your business develops?

Throughout this book, and especially in Chapters 11 and 12, there are numerous ideas about where to get information and assistance. There is not as much *low-cost* help available to importers as there is for exporters, but sometimes it is wise to get assistance, no matter what the cost.

Suppose, for example, that Customs says your Christmas merchandise cannot be released because it isn't properly marked. A good customs broker can probably get the goods released to you, *under bond.* Then if you can get them marked in a hurry, you can still deliver before Santa Claus stops working for the year.

20. How much will you invest, and how much will you earn?

You'll need to invest quite a bit of time and money; this book will help you understand how much money will be needed and where you might look for it.

To attract partners or investors, or even to make the go-ahead decision yourself, you should have a business plan that includes pro-forma financial statements. It's time now to start finding out how to prepare these statements and how they can help you.

Let's move on to Chapter 3 and begin getting detailed answers to the 20 questions just asked.

3

Setting Up Your Business

Before you can begin trading you should have a business organization, no matter how small your operation. This chapter deals with what is involved in establishing a business, from choosing a form of organization to selecting the right furniture and equipment and saving money on taxes. Although the information applies to setting up almost any kind of small business, it is of special relevance to the business of importing and exporting.

FORM OF ORGANIZATION

The form of organization to establish is an issue that new business owners must consider carefully. There are four basic options—sole proprietorship, partnership, corporation, and S corporation. We will discuss each briefly. Be sure to get all of your information together before making a decision as to which form to establish.

Sole Proprietorship

This is the quickest, easiest kind of business to establish. Normally, you simply purchase a "Doing Business as . . ."

form from a business stationery store, fill it out in triplicate, have your signature notarized, and send the form with a small check (certified or casher's check or money order) to the county clerk. This procedure and the cost vary somewhat from place to place; call your county clerk or appropriate city office to get precise information for your location.

The main purpose of this registration is to enable interested persons to identify people who do business under names that are not their own (trade names). You will make all your decisions and will be personally liable for any problems that might be caused by the business and its operations. At the end of each year, your personal income will increase or decrease for tax purposes by the business profit or loss. You can, however, deduct business losses for up to three consecutive years.

You can also deduct legitimate business expenses, including the cost of an office in your home. Be aware, however, that all such deductions must be documented, . . . to the satisfaction of the IRS should you be audited.

In general, you can get by with a sole proprietorship if you don't plan to share ownership with anyone else, if your income and expense will be small, and if you will deal only with products that are unlikely to cause any sort of illness, injury, or damage. As a sole proprietor, you bear full legal responsibility for the consequences of your business decisions.

Partnership

This form of business is as easy to start as a sole proprietorship; you simply buy a different form from the stationery store and write in more than one name. You can have one or a few partners and can work out between or among you what each of you will contribute to the business. A "full" partner will normally share the ownership, work, and liability, while a "limited" partner will not participate in management decisions and will not be liable for problems that are caused by decisions the managers make. As you can imagine, the specifics of such a relationship should be established in a written document, signed by all partners.

In general, I don't recommend partnerships. Many of them turn out to be worse than rocky marriages; the kind of person who wants his/her own business usually resists having to share decision making with anyone else. Also, a partnership must be dissolved if one or more of the partners formally leaves the business (by dying, for example).

In a partnership, each partner must pay personal income tax on his or her share of the earnings of the business. As with a sole proprietorship, legitimate losses can be deducted from earnings for tax purposes.

Corporation

A corporation is a more formal organization. It makes your business a separate legal entity, or "corpus," which can theoretically go on even if its owners cease to exist. It also allows you to attempt to raise capital by selling shares of stock. Finally, it protects your personal assets from legal judgments. This can, for example, keep you from having to sell your house to pay the medical bills of that lad who fell when a wheel broke on a roller skate you imported. Incorporation, however, will not protect your personal assets if, for example, a jury decides that you *knowingly* handled a dangerous product and incorporated specifically to protect your assets.

A corporation must be registered with your state government. The fee for registration varies but it is normally about $300 if you prepare all the forms yourself and from $1,000 up if you use a lawyer. A search should be done to make sure the name you have chosen isn't already registered in your state. There are requirements that you hold stockholders' meetings, and there are specific reports to be filed. In most states, you can buy books that tell you how to incorporate there.

The corporation will have to pay tax on its net profit. It can retain some earnings for use in the future and pay some profits out as dividends to the stockholders. The stockholders will then be liable for tax on the dividends they receive. The losses of corporations cannot be deducted from their owners' earnings for tax purposes, but can be "carried forward" to future years on the corporation's books.

Small import/export firms should be incorporated from the beginning if you are dealing with products that are taken internally or applied to the skin or that can cause harm in any way. This applies especially to products that are used by children, and applies somewhat more to importers than to exporters. Owners of other businesses can normally wait to see whether their enterprises grow and prosper before spending money on incorporation. You can save money by incorporating in one of a handful of states, such as Delaware, where the procedure is especially simple and inexpensive. The drawback is that you must then register as a *foreign* corporation in the state where you do business. A small, new firm is unlikely to come out ahead after going through this double registration procedure.

S Corporation

The S means small and is a special form of corporation created by Subchapter S of the U.S. Internal Revenue Code. An S Corporation is permitted in most states, can have only a limited number of owners, cannot make public offerings of stock, gives the same protection from liability as a regular corporation, and eliminates the corporate income tax that can lead to double taxation.

This type of business is no less expensive to set up than a regular corporation, but the advantages just mentioned make it better for most small businesses. If your business is already incorporated, you can elect, during a short time period each year, to change to the S form of organization.

YOUR TRADE NAME AND LOGO

What's in a name? Plenty if it has high recognition, like EXXON or IBM. Several years ago I saw a store in Laredo, Texas, named "Shirt on You." I would never go in there; I hated the name. There is a store in Guatemala City called "Q Kiss." I think that's a fabulous name. Ask anyone who speaks Spanish and they'll tell you what it sells.

You can choose to do business in your own name and, if the business is a sole proprietorship, you don't even have to register it. Most people, however, prefer to use a *trade name.* Pick a name that is easy to pronounce and remember and that doesn't have unfavorable connotations in the languages of the countries with whom you expect to do business. The most famous example of a name blunder was the Chevrolet Nova, which was reportedly introduced in Venezuela before anyone realized that "no va" in Spanish means "doesn't go" (although General Motors now says this oft' repeated rumor is untrue).

You will probably want to pick a symbol or logo that reinforces your company name and creates an image in the minds of persons who will see your letterhead and business cards. I suggest not using a plane, ship, or globe. They have been overused in the industry and they mark you as an amateur.

If you are willing to use a stock logo, any printer can supply a variety for you to choose from. A mail order printer that is a very good supplier to small businesses is Stationery House in Rockville Maryland (telephone 800-638-3033). It may, however, be worth your while to have a friend with an artistic bent design a logo especially for your business. This will raise the cost of your printing, but may pay dividends in increased business.

I've already explained the importance of making sure your trade name doesn't infringe on anyone else's and of registering it with the proper authorities, no matter how your business is organized.

OPENING A BANK ACCOUNT

Why have a section on something as simple as opening a bank account? Because the subject is vital to your success. Paying and getting paid are crucial aspects of international trade, and a qualified banker can give you both advice and assistance on payment matters. I was once contacted by officials of a small bank in the New York area, who said they would like me to teach them the basics of international trade because two of their clients were beginning to import and export. You don't want a banker who has to learn the business; you want one who *knows* the business already.

Select a first class, international bank. Make sure it has a Letter of Credit (LC) Department, preferably one for imports and another for exports. These major banks usually aren't eager to open accounts for new small companies, so be prepared to persuade the accounts officer that your business will be substantial in the future.

If you are forming a sole proprietorship or a partnership, just take to the bank a copy of the business certificate that was returned by your county clerk. If you have a corporation, take a corporate resolution that says you are entitled to open a bank account for the firm. In some states, you have to take the actual articles of incorporation and/or the corporate seal.

Once the account is open, try to build a good banking relationship by speaking with an officer occasionally and by never writing a check for which you don't have sufficient funds.

ESTABLISHING YOUR OFFICE

Since the first edition of this book was written, home-based businesses have become much more common. This is partly because of improved communications technology which can let you keep in touch with the world from almost anywhere in the United States.

In that first edition, I mentioned a friend who was exporting heavy construction equipment from the basement of his home. Although he reports that business is not as good as before, he has made a living that way for many years. I also mentioned home-based businesses that were unexpectedly visited by (a) a supplier from Taiwan and (b) a Dun and Bradstreet credit investigator. These things can still happen, but the visitor is not as likely to be "put off" as he might have been a few years ago by catching you at work in your pajamas.

Unfortunately, there *are* disadvantages to home-based businesses. Most residential areas have laws that restrict the use of homes for business purposes. Usually you are not supposed to keep merchandise inventories, receive business visitors, or have more than one employee. If you are on bad terms with your neighbors, they may call the authorities and cause you problems even if you are perfectly legal.

Home-based businesses usually cannot get approval to accept Visa or Master Card charges, but American Express is more liberal in this regard. Homeowner's and tenant's insurance usually do not cover business property or liability for business activities, so you may need to add a rider on your insurance policy. Finally, you may be distracted by the ever present things to do around the house.

If you decide to set up outside your home, you may be able to save money by renting empty space from an existing firm or by using one of the buildings that is set up to house small firms and that provides photocopy and fax equipment, a conference room, and perhaps secretarial services.

You don't need prime office space for an import/export business. Any safe building will do, unless you plan to import and have your office double as a showroom. In that case, location and accessibility to transportation are very important.

Office Equipment

You probably already have the basic office equipment—a desk, a chair, and a filing cabinet or two. Beyond that, you will need ways of communicating with the outside world. The June 4, 1990, edition of *The Wall Street Journal* listed basic needs and costs for a home office as follows:

IBM-compatible personal computer	$1,000
Letter-quality printer	270
Answering machine	70
Facsimile machine	480
Two-line telephone	120
Computer modem	120

You can substitute an inexpensive electronic typewriter for the computer and printer, at least in the beginning. Just make sure the type looks professional; your image is riding on it.

You need a *good* telephone and answering machine. If you can't afford a separate business phone, find out whether your local telephone company offers a *ring identification service.* That will let you have just one phone line but have a distinct ring for business callers. New York Telephone offers this service for a small set-up charge plus $4.95 a month. A good answering machine is also vital and make sure it has a "remote" feature that lets you call it for your messages. I once called my answering machine from a pay phone in the north woods of Minnesota. I got my messages, returned a couple of calls, and went right back to drowning night crawlers.

A fax machine also has become a necessity. It can work with one of the lines of your two-line phone and will let you send and receive messages across state and national borders. Cable correspondence has almost disappeared in business, and even a telex address may now be unnecessary. If you do find that you need to send and receive telexes, try using a telex service or "MCI Mail." To use MCI Mail, you will need a computer equipped with a modem. The same equipment will let you access a large and growing number of electronic databases to get U.S. export statistics, shipping rates, credit information on American firms, and other information. You will need to take time to learn how to use each of the databases you subscribe to.

Other useful pieces of office equipment include a photocopier and perhaps a postage meter. Start with a copier that's light enough to carry in for service; it is always more expensive if a repair person must come to you. The postage meter will frustrate your correspondents who may be collecting postage stamps, but will make your business look larger and more professional.

Business Printing Needs

To start with, you will need just stationery and envelopes and business cards. Your local instant printer can provide these. Consider getting lightweight letterhead if you plan to do much international mailing. If you plan to travel often to a specific country, such as Mexico, have your business cards printed with English on one side and with that country's language—Spanish—on the other. Make sure your address includes your country's name—USA.

In the beginning, you can buy any needed business forms, such as purchase orders and invoices, at a stationery store. Just type in your company's name and address. Later you might want to buy imprinted forms. You may need a few specialized international trade forms that are not available at stationery stores. Some of these are available from the consulates of the countries you trade with and others from UNZ and Company in Jersey City, New Jersey (telephone 800-631-3098). UNZ will gladly send you a catalog describing the products it sells.

When you open a business bank account, you will probably order business-size checks, imprinted with your company's name and address.

By the way, if you are working from your home and don't want to put your home address on stationery and forms, you can probably find a company that offers mail box services. The same firm will probably offer telex and fax services as well. Another alternative is a post office box. The problems with a post office box are (1) it's an extra expense, (2) you'll have to go to the post office every day to check your mail, and (3) it will look bad in some countries in which only the less reputable firms use post office box addresses.

ACCOUNTING AND TAXATION

Do you like accounting? Do accountants like accounting? Most people don't, but it is a necessity in business. You need financial statements in order to:

1. Know where your income is from
2. Know what you are spending money on
3. Know how much you are making (or losing)
4. Know whether your operating results and financial status are getting better or worse

5. Get a Dun and Bradstreet rating
6. Fill out your income tax statements
7. Apply for loans.

At the outset, you can create your own simple accounting system, but I suggest going to a stationery store and buying a ready-made one such as the *Dome Monthly Record.* With this book, you can do your accounting in an hour or two a month. It uses a *cash* system, as opposed to an *accrual* system, which means you recognize income only when you receive money and expenses only when you pay out money. This can be a small advantage if you are working as a merchant and have to pay for merchandise before you get paid for it. Your cash accounting system will show the expense but not the income for some transactions. This will make your profit slightly lower at all times, including on December 31 or whenever your tax year ends. *Note:* If your business is incorporated, the laws of your state may *require* the use of an accrual system.

When the business gets larger, you will want to have an accountant set up your bookkeeping and accounting systems and perhaps do the accounting for you. Good accountants charge $50 per hour or more, depending on the location and demand for their services, but can often save you money on income tax. For example, suppose you are a sole proprietor and take a combined business-pleasure trip to Europe. You will probably be able to deduct part of the cost, but not all of it. An experienced accountant will help you deduct the legal maximum and will then defend his decisions in case you happen to be chosen for an IRS audit.

In the import/export business as with any other business, business income is taxable and business expenses are deductible. As mentioned previously, with a sole proprietorship, a partnership, or an S corporation, you pay taxes as an individual on your share of the profits. You should pay estimated taxes quarterly, and the IRS will fine you if the estimated tax paid is not at least 90 percent of the final amount due. A corporation pays tax on its profits, then the owners pay tax on the dividends they receive.

The expense of an office at home is deductible on a square foot basis. For example, if 15 percent of your residence is used as an office, you can deduct 15 percent of your rent. If you own your home, you can deduct 15 percent of what your house could be rented for. It is also permissible to take off the same percentage of your electricity, heating oil, and utilities.

If you deduct for an office at home, the space can be used *only* for business purposes. A child's jack or marble on the floor technically cancels the deduction. If you sell your house and then buy another, thus avoiding the capital gains tax, you will still be liable for taxes on the capital gain on the space that was used as an office. Also, deducting for an office at home, may increase your chances of being audited by the IRS.

Business travel is a legitimate expense, but the rules on deducting for travel abroad were tightened a few years ago. Now a foreign business trip should be less than eight days or, if it is longer, at least 75 percent of the time must be spent on business in order for you to deduct the entire air fare. If you take a two-week trip to Budapest and only half the time is spent on business, you can deduct only half the air fare and half the living expenses.

I have a good friend who imported giftware from Europe and the Orient for several years. He took a buying trip every winter to the country of his choice and a selling trip every summer, usually to beautiful Cape Cod. He kept detailed records of all business meetings and was able to deduct nearly all the expenses. Since his wife was active in the business, her travel expenses were deductible as well.

Of course, both individual and corporate profits are subject to state income taxes. Also, there are some cities that tax home offices and/or levy "unincorporated business taxes." The rates are not high, but with a new business every penny is important.

If you plan to hire employees, you will have to contact the U.S. Internal Revenue Service for an "Employee Identification Number." This is free, and you can obtain it by mail. You will, however, be thrown into the jungle of payroll taxes and tax deductions. I suggest doing without formal employees for as long as possible.

If you plan to buy merchandise for resale in any state that has a retail sales tax, you will need to contact your state tax department for a sales tax number. For a sole proprietorship, this will probably be your social security number. Export merchants, and importers that make retail sales, must have sales tax numbers.

OBTAINING FINANCING

It is rarely easy to obtain financing for a new business of any kind. You probably have some personal savings and/or investments to draw on, and you may have friends or relatives who are willing to lend you money. If you have a well conceived business idea, but banks are not willing to finance it, you may be able to get a loan from a Small Business Investment Corporation (SBIC) or a loan guarantee from the U.S. Small Business Administration (SBA). If your business is incorporated, you can try to sell stock through a private offering. A public stock sale is too expensive for most small firms to attempt.

If your financial rating is good, you can get some credit from suppliers. You may also persuade some customers to make partial payments with their orders.

In general, you should not finance a business by borrowing on credit cards or from finance companies; their interest rates are too high. Nor should you attempt to interest venture capital firms. They usually insist on getting 50 percent of your profit and substantial management control.

Now that your business is set up, let's go on to Chapter 4 and find something for you to sell.

4

Importing: Selecting Products and Suppliers

Selecting the right product is among the most important steps in founding a successful import/export business. While an excellent choice of products does not guarantee success, a very poor choice will all but guarantee failure. This chapter will help you learn how to develop product ideas, test them for feasibility, and locate and work with foreign suppliers.

GETTING PRODUCT IDEAS

Traveling is a great way to get product ideas. A few weeks ago, I was sitting in the Hostal Los Alpes in Quito, Ecuador. That morning I had bought a fabulously beautiful wool sweater for 720 Sucres, $8.37 at the current rate of exchange. Should I have bought a hundred to sell back in the United States? Should I have taken a few to show to buyers in several stores so that, if I found a great deal of interest, I could return to purchase a great quantity?

Another excellent way to find products to import is to read specialized publications from foreign countries. Many of these are published by public and private-sector export promotion organizations abroad. Most countries have export promotion offices in New York; Washington, DC; Los Angeles; and other major United States cities, and if you call or visit them they can give you sample copies of useful publications. Some of these offices can also show you product samples, give you names and addresses of potential suppliers, and even publish your inquiries in their countries. To find these offices, try looking in the white pages of your telephone directory under the country's name or in the yellow pages under "Governments, Foreign."

There are also a number of international publications from private companies:

- There are several *Made in Europe* magazines for specific kinds of products. You can subscribe to them through a company called Tarco in New York City (telephone 212-243-3130). On the West Coast, *Made in Europe* is available from USIMCO, 17057 Bellflower Boulevard, Bellflower, CA 90706 (telephone 213-925-2918).

- There are also several *Asian Sources* magazines: *Electronic Components, Computer Products, Electronics, Timepieces, Gifts & Home Products, Fashion Accessories,* and *Housewares*. To get full information, contact Asiamag Ltd. at G.P.O. Box 12367 in Hong Kong, fax number 873-0488. Asiamag also sells booklets on importing from specific Asian countries.

- *Export Channel* is a newspaper in which anyone in the world can advertise any kind of product for export. It is available from American Business Communications in Tarrytown, NY. (Fax number 914-631-7510.) Subscription price is $176 (U.S. dollars).

To find novelty and other low-priced products to import try the International Intertrade Index, Box 636, Federal Square, Newark, NJ 07101 (telephone 201-686-2382).

Unfortunately, you are not likely to find these publications in libraries. You can, however, see them and perhaps get sample copies at some of the major trade exhibits. You can get into most trade exhibits with just a business card. You can find out about these exhibits by reading magazines related to the product line you are interested in, and you can identify the magazines by asking people in the trade what they read or from periodicals directories in your local library.

You may already know which country or countries you want to buy from, but may not know what those countries produce and sell. Or you may know which product you want to import but not which country exports it. In either case, these statistics will help you. You can consult United Nations Statistics in a major library. Look for the Food and Agricultural Organization (FAO) *Production Yearbook,* the FAO *Trade Yearbook,* the U.N. Industrial Development Organization (UNIDO) production yearbook, and the *United Nations Yearbook of International Trade Statistics.* If you want to see what specific countries are selling to the United States, visit your local field office of the International Trade Administration, U.S. Department of Commerce. There is one in most major cities. A good librarian can guide you to a U.S. government statistical publication that will show what the United States buys from each country.

Existing Products

People who are already in business have an additional source for getting product ideas—their existing products. Businesspeople are always looking for cheaper and better places to get things made. (This also applies to services, by the way.) I recently heard of a U.S. firm that was going to begin shipping valves for large engines to Central America to be re-ground. Apparently, the saving in labor cost will exceed the expense of round-trip transportation.

If you know someone who might benefit from sourcing in a low-cost country, perhaps you can make money by doing the necessary research, helping set up the business arrangement, or even importing and reselling to your friend.

Getting Samples for Testing

In the process of getting product ideas, you will have probably found several potential foreign suppliers. Contact them, by mail or fax, and ask for their catalogs and export price lists. At this stage, you don't have to give information about yourself or your company.

When the catalogs come, examine them carefully and, if possible, show them to people who are in business and can give you good advice as to what will sell. Pick out a small number of items that you think you can (1) transport to the United States at a reasonable cost, (2) bring into the country with minimum difficulty, and (3) sell in sufficient quantities to be profitable. (Future chapters will explain each of these points in detail.) Then, ask for samples.

If the items are inexpensive and you want to try to get samples for free, write a very professional letter on your new business stationery. Explain that you are an importer and that you have potential customers for products of the exporting firm. Then ask for a small number of samples, "for testing," and specify exactly which models you want and how many you want of each. If the package will be too valuable, bulky, or heavy to send by air mail, you should ask that it be shipped collect by courier or air freight. This procedure will usually get you either the samples or a quick reply explaining that you will have to pay for them.

If you don't want to risk the waste of time involved in getting a request for payment instead of a package of samples, follow this procedure: Take the lowest price quoted (which may be for a huge quantity), multiply it by the number of samples you want, add the approximate cost of insured air mail, and buy an International Money Order for the total amount. Send the check, with your letter ordering samples, by registered air mail. Registery is available to most countries. Your samples should arrive in one and a half to six weeks, depending on how good mail service is to the country you are dealing with.

There is always a chance that the exporter won't reply and you will lose your money. Consider this another cost of starting your business. It isn't likely to happen if you select exporters that have attractive catalogs and that correspond with you in a professional way.

Testing Product Ideas

The sad fact is that most foreign products, as you receive them, will not be "right" for the United States market. They may not satisfy government regulations or consumer preferences, the price may be too high, or buyers may not be interested. Therefore, you should go through a testing process to find out whether the product will sell as is, will not sell at all, or (the most likely) will sell with modifications in its design, size, package, brand, price, or other characteristics.

First, try to determine the uses of your product and who would be the consumers (actual users) and the customers (buyers). Often the two are different. Then try to determine where (from which kinds of stores or other suppliers) the customers would buy the product. Identify several of these, make appointments to see them, and show them the product. Try making appointments by saying that you are an importer of (type of product), you have a new item that you are considering adding to your line, and you would appreciate the buyer's opinion of the new item.

When you meet with buyers, ask them what they think of the product, whether they would recommend any changes in the product or its package, whether they would be likely to buy it from an importer (or from a foreign exporter through you as an agent), if so, how often they would order and in which season, how many they would order at a time, and *how much they would pay.* The question of price is critical, and you may have trouble getting honest answers. If you don't get information by asking, "How much would you pay for this?", try asking the buyers' estimated selling prices and percent mark-ups, how much they are paying for similar products, or what price you would have to meet in order for them to buy from you.

You will soon find that each buyer with whom you speak has different opinions and ideas. This is because each one has his or her individual preferences as well as a unique group of customers to satisfy. You will have to analyze the various replies to your questions and draw conclusions about the viability of your product, modifications required, the target market, the channel of distribution, and the pricing structure.

You may find, as I did when dealing with an Egyptian manufacturer of candy, that the producing firm is not willing to modify its products. The firm's managers may not think the extra profit would compensate for the cost of product modification.

As an example of this testing process, suppose you are offered some very nice rag dolls made in Colombia. They represent storybook characters such as Little Red Riding Hood. They are actually several dolls in one—turn Red Riding Hood upside down and she becomes the grandmother; flip over the bonnet and Grandmother becomes the big bad wolf. You now decide that the main customers for these dolls will not be children, or even parents who buy for their children, but grandmothers and others who purchase gifts for girls. That would make the product a gift item, not a toy. You might then decide it would sell best in high-quality gift shops. Your next step would be to identify several such stores, make appointments to see the buyers, and show them the dolls. You will be asked questions about the doll clothing (what it's made of and whether it is flame resistant), the buttons (are they toxic and how many pounds of pressure will they resist before being pulled off), and the dolls themselves (what are they stuffed with and are they hand sewn). You might be told that the labeling is inadequate, that the dolls are too big (or too little), that they are too expensive (or too cheap), that the clothing styles should be more modern, the cheeks rosier, the hair more curly, and so on. *After several interviews, you will have a good idea whether the dolls would sell, how they should be modified, how they should be packaged and labeled, to what market they should be targeted, how they should be distributed, and what prices they would bring at the wholesale and retail levels.*

FINDING FOREIGN SUPPLIERS

Let's suppose that one of the products you looked at has passed the market test with flying colors. You will probably be inclined to start doing business with the company you got samples from, but this is not necessarily the best option. You should explore other options in the same country and perhaps in other countries as well.

In the process of finding products by traveling, reading specialized publications, attending trade shows, and perhaps checking statistics, you will develop a list of potential suppliers. If you do not have such a list, you can look at foreign manufacturers or exporters directories, ask for help from the countries' trade promotion organizations, consult electronic trade opportunity services, contact import/export service firms, and/or travel abroad.

Foreign Business Directories. Business directories from most countries can be found in their trade promotion offices or embassies in the U.S. and in major libraries. Also, several can be purchased from Croner Publications in Westbury, New York, (telephone 516-333-9085). The *Kompass* directories, for example, give excellent information on substantial firms in most major countries. You should be somewhat wary of using directories of exporters from developing countries. I've seen cases in which, to make the directory look good, it is padded by putting in tiny companies that have only dreamed of selling abroad.

Trade Promotion Organizations.   As mentioned before, many countries have public and/or private sector trade promotion offices in the United States that can help you find suppliers. Two countries that do this well are Brazil and South Korea. If you write the New York office of the Korea Traders Association (KTA), and say you want to import (an example I was involved in) high-density plastic bags, you'll receive several offers over the next couple of months.

Electronic Bulletin Boards.   There are some trade opportunity electronic bulletin boards that you can use. One, called "Network," is operated by the World Trade Centers Association. You can get information about Network by calling 212-466-7196, or from any of the World Trade Centers that have been established in major U.S. cities. Another, named "International Business Network," is based in Rye, New York (telephone 914-921-1400). The cost as of early 1991 was $50 for registration plus $30 per hour of network time. Both of these systems can be accessed by computer and enable you to communicate electronically with other subscribers. The firm in Rye has other on-line services such as a worldwide list of trade exhibits.

Import-Export Service Companies.   Import-export service firms also can help you find potential suppliers, with the obvious purpose of keeping and increasing your business.

Many international banks and airlines routinely contact their foreign offices on behalf of their customers and ask these offices to suggest potential business partners. Some noteworthy examples are the Hong Kong and Shanghai Banking Corporation and KLM Royal Dutch Airlines.

Traveling Abroad.   Finally, you can identify potential suppliers by traveling abroad. Suppose you want to import artificial flowers and you get off a plane in Tegucigalpa, Honduras. Check in at the Hotel Maya, or wherever you plan to stay, then visit the Promotion Department of the Directorate General of Foreign Trade, of the Ministry of Economy, to get a list of exporters. Call them to make appointments. If you need an interpretor, the American Chamber of Commerce can help you find one to hire. There is an AMCHAM in almost every country, and the United States embassy can direct you to it. This method works in most countries, except that your first visit should sometimes be to an association of exporters rather than a government office. You can identify these organizations before your trip by looking in *Croner's Reference Book for World Traders,* which is in libraries and is for sale by Croner Publications in Westbury, N.Y. (New York City telephone 718-464-0866). In general, there is no point in visiting the commercial office at the American Embassy. It will take you 20 minutes to get past the embassy guards; then, when you say you want to import to the United States, you will be given little or no assistance.

In some cases, you can plan your trip abroad to coincide with a trade exhibit. Want to import exotic clothing? Why not visit Trinidad during the "Colour Me Caribbean" Fashion Week. Call Trinidad Express Newspapers at 809-623-1111 to ask when the next one will be held. There are hundreds of trade shows overseas. You can find out about many of them from foreign countries' trade promotion offices, the International Business Network, or books in your library such as *Exhibits Guide.* Going to trade exhibits is enjoyable and can often be profitable.

SELECTING FOREIGN SUPPLIERS

Your next challenge will be to choose among the potential suppliers, who may be located in different countries on different continents. In general, it is better to buy from a country that is politically stable, that has good transportation to the United States, and whose products can enter the country at the lowest duty. These points will be discussed in more detail in later chapters. Some U.S. importers have recently switched their sources from the Far East to the Caribbean and Central America (C/CA) because labor rates in the Far East are rising, changing currency values are making products from some Asian countries more expensive, freight rates from some C/CA countries to the United States have decreased, and nearly all C/CA products can enter the United States free of duty.

Next, you want to choose a supplier that is (1) eager to work with you, (2) competent, and (3) honest. These three criteria create a contradiction in that the most competent and honest suppliers may be less eager to work with you. They will have a wider choice of customers or will have exclusive distribution already set up. Inquire about importing Waterford Crystal from Ireland, for example, and you will receive a polite letter saying that the only authorized importer is the company-owned facility in New Jersey.

You can assess whether a foreign exporter is eager to work with you by the way it responds to your communications. By the same means, you can get an idea of the exporter's competence. Does the letterhead show a street address and a fax number? Is the catalog professionally done? When you ask for certain information, does the reply answer your questions or does it go off on a tangent?

Try *not* to judge the competence of a foreign firm by the correctness of the English used in its correspondence. A foreign executive may be top-notch, except for his or her English, but may write in English to save you the trouble of finding a translator.

Another way of assessing a foreign exporter's eagerness and competence is by the way he or she responds to requests, especially for product modifications. A friend of mine once tried to establish herself as an import agent for wooden toys from a firm in Central America. She asked for product modifications and found it took several months to receive a new sample with a slightly different design or a different color. She finally gave up on that exporter and, in fact, did her sourcing in a different part of the world.

A third useful technique is to obtain credit information on potential foreign suppliers. This is a vital topic, which will be discussed in Chapter 7.

Finally, you will want to visit a potential supplier before making a major financial commitment to it. This costs time and money, but may save you from a catastrophe like having your shipment of ski boots arrive in January or having a boot come apart on the expert slope. It is better to make appointments in advance to avoid arriving when the people you want to see are unavailable. Even then, there is a chance you'll have a problem. For example, during one week in June, 1990, Costa Rica won a game in the world soccer tournament, an ex-president of the country died, and there was a scheduled holiday. Monday through Thursday were lost for business; the only day most offices opened was Friday.

When you do get to an exporter's place of business, try to meet with key personnel, look at their financial statements if you are given access to them, and tour the plant. It is normally better to deal with people with whom you feel comfortable. Financial statements will not always help you because of differences in national accounting systems and degrees of commitment to accuracy (read between the lines here). Touring a plant can tell you a lot if you understand the production process of the product you want to import.

In most cases, you will want to import directly from manufacturers rather than from exporting, or trading, companies. This is both to save money and to have direct contact with the producers of your goods. You can usually tell the difference between a manufacturer and a trader by the company name and the catalogs it sends you. If, for example, the catalog pages have stickers with your exporter's name and address placed over some other name and address, your exporter is not the manufacturer.

You may want to make an exception to this rule:

- If your orders will be too small for a manufacturer to handle
- If you plan to order small quantities of several different items
- If you are buying from a country such as Japan in which exporting is normally done by trading companies
- If you will be dealing in handmade products. Most producers of handcrafts are too small and unsophisticated to do their own exporting.

THE SUPPLY AGREEMENT

Now that you have gone to so much trouble to find and select a supplier, you may want a formal agreement as to how you will do business with that firm. This is to give both you and the supplier some security and to reduce the range of possible business disputes. This suggestion applies whether you plan to work as an agent or as a merchant.

A young man from Thailand who lived in California was acting, without a written agreement, as an agent for a spice exporter in his country. Apparently, he did a very good job because import brokers who were also handling the product complained to the Thai exporter. The exporter promptly told our young friend that he should not call on spice packers, the market segment he had done best with, but should confine his efforts to compounders. He already knew from experience that compounders would not buy from him because he could not make them better offers than their established suppliers, the brokers. He was literally put out of business.

By contrast, a neophyte export agent entered into a written agreement to be the exclusive U.S. agent for a new kind of art supply product from Japan. She spent an entire year contacting art supply dealers, wholesalers, importers, and manufacturers before making her first sale. That sale was to a manufacturer of similar products, who already had a distribution network and could easily place the item in stores throughout the country. After the first shipment was made, the agent learned later, the U.S. importer contacted the Japanese exporter and proposed that she (the agent) be cut out of the arrangement. Her services were probably no longer essential, but she had a signed agreement and the exporter decided to honor it. Her commissions were safe for the term of her existing contract.

Supply agreements may be very brief or very long. Your supplier may have a standard agreement form that is acceptable to you (examine it carefully), or you can try to write one yourself using sample agreements in books on international commercial law. You may want to buy a copy of *Commercial Agency: A Guide to Drawing Up Contracts,* from the International Chamber of Commerce (ICC) Publishing Corporation in New York City, phone 212-206-1150. If, however, the stakes are high, financially or in other ways, you should seriously consider using an attorney. Call your local bar association to find one with international business experience, or spend $20 for a copy of the *Global Resources Directory* from North American International Business in

Rye, New York (telephone 914-921-1400). The attorney's fees will probably be at least $2,000.

The following are some topics that international trade agreements often include. Many of these are relevant to both foreign and domestic purchasing, as well as foreign and domestic selling, whether you plan to work as an agent or as a merchant.

- *The Products.* An agreement usually names the products you will handle. The supplier may, for example, give you her line of TV sets but not her computer monitors.
- *Competing Products.* Some suppliers will try to restrict you from handling products that compete with theirs. Others will want you to handle several lines, so the customers will go to you instead of to another agent or importer.
- *Sales Targets.* Suppliers often want to have sales targets or minimums written into agreements. A target tells you how much you are supposed to sell, tells the supplier how much you are likely to sell, and gives the supplier a way to void the agreement if you do not perform satisfactorily.
- *The Territory.* This is the geographical area in which you are authorized to sell the product and which you are supposed to cover. If you have exclusivity in the territory as a merchant, the supplier should not deal with any other importer who sells there. If you have exclusivity as an agent, you should receive a commission on every sale made to a customer in the area.

    As you can imagine, virtually every agent and importer would like an exclusive arrangement. Some suppliers will give it, because they feel it will encourage the agent or importer to spend time and money building up sales in the territory.

- *Prices, Mark-Ups, Commissions.* The "principal"—(the foreign supplier in this instance)—usually sets the price at which his agents must sell. The agreement will specify the percent of commission to be paid as well as when it will be paid. For example, a U.S. agent for heavy equipment from Germany might receive 5 percent of the f.o.b./ vessel value of shipments, payable when the German supplier receives a letter of credit.

It is common also to have the allowable mark-ups for import merchants included in their contracts. This is because an importer may be able to earn more by selling a small quantity, for a large mark-up, than by selling a large quantity for a small mark-up. In such a case, however, the supplier will not do well.

- *Payment Terms.* International trade agreements usually say how the supplier wants to be paid, either by an agent's customers or by his importer. If the supplier agrees to sell on other than secure terms, such as Cash in Advance, orders will be subject to approval by his credit department.

- *Shipping Terms.* Agreements between exporters and importers usually state how the exporter intends to ship, that is, to which point in the journey he will make shipping arrangements, retain title to the merchandise, and be responsible for loss or damage. This kind of clause is often omitted in an agency agreement.

- *Level of Effort.* The exporter may want a clause that gives a minimum number of person-hours or sales calls that you must devote to selling the product. More often a vague term such as "best effort" is used, but if the supplier wants to cancel the contract and finds no other grounds for doing so, you may be accused of not putting forth your best effort.

- *Promotion.* There are often clauses in a contract that state how much promotion an importer will be responsible for and/or how much assistance the exporter will provide. For example, an importer of new canned food products may get 13 cases for every 12 he orders in the first year. The extra case is for promotional use.

- *Service and Warranties.* Any product can be defective, and there should be contractual provisions that say what will happen in such instances. The exporter may agree to replace defective products at his expense, take them back for repair, or pay you for repairing them. The exporter will be very concerned about the warranty given to final buyers because, in most cases, he will end up paying the cost of repairs done under warranty.

- *Priority of Orders.* Export merchants or agents will always want their orders to be given priority over the supplier's domestic orders. This decreases the possibility that a customer tires of waiting and cancels his or her order.

- *Order Lead Times.* This is a clause similar to the above, that specifies how soon the supplier should ship after receiving an order from you. It may say, for example, that your orders will be shipped within 30 days of receipt by the exporter.

- *Reporting.* The supplier may want a clause that specifies how often you should send reports. These reports may cover your sales activities, sales results, and changes in the market country including the economy, government regulations, competition, and customers.

- *Patent and Trademark.* Foreign manufacturers' products may be patented or carry unique trade names or marks. In such case, they will usually apply for U.S. patents and/or register the names or marks in the United States, or ask you to do so on their behalf. Both registrations are with the Commissioner of Patents and Trademarks, Washington, DC 20231. Getting a patent is often time-consuming and expensive, while registering a trademark, if it is truly unique, is quick and inexpensive.

  You may want to register your own trademark and have the supplier put it on the items you purchase. Then you will own it and can use it even if you change suppliers. As an option, you can have labels printed and send them to the foreign manufacturer. Under new, simplified rules you can register a U.S. trademark without having previously used it in interstate or international commerce.

Trademarks and brand names can also be registered with the U.S. Customs Service. Then Customs will try to stop imports of counterfeit goods, such as fake Apple computers. As it now stands, however, Customs will not normally enforce business agreements. If you are the exclusive U.S. importer of "Beautiful You" cosmetics, and your supplier ships legitimate Beautiful You products to someone else in the United States, they will probably be allowed entry.

If your suppliers hold U.S. patents or trademarks, they may ask you to watch for cases of infringement. What action you must take if you hear of infringement depends on your agreements with the suppliers.

- *Relabeling and Repackaging.* Sometimes manufacturers will want you to agree not to relabel or repackage their merchandise. In other cases it will be better for them to ship in bulk and have you repackage, under their labels or yours. Suppose, for example, that you import catfish for human consumption. The market for catfish in America is comprised significantly of strong, patriotic people who buy Fords and Chevrolets no matter how much better and cheaper Toyotas are. You probably couldn't sell catfish in consumer packages that said, "Produce of China."

- *Legal Agent.* Most supply agreements have simple statements that the agent or importer is not a legal agent of the supplier. That is, you cannot enter into commitments that the supplier will be obliged to fulfill.

- *Assignment.* There is usually a clause that says you can't assign the agreement to anyone else without the supplier's approval. Without this clause, the supplier would have no control over who ended up representing him.

- *Duration and Termination.* There is usually a statement that sets forth the term of the contract, whether it will automatically be renewed if not canceled by either party, and how it can be canceled. Normally, the initial term of an agency or distributorship agreement should be for about two years. You don't want to work very hard for a year and have the agreement canceled just when you begin to write orders.

- *Disputes.* Finally, there is a clause that relates to the settlement of disputes. The agreement may say in which country disputes will be settled and which country's laws will apply. It is more common, however, to specify arbitration. International contractual disputes are often settled by arbitration under the auspices of the American Arbitration Association in Washington, DC or the International Chamber of Commerce in Paris.

   If, however, you choose your suppliers carefully and deal with them competently and honestly, you should be able to resolve any disputes with neither law suits nor arbitration. Ultimately, a long-term business arrangement will not benefit you if it does not benefit the other party. Throughout the world, business is fueled by profit, but it is oiled by friendship and trust.

5

Exporting: What Comes First, the Product, or the Market?

Let's suppose now that you want to begin exporting. You may have been inspired by federal and state departments of commerce or other organizations, which are constantly encouraging American firms to export. Governments are usually eager to increase exports, mainly to create jobs and bring in hard currency from foreign buyers. In a capitalist country, governments themselves can't export many products, so they have to persuade private firms to do so.

Perhaps you work for a company whose product may have export potential, or perhaps you have a contact overseas who has asked you to supply him with a particular kind of merchandise. Let's look at these two ways of getting into the export business—starting with the product, then starting with the market.

STARTING WITH THE PRODUCT

Determining Export Potential

A trade magazine recently reported that Luzianne Blue Plate Foods is using "screw conveyors" and "lift conveyors" to move ground coffee from one step in the manufacturing process to another. These pieces of industrial equipment are very efficient, and clean themselves out so well that Luzianne can easily switch from making one coffee blend to making a different blend.

Suppose, as an example, that you work for the company that makes these conveyors or are a good friend of the firm's owner. You are asked to begin to move the product into foreign markets.

How will you start? Your first step might be to use logic. Think about the characteristics of the product and of the countries in which it would be in demand. Basic *consumer goods* are needed everywhere but are produced in most countries, although American brands can bring premium prices. Cigarettes are a prime example. Basic *hard goods* are produced in fewer countries, probably because the market is much smaller; many bars of soap are sold for every soap dish. Very complex or very expensive items are produced in still fewer countries, but tend to be products of powerful manufacturing firms; you probably don't want to be competing with Daimler-Benz or Mitsubishi.

In the case of the conveyors for moving coffee, any large-scale producer of ground coffee would be a potential customer. These firms would be found mainly in countries, developed and developing, with large populations and the cultural habit of drinking coffee. Thus, there would be a finite, easily identifiable group of potential customers, and probably not too many competitors. The market potential would be even greater if the conveyors had other uses as well.

A logical second step would be to visit the nearest field office of the U.S. Department of Commerce. There should be an International Trade Administration officer assigned to the geographical area in which you live or work. Ask this person his or her opinion of the export potential of your product and how that office can help you. Also ask for the name and telephone number of the United States Department of Commerce (USDC) industry analyst in Washington, DC, who specializes in such products, and plan to contact that person. Finally, ask for statistics that show U.S. exports of similar products, by country of destination. There should be a Commerce Department librarian to provide you with this information, who may also be able to tell you which other countries export similar equipment to countries the United States sells to. Unfortunately, there is no comprehensive, up-to-date source of detailed import statistics for all the world's nations, except perhaps for data tapes from the United Nations.

You may find other experts to speak with in state or local export promotion organizations, trade associations, or export service firms such as international banks and freight forwarders. In the case of the conveyors, you might get ideas from the Society of Industrial Engineers or the editors of *Food Engineering* magazine. You could also try a direct approach to finding out whether you have an exportable product—call the production managers of coffee grinding firms in a few countries whose languages you speak. You could request the companies' names and telephone numbers from the USDC country desk officers or from the commercial offices in Washington, DC, of your selected countries.

A Bit of Investigation

Besides having a product and a buyer, you need to be able to get the product *out* of the United States, move it *to* the foreign country, and then enter it *into* the foreign country. This involves checking on U.S. export control regulations, transportation of the product, and foreign countries' import regulations. These subjects are discussed later in this book. (See Chapters 8, 9, and 10.)

If there are no serious procedural problems, you will probably want to take a more detailed look at the market potential for your product. An easy way to do this is to advertise it in *Export Channel,* on "Network," or in trade magazines published in foreign countries. Some of these can be identified in Ulrich's international periodicals directory.

If the product is a consumer good, you may want to show it to U.S. residents who came from the countries in which you intend to sell. They can comment on the product's design, size, color, and other characteristics. Some products such as film sell with little modification in many countries, but others such as toothpaste must cater to local tastes and cultures. I once bought shaving cream in Argentina that smelled like wet wheat. It may have done well in Buenos Aires, but I wouldn't try to sell it in Boston!

Industrial goods can be described to people from a country in which you plan to sell to obtain comments on their specifications. You may be told, for example, that the conveyors should be smaller and made to metric sizes. If they are electrical, they will have to use 220–240 volt current in most countries.

Finally, you should not invest a great deal of money in trying to sell a product without doing research in the target market. The best way of studying a market is to go there, identify potential buyers, make appointments to see them, show them the product (or product catalogs), and ask a series of questions. The answers to these questions will help you determine whether the buyers are interested in the product, whether there is a chance they would buy your products from you, whether the product would have to be modified and in which ways, approximately how much the buyers would pay, who the competitors are, and how you should go about trying to make sales.

Alternatively, you can hire a firm to do this kind of study for you. There are market research firms in nearly all countries, but it can be hard to identify them and find out which are really qualified. One such company, the Kebold Corporation in Paris (telephone 423-86-090 and fax 423-99-712) advertises that it can do preliminary market studies in Europe, select and supervise specialized market research firms, find and evaluate potential importers, distributors or agents, help you exhibit in trade shows, and provide other services. Before you use the services of any market research firm, get information about it from the firm itself and from some of its former clients. If a company won't give you names of any former clients, go elsewhere!

STARTING WITH THE MARKET

Let's now assume a very different situation. You know which country you want to sell to, but not which product you intend to sell. Or, you plan to find and pursue specific export trade opportunities.

If you have picked a country to sell to, you obviously had a reason for doing so. Hopefully this reason is (or includes) a good contact who is ready to buy from you. If, for example, you have a good friend in Hyundai Heavy Industries Division in South Korea, and that friend has asked you to quote on supplying certain kinds of machinery or components, you have a good reason for seeking to sell to Korea.

In addition to speaking with friends, you can look at U.S. international trade statistics to see which products your selected country is buying from the United States. If you visit that country's commercial office, usually in Washington, DC; New York; Los Angeles; or San Francisco, you can also see what the country is importing from other parts of the world. If you see, for example, that Korea is buying increasing quantities of tropical fruits from several countries, it may be a good market for mangos from Florida. If the value of imports is increasing faster than the quantity, you can conclude that prices are rising. This is another good indicator of market potential.

Besides statistics, the easiest way to see what other countries now want to buy from the United States is to read *The Journal of Commerce* newspaper. Five days a week it publishes more than 50 export trade leads from the U.S. Department of Commerce and others from the U.S. Department of Agriculture. There are lists of trade exhibits in the United States, and other information for importers and exporters. Unfortunately, a one-year subscription to this newspaper will set you back $250, and most libraries do not receive it.

You can also get information about foreign buyers' needs from *Export Channel*, "Network," and other services that advertise in import/export magazines. You can subscribe to publications of international organizations that describe opportunities to supply products for programs they finance. Such agencies include the U.S. Agency for International Development (A.I.D.) and The World Bank in Washington, DC and the African, Asian, Arab, Caribbean, East European, and Latin American Development Banks. Unfortunately, these publications describe mainly large deals and are quite expensive.

Finally, you can often uncover export opportunities by reading international publications. On July 21, 1990, the *New York Times* carried a headline that read: "London Stock Exchange Is Rocked by a Bombing." This told alert exporters that demand might increase in England for bomb detection devices. If you were subscribing to a British newspaper, you might have read about plans to increase security in the London area during the war with Iraq. If Britain were your target market and you received trade publications from there, you might have found still more information that would have helped you identify potential clients for security equipment.

Lining Up Suppliers

I recently saw a "Trade Match" notice that read, "FROZEN CANNED AVOCADO (NEW ZEALAND). QUANTITY: REFRIGERATED CONTAINERS—QUALITY SUBJECT TO MARKET TESTING. PACKAGING: CANNED. DELIVERY: WANTS TO STUDY SAMPLES FIRST. QUOTE: CIF AUCKLAND (buyer's name and address)." Suppose you received this notice and thought you could make the sale. How would you go about it? A suggested sequence of events follows.

First, phone or fax the potential buyer. Tell her or him you are an exporter of frozen food products and have seen the notice. Then ask (1) if she is still looking for the product, (2) if she would like a quotation from you, and (3) if she can give you some idea of the quantity needed. Also ask how she would like the merchandise shipped and how she normally pays for similar shipments.

If in this process you get an impression that the buyer is not serious or is not interested in receiving your quotation, you probably should not spend much time on this supposed export opportunity. If, however, you receive satisfactory answers to all your questions and have a good impression of the prospective buyer, you may want to go on to the next step.

In most major libraries you can find a three-volume set of books called the *Thomas Grocery Register*. A look in Volume 2 under "Avocados" will show two firms supplying frozen avocados, Calavo Growers of California and Parman

Kendall Corp. in Florida. Then look under "Frozen Foods: General List" and you will probably find others. For manufactured products in general, the best source is a much larger set of books from the same publisher, the *Thomas Register of American Manufacturers.*

If there are many potential suppliers and you have plenty of time, you can contact them by mail. Write letters to the Export Manager. Explain that you are an export merchant (or agent), that you have a potential customer ". . . in the Pacific area" for frozen canned avocado, and that you would like, for example, a quotation on a full container load, f.a.s./vessel, Port of Oakland. If you are not sure which of a manufacturer's products an importer will want, ask instead for a catalog and an export price list. Make sure to say "export" price list, because many firms have export prices that are lower that their domestic selling prices. Ask for two copies, in case you decide to send one to the customer. You should not reveal the buyer's name, and often not even the country; because then the supplier may contact the buyer directly and save the cost of your commission.

If there are only a few potential suppliers, or time is limited, it is better to phone or fax. You can call 1-800-555-1212 to ask whether the firms you want to call have 800 telephone numbers or, if you do this kind of work often, you can buy a directory of 800 numbers in some bookstores. This is important because you may have long conversations or may have to call several times to speak with a person who can help you. Ask to speak with someone in the Export Sales Department or, if there is none, the Sales or Marketing Department. Then explain your position as described in the preceeding paragraph.

Some manufacturers will not be interested in exporting. They may be willing to cooperate if you plan to work as a merchant and take care of the export procedures, but not if they have to assume these responsibilities. Other firms will not let you quote on their products at all, or will let you handle only certain products or sell to only a few countries. For example, Lee and Levis are already represented in most of the world. Your quotations on their products may be limited to Chad, Afghanistan, and a few other countries in which it is very hard to sell American goods. In some cases, you may have to deal with a producer's exclusive export agent or even with a wholesaler in order to get the merchandise you need.

The manufacturer's quotation or export price list may already have your markup (if you are working as a merchant) or commission (if an agent) built in. If this is not the case, you will have to add it on. This involves difficult decisions; you have to add enough to make the transaction profitable but not so much that you lose the sale to a competitor. In some cases, you can increase your earnings by getting export prices with built-in markups and then charging your customers a bit extra. In effect, you will be paid double.

The manufacturer's prices may be "f.o.b./factory" or they may include transportation to a port or airport. In either case, you will probably have to add all costs to the destination (Auckland for the frozen avocados) in order to deliver a quotation, usually in U.S. dollars, that will let the importer compare his cost from you with his cost from other suppliers around the world. Finally, you will need to send your quotation (and perhaps catalog pages) to the buyer along with a letter or fax that explains how you can help him better than any other supplier in the world. Then follow-up, follow-up, follow-up, and try to make the sale.

Protecting Your Interest

I once worked with a small company in the Boston area that acted as an import merchant for books from Africa and an export agent for American books and school supplies. We received an inquiry from a company in Haiti about desks for schools. After contacting a number of potential suppliers, we chose to quote on products of a company named Adirondack Chair. This manufacturer agreed to pay us an agent's commission. We sent the manufacturer's catalogs and prices to Haiti and, after only a few phone calls and letters, the customer wrote an order to Adirondack Chair and mailed it to us. We forwarded it immediately and followed up by phone to make sure it was acceptable to the manufacturer. The goods were shipped, the importer paid, and the manufacturer promptly remitted our commission.

Unfortunately, not all export transactions go so smoothly. It is tempting for a U.S. exporter and a foreign importer to try to save money by eliminating the middleman, especially if (1) they are experienced international traders, (2) the transaction is large, and (3) they don't know you.

It is very frustrating to be working on an export sale, have it fail to materialize, and then somehow find out that it was made without you. There are a few ways to protect yourself: First, try to deal with reputable companies; second, obtain letters or other evidence that your commissions will be paid; when this is not possible try to keep the exporter and the importer from identifying each other; and finally, try to make your services so valuable that they will be worth the money paid for them. Keeping the exporter and the importer from identifying each other usually works for only one transaction because the importer can usually identify the exporter from information on documents or the merchandise itself.

There is a type of payment document, a back-to-back letter of credit (LC), which lets a middleman use his customer's credit to guarantee payment to his supplier but does not identify either of them to the other. (See Chapter 7.) This kind of letter of credit can be arranged by banks that specialize in import-export finance, but usually requires that the middleman be experienced in international trade and have enough collateral to cover the amount of the letter of credit. In other words, if the deal you are arranging is much larger than your bank account, you just about have to try to work as a commission agent.

STOP PRESS—FOR EXPORTERS

The U.S. Department of Commerce has established a Gulf Reconstruction Center to help American firms sell goods and services for rebuilding Kuwait. The telephone number is (202) 377-5767. Also, the U.S. Small Business Administration is adapting its Procurement Automated Source System (PASS) so it will provide information on small firms to large companies that have reconstruction contracts from the Kuwaiti government. To be listed in the computer file, call any SBA office and ask for a PASS application form.

6

Choosing Target Markets and Finding Customers

This may well be the most important chapter in the book. It is about marketing and selling of both imported and exported goods. It is about how to get someone to pay money for the products you want to bring to or send from the United States.

Let's start by looking at why someone would buy from you. Then we'll look at both the import and the export sides of the business.

WHY SOMEONE WOULD BUY FROM YOU

Why would someone buy a product from you? There are several possible reasons. You have to find at least one of them that fits your situation.

First, you might be selling a desirable product that buyers can't get anywhere else. This is rarely possible, but you may be able to get exclusive rights to sell a particular brand of a product in the United States or in foreign markets. A good friend of mine was one of the first Americans to bring cloisonne artware from mainland China when trade was resumed in the early 1970s. For several months, he practically had the U.S. market to himself. By the time competition came on the scene, my friend's brand name was well established. If you can't find a unique product, you may be able to create one, like the "Chia Pet" or the "Wacky Wall Walker" (both imports) of a few years ago.

Second, you can try to offer the buyers a better value than anyone else can offer. This implies providing them with a product which, by comparison with those of competing suppliers, is of better design or quality, has more attractive packaging or a more appealing brand name, is sold more cheaply or on more liberal credit terms, is delivered faster, or is promoted more extensively. For example, Nantucket Corp., a computer software maker in Los Angeles, recently opened a sales office in Moscow. This office will surely help Nantucket provide Soviet buyers with products that are better designed for the market, perhaps sold more cheaply, and certainly delivered faster than they would be otherwise.

If you can't offer a unique product or a better value, you have to either do an excellent job of selling or have good friends who are buyers. Land in Florida is sold actively in Latin America and the Caribbean, by commission sales persons who can sell nearly anything to nearly anybody. Everywhere in the world, many business deals are made because of personal relationships. I recently advised a young couple who planned to begin trading with Brazil. After exploring a number of possible products, I discovered that they had a good friend who bought for a chain of stores in New England and had suggested that they supply him with imported merchandise. That made the product decision simple: They should handle whatever their friend was willing to buy from them.

I should sound a warning here—bribing buyers is sometimes done in the United States and is very common in numerous foreign countries. I suggest avoiding this means of influencing people, especially if you are new to the import/export business, except perhaps for lunch invitations or small Christmas presents. The reasons for this advice include: you won't know how bribing is done in a particular country and industry; in general, it is illegal; it is expensive; and there's always a chance that you'll pay money to someone who ultimately cannot throw the business your way.

MARKETING IMPORTS

Marketing Imports as an Agent

If you decide to work as a selling agent in the United States for foreign products, you will have to find buyers who are willing and able to do the importing. Beyond that, they will have to place orders that are large enough to be shipped directly to them from overseas. An order does not generally have to be very large if the goods are small enough, light enough, and valuable enough to be transported by air.

For several years, there has been a respectable trade in Egyptian paintings on papyrus. The best-known supplier, Dr. Rageb's Papyrus Institute in Cairo, established an agent in the Midwest to be responsible for selling throughout the United States. Since Dr. Rageb's papyrus paintings were of the highest quality, this agent could contact stores that sold high quality antiques and artworks. The number of such stores was not large, and they could be identified from trade sources or from yellow page telephone directories. As far as the agent was concerned, any store, art dealer, or museum gift shop could be a customer. Because of the nature of the product, it could be shipped in small quantities and imported by people who knew very little about importing.

Two people who consulted me for advice decided to become import agents for a new kind of industrial floor sweeper made in northern Europe. This product could not be imported economically in small quantities. To be practical, several had to be brought in at a time, and each cost several thousand dollars. Since neither end-users nor distributors were likely to buy several machines without seeing one in use, the importers had to bring in a sample, find a place to store it, and find a way to demonstrate it to potential buyers. They found an industrial equipment distributor to demonstrate the unit to potential users. They have since made some sales, but large orders will be hard to get until they become known in the industry.

The difficulty of being an agent comes from the fact that agents cannot make the decisions to buy or to sell, but can only influence the importer and the exporter to make these decisions. Typically, a U.S. selling agent will sign an agreement with her foreign principal. Then the agent will try to obtain orders, which will be written to the principal but given to the agent. The agent will send them to the principal, who will usually accept them as long as the terms are satisfactory. The principal will ship directly to the customer, collect from the customer, and pay the agent a commission. The agent must follow up frequently to make sure the transaction is eventually made and then to collect the commission that is due.

After the agent selects a product and reaches agreement with a principal, she faces the daunting task of finding buyers and persuading them to buy. The best list of U.S. importers is the *Journal of Commerce's Directory of United States Importers and Exporters*. This book is available in major libraries and contains useful information on thousands of companies. Unfortunately, it omits many of the companies that import, especially manufacturers and retailers.

The *Journal of Commerce* also has an electronic service of reporting information on both imports and exports, taken from steamship manifests. Note that air, road, and rail shipments are not included. This service is quite expensive, but is a way to find out which firms are really importing (as opposed to saying they import) specific kinds of products.

There are numerous other publications that either list importers or use codes to identify importing firms. These include directory issues of trade magazines, state and local industrial directories, and others such as the *Thomas Grocery Register,* mentioned in Chapter 5. In some cases, however, you may have to find companies willing to import by telephoning or going to see them.

I once assisted a company in Columbia that manufactured clothing for dolls. No directories showed U.S. importers of doll clothing but I found that nearly every U.S. doll manufacturer was importing clothing, mostly from the Far East. I had no difficulty identifying manufacturers of dolls, making appointments with them, showing them samples of the clothing, and explaining that if they imported from South America they could save money on customs duties and forget about "jet lag" both during and after their buying trips. Several manufacturers gave me samples of products they were buying from Asia so the South American firm could examine them and prepare quotations.

Another Colombian firm wanted to export a canned or bottled fruit from the palm tree that is known in some countries as "chontaduros" and in others as "pejivalles." This was a Latin American specialty food that would be retailed by small food stores that catered to an ethnic clientele, but the stores themselves would not be the importers. The technique used to identify importers was to go to Hispanic areas, find small food stores, and look at the imported products they were selling. On imported canned and bottled foods, the importers' names and locations (in this case cities or boroughs of New York City) are identified. A few of the importers were small firms that were not listed in the telephone directory; in these cases, we got the telephone numbers from the retailers by simply asking and explaining why we needed the information.

Marketing Imports as a Merchant

As a merchant, you will actually import goods from overseas, take title to them and probably (but not necessarily) possession of them, and sell and deliver them to your customers. A merchant normally invests more money and performs more functions than an agent, but has the potential to make a larger profit. Unfortunately, since a merchant loses if he or she cannot sell, or sells but cannot collect, there is also a potential for losing money.

In general, an import merchant will not sell to importers but to retailers, wholesalers, industrial users, and industrial distributors. The term *retailers* includes chain stores, independent stores, mail order retailers, flea market operators, and other kinds of businesses that sell directly to individual consumers. The term *industrial users* includes business, government, and nonprofit organizations of all types. In general, *wholesalers* are merchant (buy and sell) firms that sell to retailers and *industrial distributors* are merchant firms that sell to industrial users.

If you choose to sell directly to retailers, you can identify them from telephone directories or from specialized directories such as the *Salesman's Guide* series from the publishing company of the same name in New York City. There are similar books available from Merchandiser Publishing Company in New York City and from Phelon, Sheldon & Marsar Inc. in Fairlawn, New Jersey. These directories list the names and telephone numbers of the buyers of each kind of merchandise in major stores and store chains.

In general, the larger the store or store chain, the harder it is to get in to see a buyer. When you phone for an appointment, you may be asked to send a catalog or prices and samples. If you agree to send a catalog and do not have one, you will find that the cost of creating a professional-looking catalog costs at least $500 per page (in color). Instead you might choose to have a professional photographer take a good color picture for you. Twenty-five copies of one shot should cost about $150. Have the photograph printed on a full-size sheet of paper, type in the item number and name (and the dimensions and weight if relevant) and you have a catalog page. You can type the price on the same page or put it in your cover letter, or, if you have several models, you can prepare a separate list of prices. Your price list should mention your minimum order quantity, any discounts for large orders or prompt payment, and whether delivery charges are included.

A few retail stores have "open buying" days, when vendors can see buyers without having appointments. Some directories list these days, but you should call in advance to make sure they have not been changed. Then, be prepared to answer every possible question about your company and its product including its material composition and how it is made. Buyers from big stores are very professional. They do not want to take time to educate you, or to risk buying from you if they have any doubts about your ability to deliver.

The term *open buying* should not be confused with *open to buy*, which means that the buyer has money remaining in his or her current budget for the kind of merchandise you are selling. If you visit someone who is not *open to buy*, you will have very little chance of making an immediate sale.

Retail buyers know pretty well what will sell and what will not, and at which price each kind and quality of merchandise can be bought. They negotiate prices and specify the quantities, delivery dates, and payment terms they want to receive. They sometimes refuse to accept merchandise even after having ordered it, and they often take longer to pay than the terms agreed upon. A store that is given terms such as "2/10, Net 30" (2 percent discount if they pay within 10 days and payment due in any case within 30 days), will often pay in 20 or 25 days and take the discount anyway.

If you choose to sell to small independent stores, such as gift shops or boutiques, you will find it easier to see buyers. Sometimes you can even walk in unannounced, ask who does the buying, and show your samples. If the buyer likes the samples and prices, he or she may place a small order, ask for immediate delivery, and write a check or pay you in cash. Cash payments may indicate that some of the retailer's transactions are "off the books."

You will not, however, have time to make enough sales calls in small stores to produce a profitable volume of business. A solution to this problem is to enlist the services of manufacturers' representatives. These are agents that will book orders for your products from retail stores and send the orders to you. When you accept an order, you will ship it to the customer, request payment from the customer, and send the agent his or her commission.

Manufacturers' representatives can be hard to find; the best approach is probably to ask retail buyers which agents they recommend you speak with. The buyers will probably give you the names of the agents they deal with the most. A manufacturers' representative (rep) will usually ask you for a 10 to 15 percent commission and perhaps to pay a share of his overhead expenses (office, etc.). Also, you will need to supply him with catalogs or with product samples, price lists, and promotional literature. Thus, if you use 10 reps and they have an average of 5 salespersons each, you will have to supply 50 copies of your catalog.

Wholesalers of most kinds of goods can be identified from the telephone directory or from directory issues of trade magazines. Wholesale buyers can be approached directly. They are generally very experienced and negotiate hard on prices and terms of sales. Wholesalers normally buy in quantity and pay their bills promptly, but do not invest heavily in promotion. It will be up to you to persuade retailers to buy your product from the wholesalers, and perhaps to persuade customers to buy it from the retailers.

The best way to persuade either manufacturers' reps or wholesalers to handle your product is to prove that retailers will buy it and can resell it. For example, a woman interested in importing high quality wooden furniture from France began by locating a few stores that sold products similar to hers and persuading each one to stock a few pieces. Then she could import a container load of furniture, place it in stores, and tell wholesalers that the product *would* sell because it was already selling.

Many new importers plan to sell their products by mail order. This is usually not as easy as it sounds. There are essentially three ways to go about it.

First, you can identify your most likely target market, buy a specialized mailing list from one of the many list dealers such as Dunhill, prepare your mailing, and send it out. Most Dunhill lists sell for $50 per thousand mailing labels. You should get professional help in preparing your mailing pieces, or at least read books on mail order selling. You will learn techniques such as writing "Personal and Confidential" on your envelope, using a P.S. in your sales letter to communicate an important point, and putting a real stamp on your reply envelope. People hate to throw away real stamps. For large mailings, you can save money by getting a bulk mail permit, but many experts say the extra cost of using First Class Mail is a good investment.

You should send a series of three mailings to the same addresses. Most people will throw away the first one because they have never heard of you. The second one may catch their attention, and the third time they may buy. The rates of response in mail order are very low. A major organization that markets seminars by mail is said to be satisfied with a rate of about 0.0025, or a quarter of 1 percent. Some reasons for this are that even the best mailing lists contain errors (wrong addresses, names of people who have moved, etc.) and that your tiny, unknown catalog must compete for attention with the likes of Spencer Gifts and Hanover House. You will be very lucky to break even, especially when you consider the labor involved in sending the catalogs and processing the orders. (*NOTE:* If you want to mail to Japanese manufacturers, contact the Jumbo Company Ltd. for Japanese industrial databases. The fax number is 081-44-555-3850.)

A second mail order option is for you to advertise in newspapers or magazines (at least three issues of the same publication). You can ask respondents to order immediately, or to contact you for more information. Advertising in general interest publications is unlikely to pay off (although *The Wall Street Journal,* for example, carries ads over and over again for products like fresh fruit that do not seem to be high potential mail order items). But if you have a specialized product and can find a publication aimed at precisely your target market, this kind of marketing will work well. I once met an importer of Scottish bagpipe regalia who told me there was only one magazine written for bagpipe enthusiasts in the United States. He was receiving numerous orders from his advertisements in that publication.

A third mail order option is to import products and try to persuade established mail order houses to include them in their catalogs. Save all the catalogs that come to you and try to identify firms that sell products similar to yours. Also, you can look in books such as *Facts on File Directory of Mail Order Catalogs* (in many libraries) to identify companies that might want to handle your products. Then contact them, preferably by phone. Describe your product and say that you feel it would sell very well in their catalogs. If the buyer you are speaking with is interested, he or she will probably ask for a sample and prices. Your sample will not be returned unless you provide a self-addressed label and offer to accept the shipment collect from a parcel service such as UPS, and sometimes even that will not be sufficient.

Professional mail order firms place a high value on every square inch of every catalog page and are very selective about the products they include. Also, they keep their own inventories to a minimum. They won't want to take a chance on putting an item in a catalog and getting orders for it, only to find that you do not have the product. Therefore, they will probably insist that you invest in a substantial inventory in the United States. A few will send you mailing labels and ask you to "drop ship" directly to their customers, but this is becoming less common.

If you have an inexpensive, mass merchandise type of product, you may want to try selling it in flea markets or, better yet, to flea market vendors or wholesalers. Flea marketing in the United States is now an established industry with its own associations and publications, but they tend to go in and out of business quickly. Try going to flea markets in your area, speaking with dealers, and asking them which wholesalers they buy from. These same wholesalers usually sell also to street vendors, house party dealers, and other kinds of nonstore retailers.

Be warned, however, that the flea market industry works on low prices. People who shop at flea markets expect the dealers to sell cheaply. That means the dealers have to buy cheaply from the wholesalers, and the wholesalers have to buy cheaply from you. Some people consider flea marketing to be the method of selling of last resort.

Industrial users include manufacturers, wholesalers, retailers, schools, libraries, hospitals, government offices, military installations, and so on. They all have people or departments in charge of purchasing, and you can usually see them by appointment to do research on new products. It is harder to get through the door when you are actually selling something because they have established suppliers of known brands, and they don't have time to deal with numerous small manufacturers and importers. If you have a new and better paper clip, don't try to sell it to IBM. Sell it instead to a distributor that sells to IBM.

Industrial distributors are similar to wholesalers except that they buy from manufactures or importers and sell to industrial users. To reach smaller users, there are often two levels of distributors. A familiar example is the automotive parts trade in which numerous specialized companies make virtually all parts available to a myriad of repair facilities. Industrial distributors can usually be identified through telephone directories, state industrial directories, and directory issues of trade magazines, or by asking industrial users which distributors they buy from. In general, they buy in good quantities, stock merchandise, pay their bills on time, sell and do some promotion, and deliver to their customers.

While I've never worked with paper clips, I did have a friend who was importing a new kind of stapler from Japan. It was small, light, inexpensive, durable, and effective. Unfortunately, my friend's business did not last long. He didn't do a good enough job of identifying his target market, selling to appropriate distributors, or promoting to potential users.

MARKETING EXPORTS

Less is said in this book about export marketing than about marketing imported products. This is not because export marketing is easier but because (1) most readers of this book will be more interested in importing and (2) many books on export marketing are available. These include publications of the U.S. Department of Commerce and the Small Business Administration, trade books available in public bookstores, and college textbooks. See Chapter 11 for sources of information.

Assuming you are not a manufacturer, but choose to export products made by other firms, you will have to select and test products, select market countries and perhaps market segments, decide how to make your product available to each market segment (which kind of distribution channel), develop the channel, and price and promote the products so as to maximize your profit. All these activities are critical to your success.

Suppose, for example, that you have worked as a head nurse and want to become an exporter of nurses' uniforms, from the cap to the shoes. You begin by contacting the sales representatives, whom you already know, of several American manufacturing firms. You find several who are willing to work with you, select three or four whose products will give you a complete line, and sign a preliminary agreement with each one. In speaking with them you find that very few have substantial export experience and are willing to perform the export function. Thus, you will probably have to work as an export merchant. This will make it easier for you to combine products from various manufacturers in the same shipment in order to serve your customers better.

Next, you must select market countries in which there are substantial numbers of nurses, competition is not overly severe, and there is money to pay for imported goods. You can find the number of nurses in each country in publications of the World Bank or the United Nations World Health Organization. Eliminate from the list those countries that will clearly not be appropriate for your purpose, these include Iraq, which is under a U.S. embargo; India, where you can assume that local producers supply the market and imports are restricted; and Peru, which is technically bankrupt. The UNIDO *Industry Yearbook* will give you a rough idea of competition in each country, which can be refined by looking at industrial directories and import statistics. The World Bank's *World Development Report* will give you information on each country's ability to pay.

Your main markets will be nurses in public and private hospitals, and private doctors' and dentists' offices. The relative importance of these will vary from country to country. In most countries, public hospitals will buy through government purchasing offices, private hospitals through their own purchasing departments, and private medical offices from hospital supply stores. A commission agent might be best for selling to government purchasing offices, while an importer/distributor might be needed to reach private hospitals and medical offices. You might choose to work with an agent in Canada, for example, and with an importer/distributor in Germany.

Your minimum prices, f.o.b. U.S. Port (see Chapter 8) would be your cost from the manufacturers plus a mark up that will cover your operating costs and leave a reasonable profit. To enter markets in which prevailing prices are low, you may obtain temporary low prices from your suppliers and reduce your mark-up percentage. For a few high price markets, you may be able to increase your mark up. Prices can usually be quoted in U.S. dollars. Your agents may ask that price quotations include all costs up to and including delivery to their customers, while most of your importers will probably ask for Cost, Insurance, Freight (c.i.f.) quotations. See Chapter 7 for more information about methods of payment.

Your foreign representatives are likely to ask you for help in promoting sales of the products. They will need product samples, catalogs, and other promotional literature. Some may ask you to help pay the costs of advertising in trade magazines and/or exhibiting in trade shows. Also, some may ask that you send "missionary salesmen" to go with them on visits to prospective customers. As a small exporter, you will not be able to help promote the line of nurses' clothing in more than a few markets. This suggests that you should concentrate on just two or three market countries until your sales there have become profitable.

Establishing Distribution Abroad

Note that the emphasis here is on setting up long-term distribution arrangements rather than on making *ad hoc* sales that may never be repeated. Some ways of finding foreign representatives are using the "Agent/Distributor Service" (ADS) of the U.S. Department of Commerce, contacting firms listed in the USDC "Foreign Trade Index," advertising in foreign trade magazines, and exhibiting in trade shows in your target markets.

Several years ago I used ADS to help me find potential agents for office products in Nigeria. You can do likewise for any product and country. For a small fee, U.S. commercial officers will select and send you information on three potential agents or distributors. You can also identify potential "reps" by having a computer run done from the Foreign Trade Index. You can ask, for example, for medium and large importing firms in Italy that handle machine tools. You will be charged according to the number of firms on your computer printout.

If you choose to advertise for agents or distributors you can use a variety of international, regional, or local publications. Some of these are published in foreign languages in the United States, for example, by Johnson International Publications in Great Neck, New York. Many more are published overseas, some in multilingual versions. If you want to find European importers for carambola (starfruit) from Florida, *EuroFruit* magazine, published in England, will spread your message throughout the continent.

There are hundreds of trade exhibits overseas, and the U.S. Department of Commerce as well as some state and local governments can help you participate in them. Some of the best known are the Paris Air Show and Anuga (for food products) in Germany. Often you don't need to send personnel, only your products, and in a few cases you can simply exhibit your catalogs or other sales literature. Look for specialized, not general, fairs that are open only to the trade. The main disadvantage to exhibiting is the cost—usually around $2,000 for space and significant amounts for shipping product samples, your air fare and living expenses, personnel to work in your booth, and miscellaneous cost items.

By the way, importers often exhibit in trade shows in the United States. You can do this, but, to save money, find an exhibitor whom you can persuade to display your products for a small fee or commission. To find exhibitors, just contact the show managers and buy a copy of the previous year's exhibit catalog.

Selecting Foreign Representatives

When you have candidates to represent you in a country, correspond with each to exchange information about your companies and ideas about how you can work together. Then you will probably want to travel abroad to make the final selection and, hopefully, sign an agency or distributorship agreement. This is not as easy as it sounds. The firms you would most like to work with will probably not be available to you. Try to interest the best ones by showing that you are a valuable supplier with products that will sell well in the target country.

If you select an agent or distributor who has a poor reputation in his/her own country, your reputation will suffer, and if you select one who cannot sell effectively you will be wasting time and money. Also, if you pick the wrong representative, local laws may make it nearly impossible for you to let him go. I once heard of an American exporter who traveled to Saudi Arabia and fired his local agent, and was later detained at the airport with the accusation that he had violated Saudi law.

Your main criterion for choosing foreign agents or distributors should be how well equipped they are *to do the job you need done.* If you are exporting electronic products that will need servicing, your distributor must have service facilities and trained personnel. If your product is a line of expensive clothing that will be sold to high-quality department stores, you agent needs good contacts among the buyers of this kind of store.

When you have selected a foreign agent or distributor, enter into a contract with that person or firm. Make sure the key personnel understand your product thoroughly, by sending them literature and by training them either in the U.S. factory or in their own offices. Then keep in contact with them, both to motivate and to assist them. Suppose you were representing a foreign firm and, for several months, did not receive information, ideas, or encouragement from it. You would probably not spend your time selling the products of that exporter. Make sure you don't make the mistake of ignoring those who represent you in foreign markets.

7

Credit, Payment, and Related Concerns

Suppose you ask an exporter in Taiwan for a quotation on his products and he sends you the following telex message:

RCA AUG 10 0343
226078 AEGIS UR

ATTN: KENNETH D. WEISS

RYL 6/29 RE A-6825 AUTO FLOOR MATS, RUBBER WI TEX-
TILE BACKING, SIZE 26 × 18 INCH PACKED 36 PCS/CTN(1.95
CUFT/22KGS) AT FOB US# 4.21/PC BASED MIN QTY 500 PCS
OR 3.89/PC IF QTY OVER 1,000 PCS, APPROX SEAFT TO N.Y.
#0.23/PC, SHPMT W/IN 45 DAYS AFT L/C RECD.

RGDS, PETER CHEN
68934 AUTOPART

DURATION 111 SECS LISTED 06:50 EST 07/10/91

This is an actual telex, and you must be able to understand it clearly if you are going to do business with Mr. Chen. It seems like a foreign language, but it is not; it is "cabelese," an abbreviated form of English developed when most international correspondence was by cable and each word was expensive. It carried over into telex messages and to some extent even into facsimile transmissions.

This message was sent on July 10 to an RCA telex address, 226078. AEGIS is the "answerback," and UR is a telex code for the United States of America. In plain English, the message reads as follows:

Regarding your letter of June 29 about model A-6825 automobile floor mats, rubber with textile backing, size 26 by 18 inches, packed 36 pieces to a carton (a carton measures 1.95 cubic feet and weighs 22 kilograms) at Free of Board US $4.21 per piece, based on a minimum quantity of 500 pieces, or $3.89 per piece if the quantity is over 1,000 pieces, approximate sea freight to New York is $0.23 per piece and shipment will be made within 45 days after your letter of credit is received.

This telex came from Peter Chen, telex number 68934, answerback AUTOPART. It took 111 seconds to transmit and reached RCA in the United States at 6:50 A.M.

Read the original message again and see how much you have learned already. The message begins by saying which letter it refers to. It gives the product's model number, description, size, and number of pieces per carton. It gives the size and weight of each carton, which might be needed to calculate freight rates, the prices at various quantities, the approximate shipping cost, and the number of days needed to ship. "FOB" is the suggested shipping term, and "L/C" is the suggested payment term. This chapter explains the various payment terms, and Chapter 8 deals with the shipping terms.

CREDIT DECISIONS WITH SUPPLIERS AND CUSTOMERS

Whether you plan to sell domestically or to export, as a merchant, you will have to decide between taking the risk of selling on credit and losing sales by insisting on payment in cash. Your suppliers will face similar decisions about selling to you. If you work only as an agent, you will still be involved in credit decisions. You will negotiate sales for your principals and will then have to convince them that the terms of sale you have worked out with the customers are acceptable. In order to make credit decisions, you must know how to obtain and use credit information.

Bank and Trade References

The least expensive way to check on the credit-worthiness of a domestic or foreign firm is to ask for bank and trade references. A company that will not give you references is not likely to be a good paying customer.

To check a prospective customer's bank reference, give your bank (in writing) the company's name and address, its bank's name and address, and its account number. If you are checking on a foreign company and want the information quickly, ask your bank to communicate by telex or fax at your expense. You should receive a report that tells you how many years the company's account has been open, the approximate average balance, the amount of its credit line, and in general terms how satisfactory the account has been to the bank. This is not a great deal of information, but it will be helpful.

To check with trade references, send each a letter or fax that reads something like the one in Figure 7.1.

If you are checking on a potential supplier, the letter will be almost the same, but the questions will be something like the ones at the bottom of page 92.

Nearly all companies will answer this correspondence if it looks professional. If you send it by mail, it can help to enclose a stamped, self-addressed return envelope. If you want a quick reply by fax, you can offer to reimburse the sender for the expense of sending the facsimile message.

Dear Sir or Madam:

The company named below has listed you as a credit reference. We will be very grateful if you will answer the questions at the bottom of this page and return this letter in the enclosed self-addressed, stamped envelope. Your prompt attention to this request will help us make an appropriate credit decision. We will be pleased to assist you in the same way if the occasion should ever arise. Thank you very much.

Sincerely,
(your signature)

Name and Address of Applicant: (You will fill this in) _____

Number of years you have sold to this company: _____

Highest recent balance: _____

Current outstanding balance: _____

Terms you extend this company: _____

Payment record: Discounts ( ) 30 days ( ) 60 days ( ) Over 60 ( )

Your rating of account: Excellent ( ) Good ( ) Fair ( ) Poor ( )

Additional comments: _____

Your name: _____ Title: _____ Date: _____

Figure 7.1.   Letter Requesting Credit References.

Number of years you have dealt with this vendor: _____
Please comment on:

—Size of order supplier can fill: _____

—Adherence to shipping schedules: _____

—Accuracy in filling orders: _____

—Any problems experienced: _____

Other comments: _____

Your Name: _____ Title: _____ Date: _____

Credit Reporting Services

The credit reporting business in the United States is growing and changing rapidly. Unfortunately, in most foreign countries it is less well developed. Still, you can almost always get some information. Inaccuracies can creep in, however. Information in credit reports is usually a few months old and is not well verified by the credit reporting agencies. Also some privately owned firms do most of their business in cash, and little information about them may be available. Finally, in some countries, for tax purposes, most income and assets may be in the owner's name and not in the company's name.

The main credit reporting agency in the United States is the Dun & Bradstreet Corporation (D&B), and TRW has recently gained importance in this field. Unfortunately, both provide domestic reports only on a subscription basis that makes them too expensive for most readers of this book. D&B also supplies information on foreign firms, but the charge is quite high. The harder it is to get credit information in a particular country, the more a report will cost you.

For firms in the USA there is another option—look in your telephone directory under "Credit Reporting Services" for companies that can use their contacts to provide the reports you need. Their charges vary from about $20 to $50 per report. I recently used a credit reporting service in Miami, Investigators Inc., to check on a produce importer. The resulting report helped a Bolivian supplier make a very wise decision against selling to this importer on credit.

To give you information about prospective foreign companies there is a U.S. Department of Commerce service called "World Trader Data Reports." For less that $100 you can buy a report on virtually any foreign firm. If there is a current report in Washington, DC, on your prospective customer or supplier, you can get it in about two weeks. If there is no current report, the Commerce Department will have one of its foreign representatives prepare one for you, and it will take about two months. The information you get will not be as detailed as in a D&B or TRW report, but it will help you decide whether to deal with the firm you are inquiring about.

Finally, a visit to the potential supplier or customer can be very useful in making credit decisions. Sometimes you will be given access to the accounting statements and/or can speak with an accountant or auditor. At the least, you can assess for yourself the quality of the company's offices, factory, equipment, and personnel. Whenever it seems that a company is trying to hide something, it probably is, and you should be wary of dealing with it.

METHODS OF PAYMENT IN INTERNATIONAL TRADE

In international trade there are several means of payment, each of which has its costs, advantages, and risks. The most important are the following:

- Open account
- Documents against acceptance
- Documents against payment
- Letter of credit
- Payment in advance.

These means of payment are arrayed in order of risk, with open account being the riskiest for the exporter and payment in advance being the riskiest for the importer. Sometimes consignment is listed also as a payment term. It would go at the top of the list, because in consignment sales the risk is borne entirely by the exporter.

Terms of payment are a negotiable aspect of international trade transactions. Each party seeks a term that is favorable to him or her but that the other party will also accept. You need to understand the various methods, otherwise you may accept a method of payment that is riskier or more expensive than can be justified by the profit on a transaction.

Open Account

How do you pay for water? It's simple; first you receive the product, then the water company sends you a bill. Open account in international trade works the same way. First the exporters send the shipments, then they send bills for the merchandise and related costs. The importer can pay in various ways, such as by sending a form of cashier's check or an international money order. This method is very inexpensive. It does not involve any risk for the importer, but the exporter runs the risk that the importer will not pay for the merchandise. The exporter's only protection is that of the underlying contract of sale and/or the importer's word and reputation.

It may surprise you to learn that open account is the most widely used method of payment in the import/export business. This is because the great majority of international trade (in terms of value, not number of transactions) is between affiliated companies or between large firms that know and trust each other. If Toyota/Japan ships auto parts to Toyota/U.S. or to General Motors, it will not bother with costly or complex terms of payment.

As a small importer, you are unlikely to get open account terms from foreign suppliers, but your steady purchases and reliable performance may earn you this reward in a few years. As a small exporter, you will be asked to accept payment on open account. You will probably be reluctant to agree, but if your customer is a major firm or is well known to you, you may take the risk. After all, why should a foreign importer buy from you with a risky, expensive method of payment if he can get open account terms from another exporter in the United States or a third country?

As an exporter, you will want to be careful of a little game played by a few importers. They may start paying you on secure terms and then request open account for a small order. Their orders on open account will become progressively larger, and they will pay right on time. Then you will ship the big order, and the money will not arrive. I once tried to help a Long Island company that had fallen for a scam similar to the one just described. When the Long Island exporter traveled to the importing country, in West Africa, he found that most of the money had been invested in houses for the importer and his relatives.

Documentary Drafts for Collection—Against Payment and Against Acceptance

To "draft" a document is to write it. In international trade, a draft is an unconditional order in writing, signed by the seller, addressed to a foreign buyer. It orders the buyer to pay the amount specified in the draft, either when it is presented to him (Against Payment) or on a specified date in the future (Against Acceptance). Drafts as methods of payment are used only in international trade, and you may have heard them referred to by names such as sight draft, time draft, SD/DP, and others.

In brief, a draft is a simple, inexpensive means of payment that is initiated by the exporter. It works like this: Suppose I agree to sell you 100 baskets of fruit for $900, delivered to your door. I have my bank, let's say Citibank, prepare a document that looks something like a bank check. It says, "Pay Citibank $900." Citibank sends this draft to your bank, and the cashier either calls you to come in or sends it on to you. You have already received the fruit baskets, and are an honest person, so you promptly sign the draft and return it to your bank. The cashier takes the money from your account and transfers it to Citibank for my account. Technically, we wouldn't even need a sales agreement. I could select your name from the telephone directory, send you some merchandise, and have the draft sent to your bank. If you signed it, the merchandise would be yours and the money would be mine.

The kind of draft I am speaking of is also called a "bill of exchange." A bill is a piece of paper that notifies you of something, and this kind of bill notifies you of an exchange of merchandise for money. The exporter's bank "cuts" the draft, and the importer's bank "presents" it to her. If the importer doesn't sign it on "first presentation," there will later be a second presentation, and so on. When the importer writes "accepted" on the draft and signs it, she has accepted her obligation to pay the money. If the importer is supposed to pay the draft on presentation (as soon as she sees it), it is a "sight draft." If the agreement is that she does not have to pay immediately, but some time after seeing it, it will be called a 'time draft." If payment is due a certain number of days (usually 30 or 60, but sometimes as much as 180 days) after the date of the draft, it will be called a "date draft."

This method of payment, as described so far, puts the risk entirely on the exporter. If the importer refuses to accept a draft for any reason, it is the exporter who must sue the buyer to accept it, find a new buyer in the same or a different country, pay for return transportation of the goods to their point of origin, or simply abandon the shipment. All these options are time consuming and expensive. If goods are abandoned, they are usually sold at customs auctions, and there is nothing to prevent the supposed importers from bidding on them. Beware of any foreign importer who wants essential parts of an item, such as axe handles and axe heads, in separate shipments with payments by sight draft. This importer is putting herself in a position to buy cheap at the customs auctions, because only she will know where both the handles and the heads can be found.

There *is*, however, a way for the exporter to use a sight draft and still control the merchandise. It involves using a "to order bill of lading." (See Chapter 9 for a discussion of documents in international trade.) When the exporter places the goods on a ship or other vehicle for transportation, the ship's captain or his representative signs and gives the exporter a document called a "bill of lading" (an "airwaybill" if the shipment is by air). This document serves, among other purposes, as title to the merchandise. The person the goods are "consigned" to on the bill of lading can claim them. If the exporter wants the importer to receive the goods without regard to payment, as in an open account shipment, he uses a "straight" bill of lading. If, however, the exporter wants to impose conditions on delivery of the goods, he uses a "to order" bill of lading. It is usually "to order of shipper" (the exporter). Then the shipper can "order" that the goods be delivered only under certain conditions, as when the importer has accepted the draft. In practice the shipper usually endorses the bill of lading "in blank" on the back and trusts the banking system to give it to the buyer, endorsed to him, only when he has accepted the draft. With a properly endorsed bill of lading, he can receive the merchandise.

Now the risk is not all on the exporter, but is shared. If the payment document is a sight draft, the exporter still bears the risk that the importer will not pay and pick up the merchandise, but the importer bears the risk that the goods will not be as ordered. With a time or a date draft, the importer has the option of picking up the goods, examining them, and if they are faulty, instructing her bank not to pay the draft. Fortunately, this is not done very often.

In summary, a documentary draft is a simple payment instrument, initiated by the exporter, that goes through banking channels but is not guaranteed by the banks. It can be used for transactions of any size but is often favored for those in the range of about $500 to $2,500, between companies that know and trust each other. There is always some risk for the exporter, and there is also risk for the importer when a sight draft is combined with a to order bill of lading. The cost is low—usually about $50 for each party to the transaction and it is common for each party to pay his own charges.

Figures 7.2 illustrates a bill of exchange transaction with a to order bill of lading. Note that there are six parties involved—the exporter, his bank, and his freight forwarder, and the importer, her bank, and her customs broker.

Figure 7.3 is a copy of a sight draft for a shipment from New York City to Seoul, Korea. Numbers 1–30 indicate features of the document.

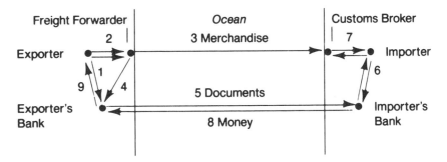

1. *Exporter* fills out form at his bank.
2. Sends goods and documents to freight forwarder.
3. *Freight forwarder* sends merchandise.
4. Sends documents to bank.
5. *Bank* sends them to importer's bank.
6. *Importer* pays or accepts; gets documents.
7. Hands over documents; gets merchandise.
8. Importer's bank transmits funds.
9. Exporter's bank credits his account.

Figure 7.2.   Bill of Exchange Transaction.

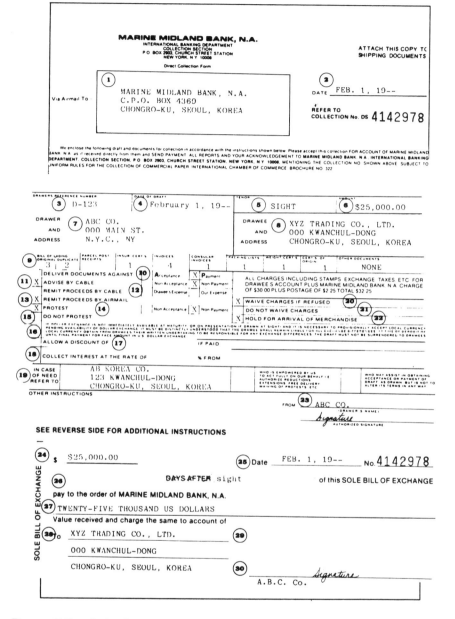

Figure 7.3.   Sight Draft. (Reprinted from *Introduction to International Banking Services*, 1983 Edition, page 13, Published by Marine Midland Bank. Reprinted with permission.)

Letters of Credit

By now, or perhaps long before now, you have heard the words letter of credit. There are various types of "LCs," but the one we will discuss here is the commercial documentary letter of credit. The word "commercial" means it is used in a business transaction, and "documentary" means it is payable upon presentation of specified documents.

You can think of a letter of credit as a letter that is written by the importer's bank to the exporter, and communicated to the exporter through banking channels. Your bank (you are the importer now) is telling the exporter that, when he presents specified documents containing specified information, he will be paid for a shipment.

Suppose an exporter in Somalia sells you flags from the civil war of 1991 for the sum of $40,000. The seller wants to be sure of being paid and therefore asks you for a letter of credit. If you agree, you must apply to your bank to open your LC, in favor of the exporter. This means that the bank is pledging to pay the exporter if he does exactly what the LC specifies. An LC normally specifies that an exporter provide "documentary evidence," that he or she has shipped the merchandise ordered, by the time and in the manner stated in the LC, including fulfilling any other specified obligations such as purchasing insurance.

The fact that you apply to your bank for a letter of credit does not mean you will get it. Your bank will not want to take the risk of paying the exporter and then not being able to collect from you. Therefore, it will look for strong evidence of your ability to pay—such as an account with an average balance that will easily cover the credit or other evidence of financial strength and stability. In some cases, a bank will allow you to pledge assets, such as a certificate of deposit, to guarantee payment on a letter of credit. The "bottom line" is that it is very hard to get a letter of credit for a larger sum than you are able to pay. That

$40,000 deal will be hard to swing with only $400 in your bank account.

The importer's bank is known as the "opening" bank. When it agrees to write a letter of credit it usually transmits it to its branch or correspondent nearest the exporter, which is known as the "advising bank" because it advises the exporter that a credit in his or her favor has been received. The banks' relationships serve, among other purposes, to protect the exporter because branches and correspondents can more easily ascertain that LCs are genuine. There have been instances, usually in developing countries, of importers using counterfeit LCs and LCs of fictitious banks.

Importers *can* specify that their own banks be used as the advising bank. In other cases, importers use their own banks as intermediaries between themselves and the advising banks, although this increases the cost to them because more banks are involved.

When an exporter is advised of the LC and receives a copy, he should study it carefully to make sure that each of its terms and conditions can be met. Otherwise, there will be a problem. For example, if the LC calls for 100 boxes each containing 400 civil war flags, and the shipping documents show that the cargo consisted of 400 boxes each containing 100 civil war flags, there will be a "discrepancy." This will probably cause the payment to be delayed until the discrepancy is "waived" or otherwise resolved.

When the exporter ships and gives the required documentary evidence to the advising bank, with no discrepancies, payment is due. In some credits, the advising bank is also the "paying bank," and can pay the exporter very quickly. In other credits, where the opening bank is the paying bank, there will be a delay of a few days.

The letter of credit is an extremely flexible method of payment because the importer can ask her bank to make any legal stipulation. If an LC states that the exporter must personally load the baskets on the ship while wearing nothing but a civil war flag and that this must be tied around his ankles, payment will not be made unless he presents documentary evidence of having done exactly that.

Nearly all LCs are "irrevocable," which means they cannot be changed or canceled without the consent of the beneficiary. In other words, once you open an LC and the exporter is advised of it, you can't back out unless the exporter agrees to let you. If the exporter has any doubt that the opening bank is solvent, or that the country in which it is located will have "hard" (convertible) currency with which to pay, he can ask to have the LC "confirmed" by the advising bank or even by a different bank in the same or a third country. For example, LCs opened in some African and Middle Eastern countries are often confirmed in the United Kingdom. Confirmation means that, if the opening bank is obligated to pay and for some reason cannot do so, the confirming bank will pay. It usually costs the exporter less than 1 percent of the value of the LC, and gives him extra assurance of being paid. If you as an exporter receive a letter of credit and no bank will confirm it, there is probably a large amount of risk involved in the transaction.

There are numerous variations of letters of credit. Some operate like revolving lines of bank credit, and others permit partial payment for parts of an order. Still others allow a trading company to use its customer's credit to guarantee payment to its supplier. Your bank can advise you on the appropriate variety for each situation.

Many exporters customarily ask for letters of credit on all transactions, but as an importer you do not have to accept the terms that are proposed to you. Come back with a counter offer and negotiate. Better yet, be the first to propose the method of payment and propose one that is more to your advantage. Then the other party may accept your terms or make a counter offer.

To summarize, a letter of credit (LC) is a formal payment document opened by the importer and communicated through banking channels. The party obligated to pay the exporter is the opening bank. The cost for this service is often a fixed fee plus a percentage, for example, a $70 opening fee plus a commission of at least 0.25 percent (a quarter of 1 percent), with a minimum commission of $60. Since the advising bank charges for its services too, the minimum total cost of a letter of credit is close to $200. This charge is higher if an LC is not payable at sight, if more than two banks are involved, or if the exporter wants the credit confirmed.

Figure 7.4 shows the steps in a typical letter of credit transaction. Note that some of the steps include more than one closely related activity.

Figure 7.5 is an example of an irrevocable documentary letter of credit for a shipment from Korea to the United

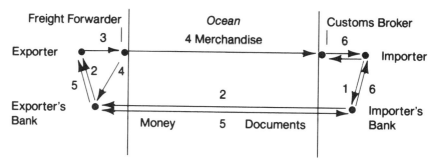

1. *Importer* applies for letter of credit.
2. *Opening bank* sends LC, through correspondent or branch, which advises exporter of receipt of LC.
3. *Exporter* sends goods and documents to freight forwarder.
4. *Freight forwarder* dispatches merchandise and provides documents to the advising bank.
5. *Advising bank* forwards documents to negotiating bank, which checks documents against LC, and authorizes payment if no discrepancies are found. The importer's account is debited.
6. *Importer's bank* gives him the documents with which he can claim the merchandise.

Figure 7.4.   Letter of Credit Transaction.

MMB NUMBER I-00000

MARINE MIDLAND BANK, N.A.
140 BROADWAY, NEW YORK, N.Y. 10···

IRREVOCABLE DOCUMENTARY LETTER OF CREDIT

PLACE & DATE OF ISSUE
NEW YORK, FEB. 1, 19--

DATE & PLACE OF EXPIRY
KOREA, MAY 1, 19--

APPLICANT:

A.B.C. Co.
000 Main Street
New York City, New York

BENEFICIARY:

XYZ Trading Co., Ltd.
000 Kwanchul-Dong
Chongro-Ku, Seoul, Korea

MAIL TO

ADVISING BANK:

Marine Midland Bank, NA
C.P.O. Box 4369
Chongro-Ku, Seoul, Korea

AMOUNT:

TWENTY EIGHT THOUSAND FIVE
HUNDRED TWENTY FIVE AND 00/100
U.S. DOLLARS
$28,525.00

PARTIAL SHIPMENTS: ALLOWED
TRANSHIPMENTS: ALLOWED
SHIPMENT/DISPATCH TAKEN IN CHARGE
FROM/AT: FOB GLOBAL KOREA NOT LATER
THAN APRIL 15, 19_ _ FOR TRANSPORTATION
TO: N.Y., U.S.A.

CREDIT AVAILABLE WITH:
BY: PAYMENT, AGAINST PRESENTATION OF
THE DOCUMENTS DETAILED HEREIN AND OF
YOUR DRAFT(S) AT SIGHT DRAWN ON MARINE
MIDLAND BANK, N.A., NEW YORK, N.Y.

Commercial invoice in 4 copies.
Customs invoice.
Packing list.
Invoice must carry percentage of stainless steel composition
on stainless flatware and overall length of each item.
On board ocean bill of lading (if more than one original has
been issued all are required) issued to order of MARINE MIDLAND
BANK, N.A. notify DEF Freight Forwarders marked freight collect
and showing letter of credit number.
Insurance covered by buyers.
This refers to our cable of today.

COVERING: 12,500 DOZ. SONNET PATTERN STAINLESS FLATWARE BUYER
P.O. #13455 DATED OCTOBER 17, 19-- F.O.B.

DOCUMENTS TO BE PRESENTED WITHIN 10 DAYS AFTER THE DATE OF ISSUANCE OF THE SHIPPING
DOCUMENT(S), BUT WITHIN THE VALIDITY OF THE CREDIT.

WE HEREBY ENGAGE WITH YOU THAT ALL DRAFTS DRAWN UNDER AND IN COMPLIANCE WITH THE TERMS
OF THIS CREDIT WILL BE DULY HONORED ON DELIVERY OF DOCUMENTS AS SPECIFIED IF PRESENTED
AT OUR COUNTERS ON OR BEFORE THE EXPIRATION DATE INDICATED ABOVE.

EXCEPT SO FAR AS OTHERWISE EXPRESSLY STATED THIS DOCUMENTARY CREDIT IS SUBJECT TO THE
"UNIFORM CUSTOMS AND PRACTICE FOR DOCUMENTARY CREDITS" (1974 REVISION) INTERNATIONAL
CHAMBER OF COMMERCE (PUBLICATION NO. 290).

Figure 7.5. Commercial Letter of Credit. (Reprinted from *Introduction to International Banking Services,* 1983 Edition, page 105, Published by Marine Midland Bank. Reprinted with permission.)

States. (Note that ICC [International Chamber of Commerce] publication number 290, named in the last line of the LC, has now been replaced by ICC publication No. 400.)

Payment in Advance

Suppose you make a small sale to an importer in Africa, who has no doubts about your honesty or ability to ship. The importer may have trouble getting foreign exchange in his country, but have a bank account in London or Paris. He may ask you to quote in British pounds or French francs and then send you a check.

This importer's sister in the Caribbean may ask you to find some parts that are urgently needed to keep machines in her factory running. She can't afford to have you hold up the shipment until you get paid, and so may simply send a check on her Miami bank account. If the importer wants you to ship without waiting for the check to clear, she can have it certified. She would prefer to send a check drawn on a bank in her country, but such a check can take several weeks to clear and many foreign currencies are not convertible to U.S. dollars.

As an importer, you may be asked for cash in advance in some cases. If you order a suit from Hong Kong, your supplier will probably ask for half the amount in advance. If you order a small quantity of samples, the easiest way to pay is to simply buy an international money order from your bank. Of course, this means that you are taking all the risk. It is possible that the foreign exporter will simply pocket your money and not respond to your frantic phone calls and faxes.

Credit cards are being used now in several countries as a means of paying for small international purchases. This system seems to be working well, and I would classify it as a variation of payment in advance.

Consignment

Consignment is not actually a form of payment but a type of agency arrangement in which the buyer takes possession of goods but does not take title to them. Suppose, for example, that you buy a $1,000 dress, wear it once at a party, and then decide you do not want it anymore. You may take it to a high quality used clothing shop and leave it there, on consignment. You might agree with the store owner to pay you 75 percent of what she sells it for, but no less than $250. If and when the dress is sold, you will receive your 75 percent of the revenue. If it is not sold within a set period of time, you may reclaim it or the store owner may ask you to take it back. If it is somehow lost or damaged, you will be paid the $250 minimum.

Consignment in international trade works much the same way. It is often used for U.S. imports, especially of fresh produce and works of art. If you decide to import fresh asparagus, for example, you cannot be sure how much of what you import will be of excellent quality or what the market will pay when your shipment is through customs and ready for sale. You will probably respond by seeking to import on consignment. When a shipment is about to arrive, you will make contacts to try to sell it. When it actually arrives, you will inspect it and, assuming it is of the expected quality, deliver it and collect from your customers. Then you will deduct your actual expenses and perhaps a 15 percent commission, and remit the remainder of the proceeds to your supplier. If you have to destroy part of the shipment because it cannot be sold, or if part of it is seized by U.S. regulatory agencies because of illegal pesticide residues or infestations, you will inform the exporter and will not pay for that part of the shipment. The exporter must trust you completely, or must pay to have someone in the port of arrival verify your report of the quality of the goods and the price at which they are sold.

I once heard of a Brazilian exporter of baler twine who used consignment selling to make sure he sold all his production every year. He shipped to a distributor in the midwestern United States, on consignment, for the entire haying season. His instructions to the distributor were to keep reducing the price until every roll was sold. The distributor, by pricing to maximize his own profit, automatically maximized the profit to the exporter.

In the U.S. export trade, the main use of consignment is to help distributors of heavy machinery and equipment. If a manufacturer of construction equipment wants to sell in Jamaica, its distributor there will need floor models and demonstrators as well as an inventory of equipment for sale. Part or all of this may be in Jamaica on consignment. If and when it is sold, the distributor will pay the manufacturer.

This system of paying for merchandise definitely favors the importer. In the worst case, for example, a shipment of fresh strawberries that cannot be sold because the plane that was carrying them had mechanical problems and the berries all spoiled, the exporter will lose both his produce and the money he paid for transportation. If the shipment is not insured, the exporter may not recover any money at all.

Export Credit and Credit Insurance

Whenever the importer does not have to pay for merchandise upon receiving it, he/she is buying on credit. Credit terms can be even more important to an importer than the actual selling price. Why should an importer in Argentina pay cash to you when an exporter in Japan will sell equally good merchandise on three months terms, especially when the cost of money (the interest rate) in Argentina is very high?

Exporters who provide financing normally do so from company funds or with bank loans or credits. There is a

U.S. Export Import Bank (EXIMBANK), in Washington, DC, which has a variety of programs for helping U.S. exporters provide credit. These are normally for transactions of about $10,000 and up, and a few very large exporting firms receive the bulk of EXIMBANK assistance. For information, call 202-566-2117.

A few states, such as California, have established special funds or banks to help finance export sales of goods made in those states. To find out if your state has such an organization, call the department of commerce, international trade, or development. Also, the U.S. Small Business Administration (SBA) has an export credit and guarantee program for small exporters. For information, contact the SBA office nearest you. For export shipments of agricultural products, the Commodity Credit Corporation in Washington, DC, has some financing available. Another financing organization, the Private Export Funding Corporation (PE-FCO) in New York City, is only for huge transactions.

Suppose your foreign importer needs time to pay and does not want to open a letter of credit. Even if you can somehow finance the transaction, you will not be sure of receiving your money in the future. You may be able to insure against this risk through the Foreign Credit Insurance Association (FCIA), which is now effectively a part of EXIMBANK, or through private companies that write export insurance. They normally sell through insurance brokers, such as Cook & Miller International and Marsh & McLennan, both in New York City.

Export credit insurance, however, has several disadvantages. The FCIA is prohibited by law from insuring shipments to a few countries, and no one will insure if your customer seems unreliable. Any insurance is expensive, and you can rarely get full coverage. You may be able to insure against 100 percent of losses that are caused by political problems, but only 90 or 95 percent of so-called "commercial" losses.

On the import side, it may be worthwhile for you to explore the export credits and credit insurance that are available to your exporter. For example, if you buy from a supplier in England and ask for credit, and the supplier says he can't afford to give it to you, you might suggest that he explore the help available from the Export Credit Guarantee Division (ECGD) of Her Majesty's Government. ECGD may become a private company by the end of the year, 1991.

FOREIGN CURRENCY TRANSACTIONS

Most international transactions are paid for with currency, and the U.S. dollar is used far more often than any other nation's currency. Many Japanese and other exporters, however, prefer to be paid in the money of their countries. As of this writing the ECU (European Currency Unit), is used mainly for accounting, but in the future we will probably see European companies seeking to pay or to be paid in ECUs.

As a U.S. importer, you can nearly always pay in dollars. If a foreign exporter insists on receiving some other currency, you have several choices. The best is probably to stand your ground and pay in U.S. dollars; if the exporter wants the sale, he will have to concur. A second option is to agree to pay in a foreign currency, such as Swiss francs, but to get a somewhat lower price to compensate you for the risk of having to pay more dollars than you expected for the stated amount in francs. Of course, the further in the future you will be paying, the greater the likelihood that your cost in dollars will vary significantly one way or the other.

For larger amounts, you may be able to use the foreign exchange forward market. This means entering into an agreement now, with your bank, to buy the foreign currency you will need, at a predetermined rate, on a specified date in the future. This is a form of "hedging." The more the market expects the foreign currency to rise against the dollar, the more you will have to pay for your hedge.

Large companies that have "exposure" in foreign currencies use other hedging techniques, such as playing the futures market. This involves buying contracts, for fixed amounts and fixed time periods, through foreign currency exchanges. International finance managers that are professionals at this game earn very good salaries.

On the export side, it is very common to be asked to take payment in foreign currencies. This can be dangerous, because many developing countries have currency that is not convertible or whose actual value is worth much less than its official value.

If you are asked to take payment in foreign currency, check with your banker to find out the strength of the currency in question. Also, newspapers such as *The Wall Street Journal* report both current exchange rates and the values of futures contracts, so you can see whether the market expects the currency in question to rise, or fall, against the dollar. If it looks as if your transaction is risky, you may be able to negotiate other terms such as more time to pay but with payment by letter of credit in U.S. dollars. Or, perhaps you can agree to accept the foreign currency but at a rate that gives you a certain amount in dollars. That way the importer can pay in his or her currency, but may have to pay more to give you the number of dollars agreed upon. Finally, it may be worthwhile for you to use one of the hedging techniques mentioned in the preceding paragraph.

In brief, try to avoid dealing in foreign currencies. For importers, this is usually not a problem. Exporters, however, may lose sales if they are not somewhat flexible. Also, there is often a chance that you will profit from the exchange rate fluctuation. If you agree to take payment in Danish kroner three months in the future, and during those three months the kroner rises 10 percent against the dollar, you will receive 10 percent more dollars. This may double your profit on the transaction.

COUNTERTRADE

The term *countertrade* refers to international shipments that are not paid for entirely in cash. There are several variations, known as "barter," "compensation trade," "buy-back," "counterpurchase," and "offset." No one knows for sure the percentage of international transactions in which countertrade is involved, but most estimates are in the range of 10 to 25 percent.

Countries often try to pay for merchandise with countertrade when they are short of hard currency. This has been and still is the case with most Eastern European and most developing countries. Colombia, Malaysia, and other nations have passed laws that regulate countertrade transactions.

Suppose, for example, that you agree with a Peruvian businessperson that you will exchange outboard (boat) motors for alpaca sweaters. After considerable discussion, you determine how many motors, of which brand and horsepower, you will ship and how many sweaters, of which quality and sizes, the Peruvian will ship. Then you agree as to when and how each commodity will be shipped and who will pay for the transportation.

To put this transaction in motion, the Peruvian will have to obtain government permission to ship the sweaters without receiving hard currency for them. She may also need approval to import the outboard motors. Then there will be two shipments of merchandise, either of which could confront problems of loss, damage, poor quality, and so on. Finally, you will have to sell the sweaters for more than your total cost, including what you paid for the motors, in order to make a profit.

The hypothetical transaction just described is an example of simple barter. More often, there is a monetary value placed on each shipment, such as $20,000 worth of motors in exchange for $20,000 worth of sweaters (or $15,000 in sweaters and $5,000 in currency, etc.). Sometimes more than one country is involved in a countertrade deal, as for example, engines from the United States to Peru, sweaters from Peru to Canada, and cash from Canada to the United States. This kind of triangular deal is both more expensive and more difficult to arrange. There are specialized companies, mostly in Europe but some in the United States as well, that specialized in arranging countertrade transactions.

I once met a New York businessman who was exporting cigarettes to Rumania and receiving clothing in return. His explanation for this was that the cigarettes were so valuable in Rumania, he was able to make more profit than if he paid for the clothing in cash. Still, countertrade has so many pitfalls that I don't recommend it for the beginner. Remember that even a simple barter deal is really two transactions instead of just one. That means there are twice as many chances for something to go seriously wrong.

8

Shipping and Insuring Your Goods

International transportation, moving goods from one country to another, is a vital function that can get quite complicated. Importers or exporters are inevitably involved in some transportation functions such as packing, shipping, and insurance. If these functions are not handled properly your goods can arrive too late, in poor condition, or not at all. The cost of shipping can sometimes be even more than the cost of the products. Fortunately, there are commercial organizations, like customs brokers and freight forwarders, ready and able to help you—for a price.

PACKING FOR INTERNATIONAL SHIPMENT

You may not ever have to pack goods for shipment abroad. If you work as an import or export agent, your principal will do the packing and, if you work as an import or export merchant, your suppliers will perform this function.

You may, however, buy from U.S. suppliers who are unable or unwilling to pack for export. Or you may import goods in large quantities and have to repack them in smaller units for your domestic customers. In these cases, you can do the packing yourself, in your office or living room, or hire a specialized firm to do it for you. Even if your principals or suppliers do the packing, you should know how they do it and you may want to give them instructions. If the packing is inadequate to protect the goods, your risks of loss and damage will be greatly increased; if the packing is grossly inadequate, the insurance company may cite that as justification for not paying a claim. At the other extreme, excessive packing will add weight and bulk to the shipment and thus increase your transportation costs. Finally, if your customer asks for a certain kind of packing and your principal or supplier does it differently, the shipment may be rejected and you will lose your commission or markup.

Insurance companies can often provide information on how specific kinds of goods are normally packed. One free book, *Ports of the World,* from a major insurance company called SIGMA (P.O. Box 7728, Philadelphia, PA 19101) depicts various kinds of export packs and their specifications.

Kinds of Packing

Until a few decades ago, most products moved overseas in individual boxes or barrels. This was known as "break bulk" shipping. It has all but disappeared in the foreign commerce of the United States, but is still very common in most developing countries. (Dividing a large shipment into several smaller ones is still known as "breaking bulk.")

When several boxes are put together to make one unit, perhaps with steel straps or plastic shrink wrap, you are dealing with "unitized cargo." Since units can easily become too large and heavy to handle easily, they are often put on wooden platforms made so that forklift trucks can pick them up. These platforms are "pallets" and the cargo is said to be "palletized." All the methods just described are known as LCL (Less than Car Load) cargo.

The real revolution in export packing came with containerization. In shipping language, a container is a large metal box that can be loaded with cargo. There are various sizes, but the most common for shipment by sea are "20s" and "40s." A typical "40" is 8 feet wide, 8 1/2 feet high, and 40 feet long. It can hold about 2,347 cubic feet or 42,000 pounds of cargo.

Export shippers can own or rent containers, or can use "boxes" (as they are often called) that belong to steamship companies. Typically, a container is cleaned and checked for soundness (no water leaks, etc.), packed, locked and sealed, and sent to its destination. It may move by road or rail and then by ocean, and is usually not opened until it reaches the importing country or sometimes even the importer's warehouse. The numbers of the seals are recorded, so that it is nearly impossible for a thief to break into a container without leaving evidence of having done so.

Containers are used also for air freight. There are several standard sizes because of the large variation in the inside dimensions of aircraft. For fast turnaround, some airlines will have a string of containers waiting when a plane arrives. Essentially, they push out one string of metal boxes and then push in another.

Break Bulk Packing

If your shipments are small, they will probably be sent break bulk, which gives you a higher unit cost than that of larger volume shippers. Also your packages will be subject to the potential risks of being dropped by handlers or handling equipment, crushed by heavy cargo, or soaked in sea water. Even cargo inside waterproof boxes can get wet if the ship sails through cold areas and moisture in the air inside the box condenses. That's why, in the old war movies, we used to see shipments of firearms coated with grease and wrapped in waxed paper. Now firms can shrink-wrap cargo and/or add materials to the packages that absorb moisture.

Logic tells us that heavier boxes should be loaded on the bottom and lighter ones on the top, but most steamships call at several ports. What goes in first, or what will come out last, usually ends up on the bottom. That means there may be a bulldozer resting comfortably on top of your ping pong balls.

Finally, some kinds of packing materials may get you in trouble with regulatory authorities. One importer wanted to bring wooden bowls packed in straw to the United States from Grenada, but was prohibited from doing so because straw can harbor insect pests that might harm American agriculture. I once heard of a South American exporter who was packing fresh garlic in mahogany boxes and was fined by his country's authorities for illegally exporting precious wood.

All this means that you should pay attention to how your cargo is packed, even if you don't personally do the packing. Find out how the first few shipments from a principal or supplier are protected from hazards and, if you don't like what you see, try to get it corrected. Your Christmas ornaments packed in thin cardboard boxes may arrive intact the first time, but what might happen to them next time?

AFTER YOU PACK IT, MARK IT

Companies that frequently pack goods for export should know how to mark them, but new exporters may have to be taught. There are several kinds of marks, which are usually printed or stenciled on boxes. In some trades, such as fresh produce, shipping boxes are being printed with colorful pictures of the products they contain.

Shipping boxes are usually marked, "Made in (country of origin of merchandise)." They also give the gross weight, net weight, and outside dimensions, often in both metric and English systems. A few countries have special regulations—Libya, for example, frowns on the use of any language other than Arabic and any measuring system other then metric.

If there is more than one box in a shipment, each one is numbered. Often a box bears the exporter's name and the importer's (or his agent's) name, address, and order number. For cargo that is especially subject to pilferage (cameras, watches, etc.), however, there is a system of blind marks that supposedly prevents thieves from knowing the contents of boxes. Blind marks should be changed often because thieves have ways of learning which shippers they belong to. Fortunately, much of the cargo that thieves especially like is now shipped in sealed containers.

There are also cautionary markings on shipping boxes, sometimes in more than one language. Perhaps the most common ones are "HANDLE WITH CARE," "GLASS," "USE NO HOOKS," "THIS SIDE UP," "FRAGILE," "KEEP IN COOL PLACE," "KEEP DRY," and "OPEN HERE."

Since cargo handlers in many ports cannot read, however, the same instructions are communicated with symbols. A champagne glass means "fragile," a hook with an X across it means "use no hooks," and so on. (See Figure 8.1 for selected examples.) Specialized books on export traffic show pictures of all these symbols.

Finally, there is an even more extensive set of symbols for marking boxes that contain hazardous materials. If you plan to deal in any product that is (1) explosive, (2) flammable, (3) spontaneously combustible, (4) water reactive, (5) oxidizing, (6) poisonous, (7) radioactive, or (8) corrosive, you need to be sure your packing and marking are as required by the U.S. Department of Transportation, the Coast Guard, and/or the Civil Aeronautics Board. The captain of a vessel is the final authority with regard to carrying hazardous materials. If he thinks a shipment is unsafe, he can reject it, even though it may be in compliance with all regulations. Port authorities are also concerned

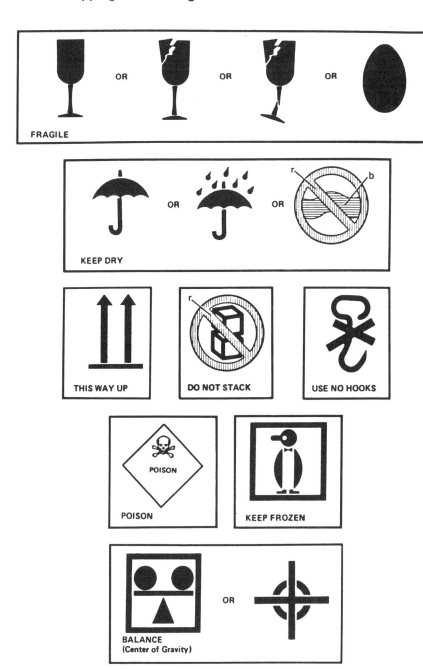

Figure 8.1.   Symbols Used in Handling of Goods.

about hazardous materials, and some ports prohibit loading or unloading the most dangerous kinds.

On the subject of hazardous materials, the risk of carrying them gives carriers an excuse to charge higher rates. An exporter told me recently that one drop of mercury in a container can cause that whole 40 foot box to be considered "hazardous" and thus increase the shipping rate.

INTERNATIONAL TRANSPORTATION

Air Mail

If your shipments are small, light, and inexpensive, the best way to send them is probably by international air mail. A mail shipment must be within the size and weight limits of the postal services of both countries, registry and certification are often not available, and the maximum value of insurance that can be obtained is small. Under current U.S. regulations, however, you can import a shipment (except most textiles and apparel) up to $1,250 in value every mail day and the postal authorities will do the customs work for you. You may still have to pay customs duty, but not a penny for clearance.

I know of an importer who had developed a catalog of light weight, low-priced consumer goods from Taiwan. He planned to mail his catalog in the United States and forward the orders received to an agent in Taiwan, who would pack each order and ship it by mail. Each customer could decide whether he or she wanted the speed of air mail or the low cost of sea mail.

Courier Services

Courier companies, of which the best known is probably DHL, offer excellent service for very small shipments. They are used often, especially for urgent or high value packages. Most courier companies will pick up packages, insure them, transport them, clear them into the importing countries, and deliver them to the consignees. Overnight courier service to Europe is now available, in spite of the fact that Europe is about six hours ahead of U.S. Eastern Standard Time.

In addition to the major firms, there are small courier services that work in just a few cities. For example, a small company called JB carries letters and small packages only between Ecuador and Miami. It is known as "the DHL of the poor people."

Shipping by Air

A monthly publication, *International Air Cargo Guide,* gives schedules for flights that carry cargo. Air freight is no longer just for rush, perishable, and compact but high-value cargo. Its use has expanded and continues to expand enormously. It has special advantages for shipments of cargo from an inland city in one country to an inland city in another country because most important world cities have airports, but many do not have seaports.

Air freight rates are usually higher than steamship rates, but other costs are often so much lower that air becomes the cheaper way to ship. Figure 8.2 gives you a format for comparing air and sea to see which is cheaper overall. Note the last item, "interest on value of goods in transit." If your $100,000 export shipment arrives 10 days earlier because it was sent by air, you may get paid 10 days earlier—$100,000 in 10 days, at 18 percent interest, is worth $500.

Shipping by Surface

A large part of the shipping between the United States and its neighbors, Canada and Mexico, is by rail and road.

Cost Item	Air	Sea
Export Packing	$ 300	$ 800
Inland freight, country of origin	100	500
Freight forwarding	100	150
Shipping	3,800	2,000
Insurance	100	300
Customs clearance	80	150
Inland freight, country of destination	50	200
Interest on value of goods in transit	50	300
Total	$4,580	$4,400

(Note: Assumes merchandise value approximately $50,000.)

Figure 8.2. Air-Sea Freight Cost Comparison.

These modes of transportation have become more important with the signing of a free trade agreement between the United States and Canada and with the increase in trade with Mexico. There is much talk of a free trade area encompassing all three countries, and this might come about as early as January, 1993.

In trade with Mexico, rail cars roll across the border for customs inspection and then are often interchanged with rail services of the other country. Trucks are often unloaded and their contents transferred to carriers of the importing country, although the proposed free trade agreement will include "right of passage" for each country's trucks in the other country. There are frequent problems of shortages of rolling stock or special customs inspections. Trade to and from Canada usually flows smoothly, although since the free trade agreement was signed, some groups of producers have blocked traffic temporarily to show their unhappiness with duty free imports that compete with their products.

Sea freight usually takes longer than air freight at both terminals and in transit. For most shipments, its only advantage is cost, but that can be a very big advantage. If Hyundai had to ship cars from Korea by air, it could not compete in the U.S. market.

Steamship services (the word "steamship" is still used even though the ships are no longer powered by steam) are either scheduled, nonscheduled, or charter. Nonscheduled lines are usually cheaper but less reliable. Most of the major lines sail on regular schedules. You can find out about sailing dates from shipping lines, freight forwarders, or any of several magazines. One is *Brandon's Shipper and Forwarder,* published by a company of the same name, and another is *Shipping Digest,* published by Geyer-McAllister Publications, both in New York City. Also the newspaper of world trade, *The Journal of Commerce,* carries shipping schedules, in addition to trade news and export opportunities.

Figure 8.3 is a page from *Brandon's Shipper and Forwarder.* Note that Nedlloyd Lines appears to be the only one on the page that has its own office in New York. United Arab Shipping Company is represented by Kerr Steamship Co., Transafrica Line by Ariel Maritime Group, and so on. Note also some of the terminology used. Ro-Ro is a special ship that cargo can be rolled onto and off of, FCL means full container load, LCL means less than container load, and BB means break bulk.

Shipping lines may also be classified as conference lines or independents. Lines sailing on many routes, as from the U.S. Atlantic and Gulf ports to West Africa, have banded together to form conferences. The lines in a conference compete with each other, but maintain similar standards and charge the same rates. They have lower rates, known as contract rates, for shippers that agree to use conference carriers for most of their shipments on a given route, but even these rates are usually higher than those charged by independent steamship lines.

U.S. law also provides for nonvessel owning common carriers (NVOCCs) and for shippers' associations. An

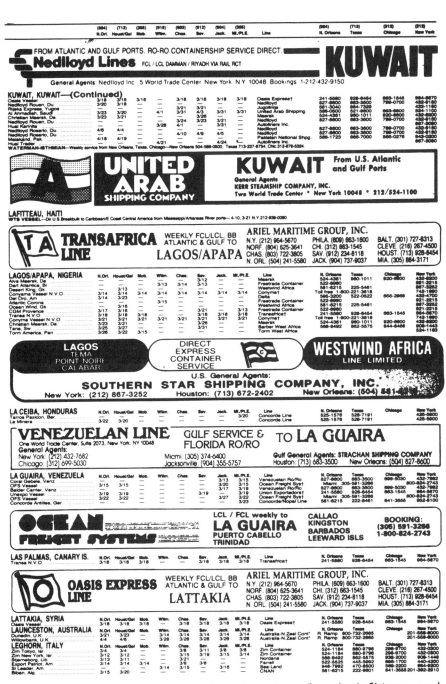

Figure 8.3. Shipping Schedule. (Reprinted from Brandon's Shipper and Forwarder, March 11, 1985. Copyright 1985 by International Thomson Transport Press.)

NVOCC is a freight forwarder who reserves fixed amounts of space on certain vessels and then resells it to individual shippers, at lower rates than they would pay directly to the steamship line. A shippers' association is a group of shippers who pool their cargoes to make larger quantities and therefore obtain lower rates. Freight forwarders can tell you whether either of these kinds of service is available in your area.

Using charter vessels is feasible only for very large quantities, although sometimes a ship charterer or broker will know of a chartered vessel that has extra space and can carry your cargo for a low rate. It is worth exploring all avenues to find the lowest prices for acceptable service.

Actually, most international shipments use more than one mode of transportation. There is a term for this—multimodal. Suppose you arrange for a steamship company to pick up your container at an inland point of origin, move it by road to a seaport, and then move it to a foreign country by sea. If the steamship company carries the goods through to their final destination and gives you just one shipping document (a "through bill of lading"), it will be providing a multimodal transportation service.

SHIPPING RATES

Your shipping rate is the price you pay per unit of cargo. A unit is usually a pound, kilogram, ton, cubic foot, cubic meter, or container. Be careful with tons because there are three kinds. A short ton is 2,000 pounds, a long ton is 2,240 pounds, and a metric ton is 2,204 pounds or 1,000 kilograms.

Shipping rates vary with the kind of service, the kind of cargo, and the route. Actually, distance is only one of the factors used in making up shipping rates. Other important factors are the amount of traffic on a route and the strength of the competition. Thus, it can cost less to bring a container of shirts to Boston from Hong Kong than from an island in the Caribbean.

Both airlines and steamship lines have rate books, known as tariffs, that show the rates for different kinds of cargo between specific areas of the world. Figures 8.4 and 8.5 show sample pages from air and ocean tariff books. Note that the first part of Figure 8.4 shows the minimum price for shipping each type of standard air container (of general merchandise) from the west coat of Taiwan to specific U.S. cities, the maximum weight that can be sent for that price, and the cost per kilo in excess of that maximum weight. The second part of Figure 8.4 shows costs for shipments of different weights between Taipei and several U.S. cities. For example, according to this rate schedule a shipment of 100 kilos or less, from Taipei to Honolulu, costs 254.80 new Taiwan dollars per kilogram. Figure 8.5 shows conference rates (the Asia North America Eastbound conference) for shipping electrical and electronic goods by sea from South Korea to ports in the United States. A shipment to West Coast (WC) ports costs $122 per cubic meter (M), $166 per metric ton, $1,720 for a 20-foot container (D20), or $2,450 for a 40-foot container (D40).

Note that the air tariff shown in Figure 8.4 is for "general" cargo rates while the ocean tariff (Figure 8.5) is for a "specific" commodity. The general rates are usually quite high. Most kinds of cargo can be shipped under specific rates, and it is important to make sure that your shipment gets the lowest rate to which it is entitled. If your cargo is unusual or hard to classify, it may pay for you to visit the airline or steamship company and look at the tariff book yourself. If there isn't a specific rate for your goods, you can apply for one to the airline, steamship line, or shipping conference. For example, a firm in Haiti wanted to ship bars of medicinal soap to New York. Since no one had made commercial shipments of soap from Haiti to New

CONTAINER GENERAL COMMODITY ARBITRARIES

Applicable from Taiwan to points in the U.S.A.

RATE TYPE	BULK/CONTAINER TYPE	N O T E	MIN. WEIGHT IN KGS.	RATE PER KG./MIN. CHARGE PER CONTAINER	PIVOT WEIGHT IN KGS.	RATE PER KG. OVER PIVOT
from WEST COAST (XXX) to PHILADELPHIA (PHL)						in NTD
GEN						
	1	-	1	141600.00	6210	22.80
	2	-	1	73880.00	3241	22.80
	2A	-	1	68000.00	2983	22.80
	2D	-	1	60320.00	2645	22.80
	2H	-	1	90800.00	3982	22.80
	3	-	1	50160.00	2200	22.80
	4	-	1	42680.00	1872	22.80
	5	-	1	42680.00	1872	22.80
	6	-	1	32280.00	1415	22.80
	7	-	1	24160.00	1060	22.80
	8	-	1	18000.00	790	22.80
	8B	-	1	18000.00	790	22.80
	9	-	1	18000.00	790	22.80
from WEST COAST (XXX) to PITTSBURGH (PIT)						in NTD
GEN						
	1	-	1	129160.00	6210	20.80
	2	-	1	67400.00	3241	20.80
	2A	-	1	62040.00	2983	20.80
	2D	-	1	55000.00	2645	20.80
	2H	-	1	82840.00	3982	20.80
	3	-	1	45760.00	2200	20.80
	4	-	1	38920.00	1872	20.80
	5	-	1	38920.00	1872	20.80
	6	-	1	29440.00	1415	20.80
	7	-	1	22040.00	1060	20.80
	8	-	1	16440.00	790	20.80
	8B	-	1	16440.00	790	20.80
	9	-	1	16440.00	790	20.80

RATE TYPE	BULK/CONTAINER TYPE	N O T E	MIN. WEIGHT IN KGS.	RATE PER KG./MIN. CHARGE PER CONTAINER	PIVOT WEIGHT IN KGS.	RATE PER KG. OVER PIVOT
from WEST COAST (XXX) to ST. LOUIS (STL)						in NTD
GEN						
	1	-	1	119240.00	6210	19.20
	2	-	1	62240.00	3241	19.20
	2A	-	1	57280.00	2983	19.20
	2D	-	1	50800.00	2645	19.20
	2H	-	1	76440.00	3982	19.20
	3	-	1	42240.00	2200	19.20
	4	-	1	35960.00	1872	19.20
	5	-	1	35960.00	1872	19.20
	6	-	1	27160.00	1415	19.20
	7	-	1	20360.00	1060	19.20
	8	-	1	15160.00	790	19.20
	8B	-	1	15160.00	790	19.20
	9	-	1	15160.00	790	19.20
from WEST COAST (XXX) to SYRACUSE (SYR)						in NTD
GEN						
	1	-	1	141600.00	6210	22.80
	2	-	1	73880.00	3241	22.80
	2A	-	1	68000.00	2983	22.80
	2D	-	1	60320.00	2645	22.80
	2H	-	1	90800.00	3982	22.80
	3	-	1	50160.00	2200	22.80
	4	-	1	42680.00	1872	22.80
	5	-	1	42680.00	1872	22.80
	6	-	1	32280.00	1415	22.80
	7	-	1	24160.00	1060	22.80
	8	-	1	18000.00	790	22.80
	8B	-	1	18000.00	790	22.80
	9	-	1	18000.00	790	22.80

Figure 8.4. Air Tariff.

RATE TYPE	BULK CONT TYPE	F N T	MIN WT LB/KG	RATE/MIN CHARGE PER CONTAINER	PIVOT WT LB/KG	RATE OVER PIVOT
TAIWAN						
from TAIPEI(TPE) to HONOLULU(HNL)					in KGS	NTD
GEN	BULK	-	1	378.80	33	-
	BULK	-	45	278.80	91	-
	BULK	-	100	254.80	221	-
	BULK	-	300	188.40	420	-
	BULK	-	500	158.40	-	-
from HOUSTON(HOU) to TAIPEI(TPE)					in LBS	USD
GEN	BULK	-	1	3.91	75	-
	BULK	-	100	2.98	191	-
	BULK	-	220	2.60	517	-
	BULK	-	660	2.05	999	-
	BULK	-	1100	1.86	-	-
from TAIPEI(TPE) to HOUSTON(HOU)					in KGS	NTD
GEN	BULK	-	1	426.40	34	-
	BULK	-	45	325.60	92	-
	BULK	-	100	302.40	233	-
	BULK	-	300	235.60	436	-
	BULK	-	500	205.60	-	-
from INDIANAPOLIS(IND) to TAIPEI(TPE)					in LBS	USD
GEN	BULK	-	1	3.97	75	-
	BULK	-	100	3.03	191	-
	BULK	-	220	2.65	517	-
	BULK	-	660	2.08	999	-
	BULK	-	1100	1.89	-	-
SCR4416	1	-	1	14451.00	12419	0.95
SCR4417	3	-	1	8350.00	5984	1.39
from TAIPEI(TPE) to INDIANAPOLIS(IND)					in KGS	NTD
GEN	BULK	-	1	429.60	34	-
	BULK	-	45	329.20	92	-
	BULK	-	100	305.60	234	-
	BULK	-	300	238.80	438	-
	BULK	-	500	209.20	-	-
from KANSAS CITY(MKC) to TAIPEI(TPE)					in LBS	USD
GEN	BULK	-	1	3.91	75	-
	BULK	-	100	2.98	191	-
	BULK	-	220	2.60	517	-
	BULK	-	660	2.05	999	-
	BULK	-	1100	1.86	-	-
TAIWAN						
from TAIPEI(TPE) to MIAMI/FT. LAUDERDALE(MIA) (cont)					in KGS	NTD
SCR9905	8	-	1	107840.00	817	132.00
	8B	-	1	108840.00	817	132.00
	9	-	1	107840.00	817	132.00
from MILWAUKEE(MKE) to TAIPEI(TPE)					in LBS	USD
GEN	BULK	-	1	3.91	75	-
	BULK	-	100	2.98	191	-
	BULK	-	220	2.60	517	-
	BULK	-	660	2.05	999	-
	BULK	-	1100	1.86	-	-
from TAIPEI(TPE) to MILWAUKEE(MKE)					in KGS	NTD
GEN	BULK	-	1	426.40	34	-
	BULK	-	45	325.60	92	-
	BULK	-	100	302.40	233	-
	BULK	-	300	235.60	436	-
	BULK	-	500	205.60	-	-
from MINNEAPOLIS/ ST. PAUL(MSP) to TAIPEI(TPE)					in LBS	USD
GEN	BULK	-	1	3.86	75	-
	BULK	-	100	2.94	191	-
	BULK	-	220	2.57	517	-
	BULK	-	660	2.02	999	-
	BULK	-	1100	1.84	-	-
from TAIPEI(TPE) to MINNEAPOLIS/ ST. PAUL(MSP)					in KGS	NTD
GEN	BULK	-	1	423.60	34	-
	BULK	-	45	323.60	92	-
	BULK	-	100	300.00	233	-
	BULK	-	300	233.20	436	-
	BULK	-	500	203.60	-	-
from NASHVILLE(BNA) to TAIPEI(TPE)					in LBS	USD
GEN	BULK	-	1	4.01	75	-
	BULK	-	100	3.06	191	-
	BULK	-	220	2.67	517	-
	BULK	-	660	2.10	999	-
	BULK	-	1100	1.91	-	-
from TAIPEI(TPE) to NASHVILLE(BNA)					in KGS	NTD
GEN	BULK	-	1	431.20	34	-
	BULK	-	45	330.40	92	-
TAIWAN						
from SAN ANTONIO(SAT) to TAIPEI(TPE)					in LBS	USD
GEN	BULK	-	1	3.91	75	-
	BULK	-	100	2.98	191	-
	BULK	-	220	2.60	517	-
	BULK	-	660	2.05	999	-
	BULK	-	1100	1.86	-	-
from TAIPEI(TPE) to SAN ANTONIO(SAT)					in KGS	NTD
GEN	BULK	-	1	426.40	34	-
	BULK	-	45	325.60	92	-
	BULK	-	100	302.40	233	-
	BULK	-	300	235.60	436	-
	BULK	-	500	205.60	-	-
from SAN DIEGO(SAN) to TAIPEI(TPE)					in LBS	USD
GEN	BULK	-		3.65	75	-
	BULK	-	100	2.78	191	-
	BULK	-	220	2.43	517	-
	BULK	-	660	1.91	999	-
	BULK	-	1100	1.74	-	-
from TAIPEI(TPE) to SAN DIEGO(SAN)					in KGS	NTD
GEN	BULK	-	1	414.00	34	-
	BULK	-	45	313.60	92	-
	BULK	-	100	290.00	230	-
	BULK	-	300	223.20	433	-
	BULK	-	500	193.60	-	-
from SAN JUAN(SJU) to TAIPEI(TPE)					in LBS	USD
GEN	BULK	-	1	3.73	77	-
	BULK	-	100	2.93	194	-
	BULK	-	220	2.60	537	-
	BULK	-	660	2.12	1014	-
	BULK	-	1100	1.96	-	-
from TAIPEI(TPE) to SAN JUAN(SJU)					in KGS	NTD
GEN	BULK	-	1	473.20	35	-
	BULK	-	45	372.80	93	-
	BULK	-	100	349.20	242	-
	BULK	-	300	282.40	447	-
	BULK	-	500	252.80	-	-
from TAMPA(TPA) to TAIPEI(TPE)					in LBS	USD
GEN	BULK	-	1	4.13	75	-
	BULK	-	100	3.15	191	-

Figure 8.4. Air Tariff. *(continued)*

	ORIG/REV	PAGE
	1st	313
	CANCELS	PAGE
	Original	313
	EFFECTIVE DATE	
	April 15, 1986	
	CORR.	324

ASIA NORTH AMERICA EASTBOUND RATE AGREEMENT (ANERA)

RATE AGREEMENT NO. 202-010776

COMMON RATE TARIFF NO. FMC-16

FROM: PORTS IN KOREA   TO: PORTS AND POINTS IN THE UNITED STATES, PUERTO RICO AND U.S. VIRGIN ISLANDS

(AS SPECIFIED IN RULE 1)

(R) SECTION 1—COMMODITY RATES

EXCEPT AS OTHERWISE PROVIDED, RATES APPLY PER TON OF 1,000 KGS. (W) OR 1 CUBIC METRE (M), WHICHEVER PRODUCES THE GREATER REVENUE.

COMMODITY DESCRIPTION AND PACKAGING	RB	RATES IN US$				ITEM NO.
		WC	MLB	AG	PRVI	
ELECTRICAL AND ELECTRONIC GOODS AND COMPONENTS AND PARTS, N.O.S.	M	122.00	140.00	140.00	138.00	11300
	W	166.00	201.00	201.00	181.00	
	D20	1720.00	2910.00	2910.00	3660.00	
	D40	2450.00	3885.00	3885.00	5200.00	

130

FOR APPLICATION OF RATES AND FOR RATES ON CONTAINERS NOT SHOWN, SEE RULE 2 OF BOTH THIS TARIFF AND SECTION 1, FMC NO. 15.

FOR EXPLANATION OF ABBREVIATIONS AND REFERENCE MARKS SEE PAGES 3 THROUGH 5.

ITS (703) 284-7500   ADO/7123/at

AUTHOR'S NOTE ON ABBREVIATIONS:

AG = Atlantic and Gulf   D = Container   FMC = Federal Maritime Cmsn.
M = Measurement   MLB = Mini Land Bridge   NOS = Not Otherwise Specified
PRVI = Puerto Rico and Virgin Islands   W = Weight   WC = West Coast

Figure 8.5. Ocean Tariff.

131

York, there was no rate established. The exporter completed a form for the steamship line and obtained a new special rate. This rate was then available for all companies that shipped the same product, on the same route, with the same steamship line.

Note also that both air and ocean rates are usually quoted on a Weight/Measure, (W/M) basis. Boxes that are large with relation to their weight are charged according to the amount of space they occupy, while boxes that are heavy with relation to their size are charged according to their weight. By air, the formula is 162 cubic inches = 1 pound. If the rate is $2.00 per pound, but it takes 243 cubic inches of your product to weigh a pound, you will be charged $3.00 for each pound you ship ($^{243}/_{162} \times 2$). By sea, the formula is 40 cubic feet = 1 short ton.

Each air and steamship line has a *minimum* bill of lading, which means that a minimum charge is levied on very small shipments. The minimum weight is usually quite low in air tariffs (1 kilogram in Figure 8.4) but much higher in ocean tariffs.

About the only place you have flexibility in using shipping tariffs is with the weight categories. For example, if your air shipment weighs 290 pounds you may be able to save money by calling it 300 pounds and paying less per pound to send it.

SHIPPING TERMS

In the early days of international trade, exporters and importers grew tired of having to negotiate all the individual conditions of every transaction. To solve this problem, they developed and defined standard packages (or sets) of conditions. Once trading partners agreed on the definition of a term, such as c.i.f., they could sell and buy c.i.f. without discussing so many details.

Gradually, two similar sets of terms and their definitions were developed—the American Standard Foreign Trade Definitions and the International Commercial Terms, better known as INCOTERMS. Most international transactions now use INCOTERMS, which have been revised periodically to keep up with changes in trade procedures. Still, if you want to be sure there's no confusion, you should be very specific. Tell your foreign buyer that your quotation is c.i.f. his port, "according to INCOTERMS, 1990 revision."

The 1990 revision includes 13 terms, whose definitions specify essentially which party makes arrangements for shipping the goods, which party has title to them at each point in their journey, and which party is responsible for loss or damage at any point. The terms are in 4 groups, as shown in Figure 8.6.

As you move down the list, responsibilities and title to goods change hands progressively nearer the buyer. In an

Group E, Departure
    EXW   EX Works

Group F, Main Carriage Unpaid
    FCA   Free Carrier
    FAS   Free Alongside Ship
    FOB   Free On Board

Group C, Main Carriage Paid
    CFR   Cost and Freight
    CIF   Cost, Insurance and Freight
    CPT   Carriage Paid To (location)
    CIP   Carriage and Insurance Paid To (location)

Group D, Arrival
    DAF   Delivered At Frontier
    DES   Delivered Ex Ship
    DEQ   Delivered Ex Quay
    DDU   Delivered Duty Unpaid
    DDU   Delivered Duty Paid

Figure 8.6.   INCOTERMS, 1990 Revision.

Ex Works sale, the seller need only shove the goods out the door of his factory. In a Delivered Duty Paid sale, on the other extreme, the seller must actually enter the goods in the foreign country and deliver them to the buyer. Complete definitions of each term are in the publication, *Incoterms 1990,* available from the ICC Publishing Corporation at 1212 Avenue of the Americas, New York, NY 10036, telephone 212-206-1150.

The terms most often used when goods move by ocean are FAS, FOB, CFR, and CIF. They are sometimes written in capital letters and sometimes in lower case letters with periods. In an f.a.s. shipment, the seller must place the goods by the side of a ship, ready to be loaded, and pay all the costs to that point. Thus, they are free of encumbrances. With f.o.b., the seller must take care of any paperwork or expenses necessary to remove goods from his country and place them on an international carrier. Be careful of this term, though, because it is often used with other forms of transportation. If you buy f.o.b. from a handcrafts exporter in the Sahara desert, and you expect the goods to be placed on board a ship while he only expects to place them on board a camel outside his workshop, there will be quite a problem. With regard to air freight, the term f.o.b. means the goods must be placed in the custody of an air carrier at an airport. It does not mean they must actually be loaded on a plane.

CFR is the new name for C&F. It means the exporter is responsible for paying the freight bill. Ultimately, he will be repaid by the buyer. Once the goods are on the ship, however, the exporter is free of responsibility for subsequent loss or damage. With a c.i.f. shipment, the exporter must also buy insurance. Technically, however, he sells the insurance policy to the importer along with the goods. Thus, if you import beer c.i.f. and most of the bottles are broken, you will have to file a claim against insurance that was bought by the exporter. There may also be claims against that insurance by others whose cargo was damaged by the beer.

In U.S. trade by land, especially with Mexico, the d.a.f. term is used widely. For example, a shipment of bathroom fixtures from Guadalajara will be placed on the U.S. side of the international bridge in Laredo, Texas. The importer will take charge of them at that point, before they are cleared through Customs.

It is hard to tell you how to decide which shipping term to use. In the beginning, try to make it easy for yourself. Export with a Group F term and import with a Group C term. Later, when you are more sophisticated, you can choose terms that minimize your cost and risk and are acceptable to both parties. You may be dealing with a big shipper who can get lower freight rates, so let her arrange transportation. You may want to use a term that lets you select the insurance company to make sure it's a good one, in case you have to file a claim. Many countries, however, require that import (and sometimes export) shipments be insured with their national companies.

One former client of mine was buying lovely wool sweaters from a small firm in Ireland that had no experience exporting. The solution was to buy f.a.s. My client arranged, through her U.S. customs broker, for a shipping agent to take charge of the goods at the Irish port.

If you have a small export shipment to a major company in Europe, the sale may well be f.c.a. The buyer will be taking several small shipments to a specialized firm that can consolidate them into one container for ocean shipment. Many other examples could be given.

Even experienced exporters, though, hesitate to get involved in shipping beyond c.i.f. to developing countries. I was once asked to quote on an export shipment to be sent d.d.p. to an importer in David, Panama. Besides being responsible for Panamanian customs clearance and duty, I would have had to arrange and pay for inland freight in the buyer's country. While a multinational company might have agreed to that, I was willing to ship c.i.f. and not an inch beyond. As I write this paragraph, I am in a foreign country where an organization I am working with has had a new fax machine tied up in Customs for the past six months. If the exporter had shipped this machine d.d.p., and did not receive payment in advance, he would still be waiting for his money.

MARINE INSURANCE

In the early days of international trade it was common for cargo to be lost when vessels ran into trouble as with sand bars, storms at sea, or pirates. Shippers would demand compensation from the steamship companies, who often lacked the resources to make restitution in full.

Thus it was that ship's captains began sitting in Lloyds' coffee house in London, asking wealthy patrons to accept (for a small fee) the responsibility of repaying shippers when losses occurred. Finally a patron, whom others respected, would write at the bottom of a manifest the percent of the risk he would accept and the fee he would charge. He was the "lead underwriter." Other patrons, or "underwriters," would add their percentages of risk and their signatures until finally the entire value of the cargo had been "underwritten." From this small beginning, Lloyds of London and the gigantic industry of marine insurance were developed.

Nearly all international shipments are insured against loss and damage. A general cost guideline is 1 percent of the insured value, but this varies enormously with the type of goods, the mode of transportation, and other factors.

There are several types of limited coverage that major shippers use to save money on premiums, but most small-scale importers and exporters purchase "all risk" coverage. This covers nearly all risks. It does not cover loss or damage caused by war, strikes, riots, civil disobedience, or "inherent vice in the cargo." This means something in the cargo that destroys it, such as moth larvae in wool sweaters or deadly bacteria in shrimp. One can pay extra for "riders" or clauses that protect against these risks.

No standard cargo insurance covers late arrival or rejection of goods by buyers or government agencies. These are insurable risks, but the rates are high and many insurance companies refuse to insure.

It is vital that your marine insurance policy contain a "general average" clause. This means that, for example, if the ship is in a bad storm and some heavy cargo is jettisoned to save the rest, every shipper who was using that vessel is responsible for a portion of the value of the jettisoned cargo. Even though your cargo may be safe and sound, you cannot get it until the steamship line has been assured of payment for your share of the loss.

Also, insurance can be "port to port," "warehouse to warehouse," or some combination of the two forms. Warehouse-to-warehouse policies cover the goods from the time they leave the exporter's premises until they are in the importer's premises. They are becoming increasingly common.

What determines who must buy the insurance? The answer is the shipping terms. The definition of each INCOTERM says who is responsible for insuring the cargo.

Many problems can arise. Suppose, for example, that you are exporting, c.f.r., on Open Account, and the cargo is lost. The foreign importer is obligated to pay you, but may not do so until he collects from his insurance company. To speed up payment, you may get involved in helping your importer settle the claim. Or, suppose you are importing c.i.f. on a letter of credit and the cargo is lost. You will have to file a claim on the insurance company from which the *exporter* purchased coverage. This will be much easier if the exporter has used a sound, reliable company that has offices in the United States.

Whenever the other party to a transaction buys insurance to protect you, and you have doubts about the adequacy of coverage, you should consider purchasing "contingent insurance." This costs about half as much as regular insurance, and pays only if there is covered loss or damage and for some reason the primary insurer does not pay.

Small-scale importers and exporters usually buy insurance supplied by freight forwarders under their blanket policies, or directly from airlines, while medium-sized shippers buy through insurance brokers. Large importers and exporters have "open" policies that automatically cover all shipments of their normal merchandise in their normal trading areas. The importer or exporter simply reports each shipment to his insurance company.

It is customary to insure for the c.i.f. value of a shipment, plus 10 percent of c.i.f. This means, for example, that if your goods are worth $9,000, the shipping cost is $900, and the insurance cost is $100, you should insure for $1,100 ($9,000 + $900 + 100 × 1.1). The extra 10 percent is to repay you for time and trouble, lost profit, and perhaps lost customers because you did not fulfill your obligations.

A few years ago, a friend of mine, a successful businessman, traveled to China and bought $5,000 worth of hand-carved wooden furniture to begin an import business. He had it shipped to the United States, but did not tell the Chinese to insure it for c.i.f. plus 10 percent. It arrived with heavy damage, and only part of the loss was recovered.

You may trade for a lifetime and never have an insured loss. If you do have to file a claim, however, you will have to present the bill of lading, the insurance certificate, and a survey report with an invoice showing the amount of damage or loss. When a marine insurance company agrees that it has an obligation to pay, it usually makes payment from one to six months after a claim is filed.

BROKERS AND FORWARDERS

If you import a small shipment by air, that has a value of $1,250 or less and doesn't include textiles or apparel, you can probably clear it through Customs yourself. Just go to your airline's cargo office at the airport, fill out a simple form (an informal entry), pay the duty if any is charged, and take the merchandise. Some possible complications to this scenario will be discussed in Chapter 10.

If the shipment arrives by sea, however, or is worth more than $1,250, or contains textiles or apparel, you should probably use the services of a licensed U.S. customhouse broker. Their functions are to locate your goods, fill out an entry form (a formal entry), and arrange for a customs inspector to clear your goods. Normally, brokers will send you one bill for services and for duty if any is paid. Brokers have two weeks to pay duty to Customs, so they bill importers immediately and hope to be paid before they have to lay out cash of their own.

A brokerage fee for a routine clearance is about $85, but these fees are unregulated and vary considerably. If your product needs approval by other agencies, such as the U.S. Food and Drug Administration, the broker will make the necessary arrangements. The cost of routine FDA clearance includes cartage to the FDA's office at the port or airport, the FDA fee, cartage back to Customs, and a small extra broker's fee—usually $25 to $50 all together. If there are problems with documents, such as a missing or incomplete commercial invoice, the broker can usually resolve them. This, again, will cost you extra.

When your broker fills out customs forms (see Chapter 10 for details), he will classify each product in your shipment by its Harmonized System number and report its value. The Harmonized System, of classifying and coding merchandise in international trade, is explained in Chapter

10. Since the broker is your agent, you can be fined for any error that he might commit.

Also, in the process of clearing goods through Customs the duty that is paid is only an estimated duty. The inspectors at ports are very knowledgeable but are not product specialists. Customs has one year from the date of an entry for a product specialist to examine the paperwork and determine whether the correct duty was paid. If you paid too much, Customs will send you a refund (it happened once in the year 1493). If you paid too little, Customs will send you a notice and then a bill. If the product specialist wants to see a sample of the merchandise so as to determine its proper classification, Customs will send you a Redelivery Notice. Customs can also ask for redelivery of a sample to check the labeling on your product, and can do this as long as a year after your shipment has been entered.

Since importers usually receive their shipments before paying duty, Customs needs a way to be sure it can collect. Also there is a logical fear that an importer will bring in goods and pay too little duty, that within a year Customs will try to collect the remainder, and that the importer will have passed away, gone broke, or gone into hiding in some faraway country. To reduce this risk, rules stipulate that, with few exceptions, each shipment that requires a formal entry must be covered by a bond. A ruling in January, 1991, raised this bond to about three times the estimated value of the merchandise.

You can go to a bonding company yourself and purchase either a *single-entry bond* to cover just one shipment, or a *term bond* to cover all your shipments for a year. The charge will be a percentage of the value of your shipment(s), with a minimum charge of about $50. Bonding companies will protect themselves by checking your income and financial position. If you use a broker to clear your shipment, however, he will get the bond for you. This may cost you as much or more, but will be easier for you because bonding companies usually accept the word of a broker that an importer is honest and financially sound.

If there is a small problem with your entry, such as a missing document, the same bond will guarantee Customs that the document will be submitted within 120 days. You have only 60 days to submit a missing Form A, a document which will be explained in Chapter 9.

In most ports, there are many licensed customs brokers. You should select one who will tell you clearly and honestly what the fees are and which services they cover. I once spoke with an importer who had been using the same broker for several years and had never received an itemized bill; as you might have guessed, the broker was overcharging but was a good friend of the company's president.

If you have special requirements, such as rush shipments or highly perishable cargo, look for a brokerage firm that can guarantee the kind of service you need. I once had an urgent shipment of product samples land at Kennedy Airport on a Saturday with everything mixed up. The shipment was consigned to the wrong party, it contained quota goods and even a prohibited item, and *there were no documents at all.* My brokerage firm sent its number-one broker, a middle-aged lady about five feet tall with a voice like a Bengal tiger, and believe it or not the goods were out of customs and in Philadelphia by 6:00 P.M. on Sunday.

Once your goods are cleared through Customs you can pick them up, but an easier choice is to have the broker get them on a truck and delivered to your door. He or she will then be performing the function of a domestic freight forwarder. Some broker/forwarders have their own trucks for delivery, but more often they use the services of private trucking companies. In either case, you will be billed for forwarding, trucking, and perhaps insurance if the policy in force does not cover through to your warehouse.

I recently met an importer who was having small shipments sent to him from Kennedy Airport by UPS. He said the charge was about $5.00, compared with $140 by truck. The moral is: Examine *all* your options.

On the export side, air and ocean forwarders can help you by:

- Supplying costs needed to prepare c.i.f. quotations
- Booking space on vessels or aircraft
- Taking charge of cargo at the port or airport
- Arranging for packing if this is needed
- Preparing export documents
- Making sure the cargo is loaded on the vessel
- Collecting or assembling the documents and sending them to you or to your bank
- Tracking shipments that do not arrive as scheduled.

These are very valuable services. For example, if you receive a letter of credit that says you must ship by July 1, and your cargo reaches the port on time but cannot be loaded because you didn't book space on the only vessel available, your payment may no longer be assured.

Freight forwarders are paid by fees from their clients (usually exporters), plus commissions from the carriers they use. Fees are not regulated and vary considerably, but are usually about $65 for an air shipment and $150 for an ocean shipment. Commissions are around 5 percent but vary greatly, especially for ocean freight. It is illegal for forwarders to "kick back" any of their commissions to the shippers, but this is certainly done at times.

It *is* legal, however, for air forwarders to charge you, the shipper, whatever rate they care to set. For example, an airline could quote a price of $2,000 for a shipment and pay the forwarder 10 percent of that as a commission. The forwarder could charge you, the shipper, only $1,900, thus effectively giving you half the commission. You may come out better than if you dealt directly with the airline.

Foreign freight forwarders (and brokers as well) are listed in telephone directories, port handbooks, and some trade magazines. You will want to pick a forwarder who has offices near the ports or airports you use, who has experience with the kinds of cargo you will be shipping and with the destinations you will be shipping to, and who has friendly, competent personnel and good financial standing. This last criterion is especially important. If a forwarder should handle a shipment for you and you pay him for it, only to have the forwarder go out of business before paying the carrier, you will still be liable. This happened to me once, when I used a not-so-stable forwarder to air freight a friend's dog from Boston to Jakarta.

Also, it is worth checking directly with carriers from time to time to make sure your forwarder is giving you the lowest rates to which your cargo is entitled. All it takes is a phone call or two.

Many forwarders pick up freight at inland points of origin, and several can save you money through their roles as freight consolidators or nonvessel operating common carriers (NVOCCs). The moral, again, is to look at all your options.

9

Documents, Documents, Documents

Question: Why is smuggling so common? Answer: It has no rules, no taxes, and no documents. A single international shipment can use as many as 70 different documents. And documentation is a no-win matter; no one gets praised for having perfect documents, but international traders can have serious problems because of imperfect documents.

Fortunately many of the requisite documents, like those between airlines and the airports they fly into and out of, are never seen by the importer or the exporter. Also, most shipments are reasonably uncomplicated. If you send toothpicks from the United States to the United Kingdom, by air freight under Open Account, documents aren't much of a problem. On the other hand, if you want to ship repeating rifles from the United States to El Salvador, by sea freight on a letter of credit, you'd better be prepared for reams of paper.

Most international trade documents can be placed into four categories:

- Commercial documents
- Banking documents

- Transportation and insurance documents
- Government formalities documents.

In general, the purposes of all of them are to facilitate, control, and keep track of international cargo movements. We will discuss each of them in turn.

COMMERCIAL DOCUMENTS

The commercial documents we will discuss are as follows:

- Request for Quotation
- Quotation
- Pro Forma Invoice
- Terms and Conditions of Sale
- Purchase Order
- Order Acceptance or Confirmation
- Sales Contract
- Commercial Invoice

How The Process Begins

Buyers and sellers can exchange any number of phone calls, letters, cables, telexes, and telefax messages as the initial steps of an international transaction. This will often lead to the importer sending a *Request for Quotation,* for which some importers use special printed forms. The response will usually be a *Quotation,* for which most exporters use specialized forms. Figure 9.1 is an example of a quotation from OK International. Note that this example is more a price list than a quotation to a specific importer on named quantities of named items.

If an importer wants to know precisely what an order will cost her, usually to get an import permit or foreign

OK INTERNATIONAL LTD.

TLX: 22781 OKFRANK
CABLE: "OKFRANK" TAIPEI
TEL: (02) 3931857, 3938504

ALL LETTER PLEASE MAIL TO:
P.O. BOX 5-222 TAIPEI
TAIWAN, REP. OF CHINA

2FL., NO. 38, NINGPO W. ST.
TAIPEI, TAIWAN, R. O. C.
台 北 市 寧 波 西 街 38 號 2 樓

QUOTATION No. KQ-07/412

Messrs. TREICO

Date: July 23, 1935

Dear Sirs,

In compliance with your esteemed inquiry HAIR ORNAMENT
We are Pleased to quote you as follows:

Time of Shipment: 30 days after receipt of your L/C.

Terms of Payment: By irrevocable & confirmed L/C at sight in our favor.

Item No.	Unit Price/US Dollar FOB/DZ		Item No.	Unit Price/US Dollar FOB/DZ		Item No.	Unit Price/US Dollar FOB/DZ	
JUMBO-LACE			B-033	USD 1.25		N-007	USD 4.29	
A-1	USD1.39		B-050	0.89		N-014	10.01	
A-2	1.25		B-051	0.89		N-023	10.01	
A-3	1.00					N-024	10.01	
			BRACELET			N-025	5.00	
BROOCH			C-001	USD 2.07		N-026	4.29	
B-001	USD0.95		C-002	2.07		N-028	5.00	
B-002	0.95		C-003	2.07		N-033	3.57	
B-003	0.95		C-004	4.11		N-035	7.15	
B-004	0.95		C-005	0.71		N-036	5.00	
B-007	0.95		C-006	0.78		N-039	10.01	
B-008	0.95		C-007	3.57		N-040	5.72	
B-010	0.95		C-008	6.43		N-041	5.72	
B-015	0.71					N-042	7.86	
B-016	0.71		**EARRINGS**			N-044	7.15	
B-017	1.07		E-266	USD 1.96		N-045	3.21	
B-018	0.89		E-268	1.78		N-089	6.79	
B-019	0.89					N-090	5.72	
B-020	0.89		**HAIR-BAND**			N-091	5.72	
B-021	0.89		H-018A	USD 11.79		N-092	14.65	
B-022	0.71		H-019A	10.00		N-093	15.37	
B-023	0.71		H-020A	11.79		N-094	15.01	
B-024	0.89					N-095	14.65	
B-028	1.07		**NECK-LACE**			N-096	15.01	
B-029	1.78		N-002	USD 4.64				
B-031	1.43		N-003	7.15		**SUPER-ROLLER**		
B-032	1.25		N-006	5.36		S-001	USD 1.25	

Figure 9.1. Quotation.

147

exchange authorization and/or to open a letter of credit, she may go one step further and ask for a *Pro Forma Invoice.* This looks like a regular commercial invoice (Figure 9.4), except that it says "PRO FORMA" at the top. These words mean that the document in hand isn't the actual commercial invoice, but is almost exactly what the actual invoice will look like.

Sometimes quotations and pro forma invoices are accompanied by other documents known as *Standard Terms and Conditions of Sale.* These give important information— such as "All shipments are made f.o.b. McAllen, Texas"— that is not shown on quotations or pro-forma invoices. This information is somewhat analogous to the "fine print" when you open a bank account or receive a credit card.

If the importer is satisfied with the quotation and/or pro forma invoice, she may place an order. This can be a simple oral or written statement such as "We hereby order as per your pro forma invoice number 627." More often there are additional details, for example, "We hereby order 100 dozen Model R FILEMAST bicycle pumps, c.i.f. New York, to be shipped by ocean no later than January 1, 19XX, with payment by irrevocable letter of credit." An order can include other conditions such as documents that should be provided and even what should be said on the documents. Figure 9.2 is an example of an International Purchase Order.

The exporter should reply with a simple statement such as, "We accept your Purchase Order No. 291/91, dated May 2, 19XX." In international trade an order and an unconditional acceptance make a contract that theoretically can be enforced by either of the contracting parties. The next chapter includes some information about enforcement of contracts of sale.

In some cases, importers order informally, by telephone, although this system has been partly replaced by the telefax. The exporter then sends an *order confirmation,* (see Figure 9.3) which the importer signs and returns. This procedure creates a contract of sale.

TREICO
93 Willets Drive
Syosset, NY 11791
USA

BANK: Citibank N.A.
   Syosset, New York

TO: Exportadors Uribe
  77 Calle Inventada
  Rogelio, Panama

P.O. DATE: Jan. 8, 1986

P.O. NO.: 3/86

SHIP TO: TREICO
    93 Willets Drive
    Syosset, NY, USA

NO.	MODEL	DESCRIPTION	UNIT	TOTAL PRICE
10	S33	Cartons each containing 4 dozen Panama hats	$146.00	US$1,460.00
5	S29	Cartons each containing 4 dozen Panama hats	120.00	600.00
		TOTAL F.O.B. COLON, PANAMA		US$2,060.00
		Ocean Freight		421.15
		TOTAL C&F NEW YORK		US$2,481.15

MARKS: TREICO └ 3/86
     Syosset, NY

PAYMENT: SD/DP

SHIPMENT: By sea, C&F New York

INSURANCE: TREICO will cover

_____
PURCHASING DEPT.

Figure 9.2.   International Purchase Order.

(SELLER)
CORPORATION

TAIPEI, TAIWAN P.O.C

P. O. BOX   TAIPEI, TAIWAN
CABLE:
TELEX:
TEL:

Original for Seller

SALES CONFIRMATION

Date: Feb. 20, 19XX

Ref. No: SC-861013

Referring to   (BUYER)   LTD, U.S.A.

(Please indicate the above
  number in the covering L/C)

we confirm the following sale to you on the terms and conditions set forth hereunder and on the reverse hereof:

Item No.	Description	Quantity	Unit Price	Amount
			FOB TAIWAN NET	
	P.O. 239			
4505	5 LBS/PR WRIST/ANKLE 6PCS/CTN/0.56'/15KGS	576PCS	US$2.02	US$1,163.52
4502	2 LBS/PR WRIST/ANKLE 12PCS/CTN/0.57'/12.5KGS	456PCS	US$1.47	US$670.32
5016	16LBS DUMBBELL WTS. 4PCS/CTN/0.26'/24.5KGS	24PCS	US$7.10	US$170.40
	TOTAL........................	..1,056PCS vvvvvvvvv		US$2,004.24 vvvvvvvvvvvv
	SAY TOTAL IN U.S. DOLLARS TWO THOUSAND FOUR AND CENTS TWENTY FOUR ONLY.			

PAYMENT : By Irrevocable and Confirmed Letter of Credit available against drafts drawn at sight in favor of Seller or transferable

SHIPMENT : Mar. 17, 19XX

DESTINATION: NEW YORK

VALIDITY : 30 DAYS SUBJECT TO UPDATE

REMARKS :   IND. CO.

SHIPPING MARK

(BUYER)
NEW YORK
C/NO.
MADE IN TAIWAN
R.O.C.

SIDE MARK

STYLE NO:
Q'TY:
ORDER NO: 239
N.W.:
G.W.:
MEA'T:

Agreed and accepted by:

Buyer:

(SELLER)   CORPORATION

_____
(Buyer's signature)

_____
(Seller's signature)

Figure 9.3. Order Confirmation (Sales Confirmation). (Reprinted with permission of Jonquil International, Ltd.)

The Finishing Touches

With large shipments between non-affiliated companies, there are usually more formal contracts of sale. These can run to 30 or 40 pages. If you decide to buy or sell a shipload of copper, for example, I'd strongly suggest the services of a good attorney, expensive though they may be.

As an exporter, once you ship you will need to supply a *commercial invoice* that says how much the importer owes you (even if he has already paid), and for what. Each country has its own requirements for commercial invoices, which you can obtain from freight forwarders, consulates of the countries you are shipping to, or publications such as the Dun & Bradstreet *Exporters Encyclopedia* and *Shipper and Forwarder* magazine. For example, on c.i.f. shipments to many countries you are required to provide invoices that break out the prices of the goods, sales commissions, transportation costs, and so on.

Some countries have special forms for commercial invoices, which you can buy from their consulates or from UNZ & Company in Jersey City, NJ. The United States no longer requires a special form except for imports of steel products.

For shipments to the United States, the commercial invoice must show the following information:

- Port of entry of the merchandise
- Names of the seller and buyer, or shipper and receiver (Usually addresses are shown as well, and these are required for some kinds of products.)
- Invoice date
- Country from which the shipment is made
- A detailed description of the merchandise including the name and quality of each item, marks used in domestic trade in the country of origin, and marks and numbers on the export packing

- The quantity of each item (Some products are quantified by the number of pieces, others by weight, and others by volume, as specified in the Harmonized System.)
- The purchase price of each item, in the currency actually used for the transaction. (If the shipment is on consignment and there is no purchase price, the value must be shown.)
- Charges involved in moving the freight from f.o.b. vessel to where the U.S. Customs inspection takes place may be shown on an attachment to the invoice, which the customs broker can prepare.
- Any rebates or similar incentives the exporter will receive from his government for having made the exportation.

The invoice should be in English, or accompanied by an accurate translation. It should show any significant "assists" the importer gave the foreign producer, such as dies or manufacturing equipment.

A more detailed description of invoicing requirements is in the book, *Importing into the United States,* published by the U.S. Customs Service and available from the Superintendent of Documents. Figure 9.4 shows a computer-generated invoice for an actual export shipment from New York to Saudi Arabia. Note the statements made at the bottom.

BANKING DOCUMENTS

The processes of paying and getting paid require relatively few documents. Cash in Advance may be as simple as the importer sending the exporter a check or depositing it in his or her bank account. It is rarely more complicated than filling out a simple form to buy a bank draft or to order an airmail or cable transfer. Consignment, open account, and credit card transactions are equally uncomplicated.

CHEW INTERNATIONAL CORPORATION	**INVOICE** PAGE: 1
	ORDER NO.: A039608 DATE: 6/26/XX

| EXPORT DEPARTMENT
71 MURRY STREET, 9TH. FLOOR
NEW YORK, N.Y. 10007-2114, U.S.A.
TEL: (212) 619-4300, FAX: (212) 619-4273
TLX: 232715, 427413, 177799, 661570 | REFERENCE DATA:
  INVOICE NO.: A039608/01
  DATE: 26JUNXX
  YOUR REF.:
  ORDER DATE: 08MAYXX |

BUYER:
_____

ATTN: MR. _____
P.O. BOX _____
ALKHOBAR, SAUDI ARABIA
_____

CONSIGN TO: _____
_____
NOTIFY: _____
_____
ULTIMATE CONSIGNEE: _____

MARKS:
_____ /DAMMAM
  SAUDI ARABIA   A039608

TERMS:
  SALES: NET C&F DAMMAM
  DELIVERY: NET C&F DAMMAM
  PAYMENT: TELEX TRANSFER

SHIPMENT DATA:
  SHIP VIA: OCEAN FREIGHT
  ARRIVES AT: DAMMAM

  THIS IS A COMPLETE SHIPMENT

IT	DESCRIPTION	NO. OF UNITS	UN TP	UNIT PRICE	AMOUNT US DOLL.
1	6/10 Whole Kernel Corn	375	ctn	11.75	4,406.25
2	24/16 Oz. Whole Kernel Corn	375	ctn	8.25	3,093.75
3	24/16 Oz. Sliced Beets	350	ctn	9.50	3,325.00
	Above 3 Items—Super Fresh Brand: English/Arabic Labels with m/e date (shelf life—2 years)				
4	24/16 Oz. Kingsway Cut Wax Beans English/Arabic Labels with m/e date (shelf life—2 years)	215	ctn	9.30	1,999.50

NET C&F DAMMAM $12,824.50

THESE COMMODITIES LICENSED BY U.S. FOR ULTIMATE DESTINATION SAUDI ARABIA DIVERSION CONTRARY TO US LAW PROHIBITED.

WE CERTIFY THAT THIS PRODUCT DOES NOT CONTAIN PORK, ALCOHOL, GELATINE, SACCHARINE OR CYCLAMATE
          PER _____ , TRAFFIC MANAGER

BUYER INSURES

1-20° CONT.NO.IEAU-20845, SEAL.NO.10382
TOTAL CARTONS: 1315 CTNS
TOTAL GR.WT.: 45,728 LBS./20,742KILOS

CERTIFIED TRUE & CORRECT   _____
                    FOR CHEW INTERNATIONAL CORPORATION

Figure 9.4.   Commercial Invoice. (Reprinted with permission of Chew International Corporation.)

With payment by Bill of Exchange (Sight or Time Draft), the exporter must complete a form to instruct his bank to prepare the draft and send it to the importer's bank. The first time you do this, you should sit down with your banker and go over each of the options that are presented on the form. (See Figure 9.5.) There is a more complete example in Chapter 7.

A letter of credit sale is somewhat more complex than other forms of international payment. There are at least four documents involved, as follows:

- Application for letter of credit
- Letter of Credit
- Advice of Letter of Credit
- Drafts (drawn on a bank for payment).

$4,520.00   Date February 4, 1991   No. BE682/91

90 DAYS AFTER SIGHT

Pay To The Order Of (NAME OF U.S. EXPORTER'S BANK)

Four Thousand Five Hundred Twenty U.S. Dollars

Value received and charge same to the account of

To Importaciones El Greco

Barcelona, Spain

Weiss Export Agency

(signature)

Figure 9.5.   Bill of Exchange.

The application for a letter of credit must be completed by the importer and given to the opening bank. It is fairly complicated, and should definitely be completed only with help of your banker. Major international banks now accept applications from established customers by computer. The importer simply fills in details on a form that is in his data processing system and transmits it to his bank by modem.

The actual letter of credit (LC) is transmitted to the opening bank's branch or correspondent in the exporter's country. It tells the exporter exactly which functions to perform, and which documents to provide, in order to get paid. (See Figure 9.6.) There is a more complete example in Chapter 7.

The advice of a letter of credit is a simple form that is sent to the exporter by a bank in his country. It says that a credit has been opened in his favor, and it is followed by the actual letter of credit. It gives the exporting firm assurance that it can begin preparing the goods for shipment.

Finally, the exporter must present drafts for collection to the paying or negotiating bank. For example, if you receive an LC that is payable upon presentation of documentary evidence that you have shipped as instructed, you can go directly from the port to the bank, armed with a draft for collection and the required documents. More likely, you will ask your freight forwarder to do this for you. To save time, the forwarder will probably send the draft and other documents to the bank by courier.

Still other documents will be involved in more complicated LC transactions, for example, when partial shipments are allowed or a credit is transferred or assigned from one beneficiary to another. There are also special documents for the seller to request, and the buyer to grant, amendments to LCs.

(Export LC, Confirmed)

(NAME AND ADDRESS
OF EXPORTER'S BANK)

Their Ref. No. 68392   Our Advice LC R23259   Date 2/5/1991

TO: City Directory Company
      650 East 11th Street
      New York, New York

104-686943

Instructions
Received from: Neopolitan Bank, Florence, Italy

For Account of: Cassata Importers, Florence, Italy

Gentlemen:

Our correspondent, named above, has instructed us to advise you that they have opened their irrevocable credit in your favor, as designated above, for a sum or sums not to exceed the following:

FIFTEEN THOUSAND DOLLARS UNITED STATES CURRENCY ($15,000 USC)

Available by your draft(s):

For FULL invoice value of merchandise, to be described in your invoice as follows:

GUIDEBOOKS TO MAJOR NORTH AMERICAN CITIES

Your draft(s) must be accompanied by the following:
1. Your commercial invoice, original and 3 copies
2. Your ocean bill of lading issued to order, endorsed in blank

evidencing shipment of the goods from New York to Florence.

Partial shipments are not permitted. Insurance is to be obtained by the buyers. We confirm this credit and affirm all drafts presented against it at (bank's address) by (date) will be honored.

This credit is subject to the Uniform   Yours truly,
Customs and Practice for Documentary
Credits as described in International
Chamber of Commerce Publication No. 400.   Authorized Signature

Figure 9.6   Letter of Credit.

TRANSPORTATION DOCUMENTS

The old expression, "goods move on paper," isn't really true. Goods don't move on paper, but neither do they move without it. The transportation documents that will be mentioned in this section include:

- Packing List
- Delivery Instructions to Domestic Carrier
- Inland Bill of Lading
- Dock Receipt
- Insurance Request, Insurance Certificate
- Shipper's Letter of Instructions
- Ocean Bill of Lading or Airwaybill
- Booking Request
- Arrival Notice
- Carrier's Certificate and Release Order
- Delivery Order and Freight Release.

The purpose of most of these documents is to keep track of merchandise as it passes from one hand to another and to make sure it isn't delivered to someone who is not supposed to receive it. If a shipper delivers goods to a trucking company, the shipper gets a receipt to show they have been delivered (the inland bill of lading). The truck driver needs proof of delivery when the goods are delivered to the dock (a dock receipt), or any other location. If a shipment disappears, there should be a trail of documents that will tell investigators who had custody of it at the time it was lost.

There is another important aspect to this trail of paper. No one wants to be held accountable for damage to merchandise that was caused by someone else. Therefore, each party who receives goods is supposed to make a visual inspection of the boxes. If a steamship company receives a box with no apparent loss or damage, it will simply accept it and issue a bill of lading (or sign the bill of lading previously prepared by the freight forwarder). If the box is wet or badly dented, however, the steamship company will note this as an exception on the bill of lading (B/L). The document will then be known as a *foul* bill of lading. Letters of credit often stipulate that an exporter must present to the bank a *clean* bill of lading in order to be paid for a shipment. If a box is damaged before being loaded on the ship, and a foul B/L is issued, the exporter's payment will be held up until the situation is resolved. (You may remember reading or hearing of a California firm whose business included shipping human heads for research purposes. This illegal trade was discovered during a routine visual inspection by a transportation company.)

The *packing list* is a simple document that shows how many boxes there are in a shipment, how to identify each, and what is in each. If a box is missing, one can determine from the packing list which one it is and what it contains. Or, if you should need to find something specific in a shipment, the packing list should tell you which box it is in. The simple packing list in Figure 9.7 is from the book, *A Basic Guide to Exporting,* prepared by the U.S. Department of Commerce and available from the Superintendent of Documents. Note that there are five cases of the same goods, numbered from one to five.

As an exporter, you are likely to be shipping goods by truck to ports and airports. You must provide delivery instructions to the domestic carrier. The carrier, in turn, will provide you with a signed inland bill of lading. This document shows that the carrier has received the goods and to whom they are to be delivered. The fine print on the back makes this bill of lading also a contract of carriage.

When your trucking company delivers goods to an ocean terminal, it will obtain a *dock receipt.* This is the domestic carrier's proof of when and where it has made

PACKING LIST

........................DEC. 15........................19. XX
Place and Date of Shipment

To   X Y Z COMPANY
     LONDON ENGLAND

Gentlemen:

Under your Order No...123...the material listed below

was shipped 12/15/XX via   TRUCK AND VESSEL
To   LONDON

Shipment consists of:	Marks
.....5.....Cases..............Packages	X Y Z CO.
..........Crates..............Cartons	LONDON ENGLAND
..........Bbls..............Drums	MADE IN USA
..........Reels................................	#1/5

*LEGAL WEIGHT IS WEIGHT OF ARTICLE PLUS PAPER, BOX, BOTTLE, ETC., CONTAINING THE ARTICLE AS USUALLY CARRIED IN STOCK.

PACKAGE NUMBER	WEIGHTS IN LBS. or KILOS			DIMENSIONS			QUANTITY	CLEARLY STATE CONTENTS OF EACH PACKAGE
	GROSS WEIGHT EACH	*LEGAL WEIGHT EACH	NET WEIGHT EACH	HEIGHT	WIDTH	LENGTH		
1/5	300		250	25	25	25		SPARK PLUGS (AUTO PARTS)

Figure 9.7.   Packing List. (Reprinted with permission of U.S. Foreign Commercial Service, U.S. Department of Commerce.)

delivery. If the exporter is responsible for insuring the shipment, he or she will fill out an insurance request and obtain an insurance certificate. If you export c.i.f. under a letter of credit, the insurance certificate will have to be included in the package of documents you present to the bank for payment.

Assuming the exporter uses the services of an international freight forwarder, he must tell the forwarder which goods she should find, where and when she should find them, and what she should do with the goods and with the documents. This information is communicated by means of a *shipper's letter of instructions*. Figure 9.8, from an export information manual published in Texas, is such a letter of instructions. It tells the forwarder to ship to La Paz, Bolivia, to prepay the freight, to insure the shipment, and to present the documents to the bank. Note that the shipment is consigned to a bank in Bolivia and is probably being sent with a "to order" bill of lading.

The ocean bill of lading, or airwaybill, serves as a receipt for the goods, a contract of carriage, and a temporary title document. You may run into various types of B/Ls including "short form" and "long form," "received for shipment" and "on board," and "straight" and "to order." For example, if you ship goods by sea f.o.b. vessel, with payment by sight draft, you will probably use a long form, on board, to order, ocean bill of lading. Complicated sounding, it can be, but only until you have made your first few shipments.

Figure 9.9 is an example of a short form, intermodal bill of lading. The goods are being sent by two modes of transportation, *air* from Dallas to Miami and sea from Miami to La Paz, Bolivia. The B/L, issued by a freight forwarder, is called a forwarder's bill of lading. It would not be accepted for payment if the importer's letter of credit specified an on board ocean bill of lading.

If you and your freight forwarder are both doing your jobs, the forwarder will send a *booking request* to the

EXPORT SHIPPING INSTRUCTIONS

DATE __FEB. 9, 19XX__

Shipper's Ref. No. __78-456__

Ship in name of __ABC MANUFACTURING COMPANY, ANY STREET, DALLAS, TEXAS__

Consign to __BANCO DE AMERICA, APTDO. 666, LA PAZ, BOLIVIA__

Notify __XYZ DISTRIBUTING COMPANY, APTDO. 792, LA PAZ, BOLIVIA__

Port of Discharge __LA PAZ__   Final Destination __LA PAZ__

MARKS AND NUMBERS	NO. OF PKGS.	DESCRIPTION OF COMMODITIES	VALUE	GROSS WEIGHT (POUNDS)	MEASURE-MENT
XYZ COMPANY LA PAZ P.O. 78-456 MADE IN U.S.A. CTN. #1	1 CTN.	CONTAINING: OIL WELL DRILLING PARTS Partes para uso en la industria petrolera. 6 #2489 O RINGS @ 2.89 10 #6723 GASKETS @ 1.59 4 #8932 SEALS @ 8.79 18 #8056 BUSHINGS @ 9.30 1 #5741 SHIM TOTAL F.O.B. DALLAS	$ 17.34 15.90 35.16 167.40 12.68 $250.04		83 LBS.

Letter of Credit Expires _____

Value for Customs Clearance _____

Inland Freight to be Charged to _____

Port Charges to be Charged to _____

Air/Ocean Freight: Prepaid or Collect? __PREPAID__

Insurance Requirements __INSURE SHIPMENT__

Send Documents to __BANK__

Bank Documents Through __BANCO DE AMERICA__

License No. _____

Export Carrier _____

Point of Origin __DALLAS, TEXAS__

Name of Supplier _____

Inland Routing _____

Car No./Truck Line _____

OTHER INSTRUCTIONS

Consular Declaration or Other.

Figure 9.8. Shipper's Letter of Instructions.

A. FREIGHT FORWARDER, INC. DALLAS, TEXAS	SHORT-FORM INTERMODAL BILL OF LADING NOT NEGOTIABLE UNLESS CONSIGNED "TO ORDER"

SHIPPER / EXPORTER	DOCUMENT NO
ABC MANUFACTURING COMPANY ANY STREET DALLAS, TEXAS	EXPORT REFERENCES D-74896 P.O. NO. 78-456

CONSIGNEE	FORWARDING AGENT NAME AND ADDRESS - REFERENCES
BANCO DE AMERICA APARTADO 666 LA PAZ, BOLIVIA	A. FREIGHT FORWARDER, INC. DALLAS, TEXAS GOODS ACCEPTED FOR CARRIAGE AT DALLAS/FORT WORTH, TEXAS

NOTIFY PARTY	DOMESTIC ROUTING / EXPORT INSTRUCTIONS
XYZ DISTRIBUTING COMPANY APARTADO 792 LA PAZ, BOLIVIA	ALSO NOTIFY: HERMANOS SOLARES APARTADO 456 LA PAZ BOLIVIA

EXPORT CARRIER (VESSEL) A.N.Y. AIRLINES	PORT OF LOADING MIAMI	GOODS ENGAGED FOR DELIVERY AT
PORT OF DISCHARGE LA PAZ, BOLIVIA	FOR TRANSSHIPMENT TO	

PARTICULARS FURNISHED BY SHIPPER					
MARKS AND NUMBERS	NO. OF PKGS.	DESCRIPTION OF PACKAGES AND GOODS		GROSS WEIGHT	MEASUREMENT
XYZ COMPANY LA PAZ P.O. 78-456 MADE IN U.S.A. CTN. #1	1 CTN.	CONTAINING: OIL WELL DRILLING PARTS Partes para uso en la industria petrolera.		83 LBS.	
		6 #2489 O RINGS -Anillos @ 2.89		$ 17.34	
		10 #6723 GASKETS -Empaques @ 1.59		15.90	
		4 #8932 SEALS -Sellos @ 8.79		35.16	
		18 #8056 BUSHINGS -Bujes @ 9.30		167.40	
		1 #5741 SHIM -Planchas		12.68	
		TOTAL F.O.B. DALLAS, TEXAS		$ 250.04	
		(*) TO BE COMPLETED ONLY WHEN GOODS ACCEPTED ON THROUGH TRANSPORTATION BASIS			

FREIGHT/CHARGES	PREPAID	COLLECT	Received by_____ for shipment by ocean vessel, between port of loading and port of discharge, and from place of acceptance and/or oncarriage to place of delivery as indicated above, the goods as specified above in apparent good order and condition unless otherwise stated. The goods to be delivered at the above mentioned port of discharge or place of delivery, whichever applies, subject to terms contained on the reverse side hereof, to which the shipper agrees by accepting this Bill of Lading. In witness whereof three (3) original Bills of Lading have been signed, if not otherwise stated above, one of which being accomplished the other(s) to be void.
INLAND FREIGHT (DALLAS/MIAMI)	XXX.XX		
OCEAN FREIGHT (MIAMI/LA PAZ)	XXX.XX		
			A. FREIGHT FORWARDER, INC.
TOTAL	XXX.XX		MO. DAY YEAR B/L NO.

Figure 9.9.   Intermodal Bill of Lading.

chosen carrier as soon as you give him the information he needs to do so. Then when the goods reach their country of destination, the air or steamship line will send an *arrival notice* to the importer or his customs broker. Airlines usually phone in addition to mailing the notice. Then the carrier will provide Customs with a carrier's certificate and release order, the consignee will give his broker or the carrier a release order, and the carrier will provide the consignee with a freight release. All this may sound complicated on paper but once you begin using the forms, it really isn't.

GOVERNMENT CONTROL DOCUMENTS

The United States and foreign governments all want to know which goods enter and leave their countries. They need information, which is provided by documents, both for statistical purposes and to facilitate control. A country can't limit imports of certain goods, or restrict exports to certain countries, unless it knows what is moving in and out. In many developing countries, import and export documents serve to maintain employment in the bureaucracy and preserve the power of bureaucrats, including in many cases the power to extract bribes or "grease payments" from importers and exporters.

The government control documents we will mention in this section include:

- Import License, Foreign Exchange Authorization
- Export License Application, Validated License
- Certificate of Origin
- Inspection Report
- Commercial, Special, and Consular Invoices
- Shipper's Export Declaration
- Customs Entries.

The United States does not use import licenses (except for a few commodities) or foreign exchange authorizations. In many countries, however, importers have to present pro forma invoices to their government authorities to get permission to import goods and/or to pay for them in hard currency. Many developing countries play tricks with exporters' foreign exchange earnings such as giving them only a small percentage in hard currency and giving them the rest in local currency, at artificially set exchange rates. This subject is too complicated to go into here, but these systems affect the prices that U.S. importers must pay.

U.S. exporters have to be sure they don't ship to importers who need licenses or authorizations before these are actually in hand, unless payment is assured whether or not the importer gets his authorizations. Sometimes importers will instruct their vendors to ship, before the licenses are in hand, assuming they can *buy* the required documents from friends in high places. If you get paid up front, and have no moral qualms about this kind of arrangement, there is nothing wrong with making the shipment.

Many foreign countries require all their exporters to be licensed and/or to apply for a license to make each shipment. That way they can control what leaves the country and make sure that at least most of the foreign exchange comes into the country.

In Ecuador in early 1990, a large quantity of eucalyptus logs was stopped just before being loaded on a ship. Although it was clearly illegal to export this product from Ecuador, the exporter claimed he had the necessary permits from the country's Central Bank. I never learned whether any heads rolled, but did hear that the logs stayed in Ecuador and were then sold cheaply to local sawmills.

Like many foreign countries, the United States requires that all significant outgoing shipments be accompanied by export licenses. Unlike many countries, however, U.S. exporters can give themselves licenses to ship most goods to most countries. This is explained in Chapter 10 in the section on regulations for exporters.

In the instances when a validated license is required, the U.S. exporter must complete an export license application. This is obtained from and sent to the U.S. Department of Commerce. If your shipment requires a validated license, *do not try to send it* until and unless this requirement is met. (See Chapter 10 for more information about export licensing in the United States.)

Every national government wants to know the country of origin of imported goods, and often an exporter must provide this information by means of a formal document called a *certificate of origin.* Its purpose is to make it harder for importers to falsify the country of origin in order to pay lower duties or to bring merchandise from prohibited countries. Since there are U.S. import quotas on textiles and apparel items from many countries, but not from all countries, importers are sometimes tempted to transship in third countries and use false certificates of origin. Customs inspectors are generally pretty sharp, however, and those who try to deceive them often get caught.

A U.S. exporter who needs a certificate of origin can usually obtain it from the nearest large chamber of commerce by sending three copies of his commercial invoice, a letter stating that the goods are of U.S. origin, and a check (usually around $20) for the chamber's fee. The chamber will certify on the invoice that the goods are of U.S. origin, and the certified invoice then becomes a certificate of origin. Chambers of commerce vary in their policies toward giving certificates of origin, but most accept the declarations of exporters that their products are of U.S. origin, at least until something happens to show that a particular exporter is dishonest. Chambers usually provide better service and lower fees to companies who are members, but most will issue certificates of origin to nonmembers as well.

U.S. import shipments must be accompanied by certificates of origin if they are intended to be duty-free under the preferential arrangements that are in force with Israel, Canada, Mexico, most developing countries in general, and most Caribbean countries in particular. For imports from developing and from Caribbean nations, the form used is a Form A, Certificate of Origin. This is a General Agreement on Tariffs and Trade (GATT) form that is theoretically not available in the United States. Your foreign exporter must provide it.

Figure 9.10 is a sample of a Form A. The important part is at the bottom right, where the exporter declares in which country the merchandise was produced.

Country of origin declarations are complicated by the fact that relatively few goods are produced entirely in one country. A shirt can be made with Egyptian cotton, spun and woven in England, cut in the United States, and sewn and finished in the Dominican Republic. What is the country of origin? For Generalized System of Preferences (GSP) and Caribbean Basin Initiative (CBI) shipments, the country of origin is generally that country from which the product is shipped to the United States, provided that at least 35 percent of the value of the product was added in that country (or sometimes in a combination of eligible countries). Under CBI rules, up to 15 percent of the 35 percent can be American-made materials or components.

Suppose, for example, that the Egyptian cotton that goes into a shirt is valued at $0.40. When the finished cloth reaches the United States for cutting, the value has increased to $1.60. After the cloth is cut into parts of a shirt, and delivered to the Dominican Republic, the value has reached $2.40. The f.o.b. country of origin value of the finished shirt is $3.60. That makes the value added in the Dominican Republic $3.60 minus $2.40/3.60, or about 33 percent. By including the value of the processing in the United States, the 35 percent rule is satisfied, and

ORIGINAL

1. Goods consigned from (exporter's business name, address, country)	Reference No. 393557
(SELLER) CO., LTD., 5-8/F., KWUN TONG, KOWLOON, HONG KONG.	GENERALISED SYSTEM OF PREFERENCES CERTIFICATE OF ORIGIN (Combined declaration and certificate) FORM A
2. Goods consigned to (consignee's name, address, country) (BUYER) NEW YORK 10475, U.S.A.	Issued in HONG KONG (country) See notes overleaf
3. Means of transport and route (as far as known) "SHIPPED AS PER S.S. 'PRES. WASHINGTON' SAILING ON OR ABOUT 20 JULY 1986, FROM HONG KONG TO NEW YORK, NEW YORK, USA."	4. For official use

5. Item number	6. Marks and numbers of packages	7. Number and kind of packages, description of goods	8. Origin criterion (see notes overleaf)	9. Gross weight or other quantity	10. Number and date of invoices
21-1213	O. K. NEW YORK P.O. 29288 MODEL : BC-3-115 C/NO. 1-12 MADE IN HONG KONG	TWELVE (12) CARTONS BATTERY CHARGER	'Y' 45.79%	SIX HUNDRED (600) PIECES	E86-736/S 17 JULY 1986
		I DECLARE THAT THE COST OF DOMESTIC MATERIALS PLUS THE DIRECT COST OF PROCESSING IN HONG KONG EQUALS TO 45.79% OF THE EX-FACTORY PRICE OF THE ARTICLE.			

11. Certification It is hereby certified, on the basis of control carried out, that the declaration by the exporter is correct.	12. Declaration by the exporter The undersigned hereby declares that the above details and statements are correct; that all the goods were
COUNTERSIGNED FOR DIRECTOR OF TRADE HONG KONG 21 JUL 1986	produced in HONG KONG (country) and that they comply with the origin requirements specified for those goods in the generalised system of preferences for goods exported to
	U. S. A. (SELLER) Company Limited (importing country)
Place and date, signature and stamp of certifying authority	HONG KONG 17 JULY 1986 Place and date, signature of authorised signatory Authorized Signature

Figure 9.10. Form A Certificate of Origin.

the shirt can be considered a product of the Dominican Republic.

There are many cases in which governments or importers (and sometimes exporters as well) demand *inspection reports.* Some developing countries insist on inspection of outgoing shipments to make sure their exporters are not sending illegal or low quality merchandise. Also, some developing countries want inspection of imported goods to make sure the importers are declaring the goods they actually bring in and are not falsifying the prices paid or other costs. Finally, some importers want goods to be inspected by independent organizations as a condition for payment to be made to the exporter.

There are three major inspection companies in the world—SGS, from Switzerland, SSI, from Great Britain, and Bureau Veritas, from France. In some cases, inspections are performed by small independent firms or by government agencies, such as the U.S. Department of Agriculture and the Food and Drug Administration.

Your commercial invoice, discussed previously, is a government control as well as a commercial document. Importing country authorities use it to see types and quantities of goods, countries of origin, and values.

As discussed previously, some countries have special forms for commercial invoices or special requirements as to the information that must be provided on these documents. Both exporters and importers should take steps to ensure that their invoices contain all the required data.

There are a few countries that still require documents known as *consular invoices.* This is a special form that must be "legalized" by a consulate of the country you are shipping to. It is theoretically a device to prevent prohibited or over- (or under-) priced goods from being shipped to a country, but its main function is probably to give some countries' consulates a bit of extra income.

FORM 7525-V-ALT (Intermodal) (3-18-86)

U.S. DEPARTMENT OF COMMERCE — BUREAU OF THE CENSUS — INTERNATIONAL TRADE ADMINISTRATION

SHIPPER'S EXPORT DECLARATION

CONFIDENTIAL — For use solely for official purposes authorized by the Secretary of Commerce (13 U.S.C. 301(g)).

OMB No. 0607-0152

DO NOT USE THIS AREA

2. EXPORTER (Principal or seller–licensee and address including ZIP Code)

ZIP CODE

3. CONSIGNED TO

4. NOTIFY PARTY/INTERMEDIATE CONSIGNEE (Name and address)

5. DOCUMENT NUMBER

5a. B/L OR AWB NUMBER

6. EXPORT REFERENCES

7. FORWARDING AGENT (Name and address — references)

8. POINT (STATE) OF ORIGIN OR FTZ NUMBER

9. DOMESTIC ROUTING/EXPORT INSTRUCTIONS

AUTHENTICATION (When required)

29. THE UNDERSIGNED HEREBY AUTHORIZES

TO ACT AS FORWARDING AGENT FOR EXPORT CONTROL AND CUSTOMS PURPOSES.

EXPORTER (BY DULY AUTHORIZED OFFICER OR EMPLOYEE)

30. METHOD OF TRANSPORTATION (Mark one)
☐ Vessel ☐ Other — Specify
☐ Air

31. ULTIMATE CONSIGNEE (Give name and address if this party is not shown in item 3.)

32. DATE OF EXPORTATION (Not required for vessel shipment)

33. COUNTRY OF ULTIMATE DESTINATION

34. EXPORTER EIN NUMBER

35. PARTIES TO TRANSACTION
☐ Related ☐ Non-related

Export shipments are subject to inspection by U.S. Customs Service and/or the Office of Export Enforcement.

12. PRE-CARRIAGE BY

13. PLACE OF RECEIPT BY PRE-CARRIER

14. EXPORTING CARRIER

15. PORT OF LOADING/EXPORT

16. FOREIGN PORT OF UNLOADING (Vessel and air only)

17. PLACE OF DELIVERY BY ON-CARRIER

11. TYPE OF MOVE

11a. CONTAINERIZED (Vessel only)
☐ Yes ☐ No

MARKS AND NUMBERS (18)

NUMBER OF PACKAGES (19)

DESCRIPTION OF COMMODITIES in Schedule B detail (20)

GROSS WEIGHT (Pounds) (21)

MEASUREMENT (22)

D OR F (23)

27. VALIDATED LICENSE NO./GENERAL LICENSE SYMBOL

28. ECCN (When required)

Value — Selling price or cost if not sold (U.S. dollars, omit cents)

Quantity — Schedule B unit(s) (Nearest whole unit)

24. SCHEDULE B NO.

25. QUANTITY

26. VALUE

36. I certify that all statements made and all information contained herein are true and correct and that I have read and understand the instructions for preparation of this document, set forth in the "Correct Way to Fill Out the Shipper's Export Declaration," I understand that civil and criminal penalties, including forfeiture and sale, may be imposed for making false or fraudulent statements herein, failing to provide the requested information, or for violation of U.S. laws on exportation (13 U.S.C. Sec. 305; 22 U.S.C. Sec. 401; 18 U.S.C. Sec. 1001; and 50 U.S.C. App. 2410).

(Signature)

(Title)

(Date)

This form must be privately printed. Sample copies may be obtained from the Bureau of the Census, Washington, D.C. 20233, and local Customs District Directors. The "Correct Way to Fill Out the Shipper's Export Declaration" is available from the Bureau of the Census, Washington, D.C. 20233.

Figure 9.11. Shipper's Export Declaration.

Each export shipment from the United States worth over $2,500 ($500 for mail shipments, but this should be increased soon), whether or not it requires a validated export license, must be accompanied by a Shipper's Export Declaration. An exception was made early in 1991 for shipments to Canada that are to *remain* in that country. A Shipper's Export Declaration is a document on which exporters report their shipments to the federal government, both for statistical purposes and to help in enforcement of export control regulations. There are three versions of this form—a 7525-V for most shipments, a 7525-V-Alternate for intermodal shipments, and a 7513 for in-transit goods. They can be purchased from the Superintendent of Documents, from UNZ & Co., in Jersey City, New Jersey, or from a good commercial stationer.

Figure 9.11 is a blank form 7525-V-Alternate. Note, at the bottom of this document, the statement to the effect that both civil and criminal penalties can be imposed for making fraudulent statements, omitting requested information, or violating U.S. laws on exportation.

Finally, there is a customs entry, which you or your broker must file with customs authorities. There are many types of customs forms; however, the most important for you will probably be the Consumption Entry, the Immediate Delivery Entry, and the Entry Summary. These will be discussed in Chapter 11.

10

Regulations You Must Know About

International trade is among the most regulated of economic activities. Every shipment is subject to multinational, regional, national (both exporting country and importing country), and state and local regulations. Some of these have been mentioned earlier in this book.

The focus of this chapter is on regulations in the United States that affect the way small-scale importers and exporters do business. We'll look first at U.S. Customs, then at other federal agencies that deal with imports, then at state and local regulations, and finally at a few laws that concern exporters from the United States.

UNITED STATES CUSTOMS

The U.S. Customs Service is a powerful component of the Department of the Treasury. It is headquartered in Washington, DC, and has offices throughout the United States and in several foreign countries. Its main task is to enforce the laws of the United States at the country's borders with respect to nearly everything entering or leaving—except

171

living human beings; the Immigration and Naturalization Service (INS) takes care of them.

Customs is responsible for enforcing laws with regard to both incoming and outgoing cargo. It can inspect part or all of any shipment, and is normally not held liable for damage to products that might occur in the inspection process. It works closely with other U.S. government agencies and with the customs departments in foreign countries.

Your First Contact

You should contact Customs before attempting to import a product. There are nearly 50 district offices in the country, which means you can find one in every major air, sea, lake, river, and land port, such as Dallas/Fort Worth (air), New York (sea), Duluth, Minnesota (lake), St. Louis (river), and El Paso (land). Call telephone information in your nearest major port for a telephone number.

For simple questions, you might get by with a recorded message. Dial Customs in Washington, DC at (202) 566-8195. Then press 118 for Frequently Asked Questions, 324 for Information for Importers, or 325 for Frequently Requested Phone Numbers.

Each Customs District employs several kinds of personnel including inspectors, law enforcement specialists, and those of greatest concern to you in the beginning—Classification and Value (C&V) officers. These are the people who determine what a product is, in Customs terms, and therefore what duty is to be charged. For example, there is no special category for coulottes. A coulotte can be classified as ladies' pants, or as a split skirt, depending on very small differences. There is, however, a significant difference in the amount of duty on the two items. C&V people are concerned also with the values assigned to imported goods. Should you be tempted to ask your foreign supplier to put an artificially low value on the documents, looking to save money on duties, be aware that Customs officers know values quite well and that cheaters often get caught.

When you get through by telephone to Customs, ask to speak with a C&V specialist who handles the kind of product that you plan to import. Make sure to get the person's name and direct phone number in case you have to call again. Then describe your product and ask the following questions:

- What is the Harmonized System (HS) number?
- What is the rate of duty from your supplying country?
- How should the product be marked and labeled?
- Are there any other federal agencies that regulate imports of the product, and if so, how can you ascertain their regulations?
- Is there any other information the Customs officer can give you?

You should not ask the Customs official for commercial information such as names of importers or exporters. This is considered confidential.

The Harmonized System

On January 1, 1989, the United States adopted a new system of classifying and coding products in international trade—the Harmonized System. This new system is very logical; it is being adopted by most of the world's nations; and it replaced separate coding and classification systems that were in use for exports and imports in the United States. It greatly facilitates comparing import and export statistics from major countries. The categories can be quite fine, for example, HS 0810.10.40 00 4 is for fresh strawberries entered between June 15 and September 15 of any year. You can buy a Harmonized System book from the U.S. Government Printing Office for less than $100, but most libraries have either the *Tariff Schedules of the United States Annotated* or the *Custom House Guide.*

Figure 10.1 is a page from the Harmonized System book. Your Customs entries should use the numbers, descriptions, and units of quantity shown for the products you are importing. Also, you should tell your exporters to use the same numbers on their commercial invoices. The duty columns will be explained in the next section.

The Rate of Duty

U.S. Customs duties range from 0 to about 120 percent, but the average rate is only around 6 percent. In general, the purposes of customs duties are to raise money for the federal government and to protect domestic producers. They are set by Congress and are negotiated with other countries in meetings, or "rounds," of the General Agreement on Tariffs and Trade (GATT). There are three kinds of duties: Ad valorem, specific, and mixed or compound.

Ad valorem means a percentage of value. There are a series of ways of determining the value of a product, but the most common is transaction value, or what you pay in the country of origin. If you buy, for example, f.o.b. vessel, you will probably pay duty on the cost of the goods loaded on the ship. If you buy the same goods Ex Works, and arrange for the foreign inland freight and freight forwarding, the dutiable value should be just the price of the goods on the loading dock of the factory. In no case does the United States charge duty on the cost of international transportation, as some countries do.

The law has many intricacies, and knowledgeable importers can reduce their duties by ensuring that their transactions are structured to avoid pitfalls and take advantage of benefits. For example, importers who buy through agents overseas may be better off if the agents work for them rather than for their suppliers. This is because buying commissions are not dutiable, while selling commissions are.

Specific duties are per unit, such as 20 cents per kilogram or 60 cents per item. Since a specific duty is the same no matter what the price of the article, the duty percent is lower for higher priced items. This is supposed to encourage imports of better quality merchandise.

Sometimes a product has a mixed or compound Customs duty, such as 10 percent plus 15 cents a kilogram. This usually means that Congress couldn't agree on whether to apply an ad valorem or a specific duty and compromised by using a little of each.

The "General" column in the Harmonized System is for the "Most Favored Nation," or "GATT," rates of duty. It is applied to imports from most developed countries. On the far right are column 2 duties, which are charged on imports from a few countries with which the United States does not have good political relationships. Some eastern European countries have recently been moved from column 2 to the General or the Special columns.

The "Special" column is for special privileges that are given to certain countries, as follows:

- An "E" in the column means the product is free of duty from most Caribbean and Central American countries. Nearly all products fall into this category. The major exceptions are textiles and apparel, except certified hand loomed products.
- An "A" in the column means the product is free of duty from most developing countries. Around 1700 products receive this treatment. South Korea, Taiwan, Hong Kong, and Singapore were recently "graduated" from the Generalized System of Preferences (GSP), which means that "General" duties are now paid on their products. An asterisk after the A means that duty free entry for that product

HARMONIZED TARIFF SCHEDULE of the United States (1990)

Annotated for Statistical Reporting Purposes

Heading/ Subheading	Stat. Suf. & cd	Article Description	Units of Quantity	Rates of Duty General	Rates of Duty 1 Special	2
0801		Coconuts, Brazil nuts and cashew nuts, fresh or dried, whether or not shelled or peeled:				
		Coconuts:				
0801.10.00	20 5	In shell........	kg	Free		7.7¢/kg
	40 1	Shelled........	kg			
0801.20.00		Brazil nuts:		Free		9.9¢/kg
	20 3	In shell........	kg			
	40 9	Shelled........	kg			
0801.30.00	00 5	Cashew nuts.......	kg	Free		4.4¢/kg
0802		Other nuts, fresh or dried, whether or not shelled or peeled:				
		Almonds:				
0802.11.00	00 7	In shell........	kg	12.1¢/kg	Free (E,IL) 7.2¢/kg (CA)	12.1¢/kg
0802.12.00	00 6	Shelled........	kg	37.5¢/kg	Free (E,IL) 30¢/kg (CA)	40.8¢/kg
		Hazelnuts or filberts (Corylus spp.):				
0802.21.00	00 5	In shell........	kg	11¢/kg	Free (E,IL) 6.6¢/kg (CA)	11¢/kg
0802.22.00	00 4	Shelled........	kg	17.6¢/kg	Free (E,IL) 14¢/kg (CA)	22¢/kg
		Walnuts:				
0802.31.00	00 3	In shell........	kg	11¢/kg	Free (A,E,IL) 6.6¢/kg (CA)	11¢/kg
0802.32.00	00 2	Shelled........	kg	33.1¢/kg	Free (E,IL) 26.4¢/kg (CA)	33.1¢/kg
0802.40.00	00 2	Chestnuts (Castanea spp.)........	kg	Free		Free
0802.50		Pistachios:				
0802.50.20	00 5	In shell........	kg	1¢/kg	Free (A,CA,E,IL)	5.5¢/kg
0802.50.40	00 1	Shelled........	kg	2.2¢/kg	Free (A,CA,E,IL)	11¢/kg
0802.90		Other:				
		Pecans:				
0802.90.10	00 9	In shell........	kg	11¢/kg	Free (E,IL) 6.6¢/kg (CA)	11¢/kg
0802.90.15	00 4	Shelled........	kg	22¢/kg	Free (A,E,IL) 17.6¢/kg (CA)	22¢/kg

0802.90.20	00 7	Pignolia: In shell..............	kg......	1.5¢/kg 1/	Free (A,CA,E,IL)	5.5¢/kg
0802.90.25	00 2	Shelled..............	kg......	2.2¢/kg 2/	Free (A,CA,E,IL)	11¢/kg
0802.90.80		Other: In shell.............		2.9¢/kg	Free (A,CA,E,IL)	5.5¢/kg
	10 2	Macadamia nuts........	kg			
	90 5	Other.............	kg			
0802.90.90		Shelled...............		11¢/kg	Free (CA,E,IL)	11¢/kg
	10 0	Macadamia nuts........	kg			
	90 3	Other............	kg			
0803.00		Bananas and plantains, fresh or dried:				
0803.00.20		Bananas.............		Free		Free
	20 1	Fresh.............	kg			
	40 7	Dried.............	kg			
0803.00.30	00 3	Plantains: Fresh...............	kg......	Free	Free (A,CA,E,IL)	Free
0803.00.40	00 1	Dried.............	kg......	3% 3/		35%

1/ See heading 9903.10.05
2/ See heading 9903.10.06
3/ See heading 9903.10.07

Figure 10.1. Sample Page from the Harmonized Tariff Schedule.

177

has been taken away from one or more of the GSP countries because it was shipping too much of the product to
the United States.

- An "IL" or a "CA" in the column means the product is
either free of duty or is charged a special low duty if it was
produced in and shipped from Israel or Canada. There are
free trade agreements with both of these countries, which
are being phased in over several years.

Marking and Labeling

U.S. law requires that nearly all products be marked with
the country of origin, in such a way that the final buyer can
see and read the mark. The English country name should be
used, but the type and location of the marks vary. It should
be on a sticker glued to the bottom of a crystal ash tray, die
stamped in most metal parts, sewn in the back of the neck
of men's shirts, and so on. Be sure to ask Customs about the
country-of-origin mark for your product.

There are some products, such as clocks, for which
separate marking of each major part is required. There are
also cases of "transformation" which is not considered "substantial." For example, crude pistachio nuts from Iran, that
are roasted and bagged in the United States, must still be
identified as Iranian produce.

Proper marking is no laughing matter. If you import
100,000 candy bars, and the Swiss exporter doesn't put his
country's name on them, you won't be able to sell them until
they are properly marked. You may be able to get them
released from Customs by posting a bond, but you cannot
deliver them to a customer until you have marked them,
redelivered a sample to Customs, and received approval.
Sometimes Customs will even clear and release goods that
are improperly marked, and then (within 30 days) request
redelivery. If you can't take the shipment back to Customs,

you will be assessed a 10 percent marking duty plus a penalty.

You should also ask the C&V specialist what other information should be on the product or its package. Some possibilities are instructions for laundering (wearing apparel), ingredients (processed foods), and safety warnings (cigarettes). It is illegal to sell an imported product that lacks any of the required information.

Other Federal Agencies

You might also ask the C&V specialist which other federal agencies regulate the importation or sale of your product. There are several possibilities including the Food and Drug Administration, the Consumer Products Safety Commission, and the Department of Transportation. These will be discussed later in this chapter.

GETTING DEEPER INTO CUSTOMS

In some cases, especially with apparel products, the Customs officer won't be able to tell you with certainty over the phone the classification of your product. If this occurs, make an appointment to visit the C&V specialist in order to show your product to him or her. A Customs specialist can nearly always look at your product and tell you the exact classification and the correct rate of duty, although in some cases even specialists can disagree. Try it yourself: Are chocolate covered cherries fruit or candy? Is a pointed piece of wire, with threads but with no slot in the head, a screw or a nail? There are numerous other examples.

In some cases, a Customs specialist can help you by suggesting ways of modifying the product to reduce the rate of duty. For example, dry onion powder from developed countries is charged a 35 percent duty, while dry onion *flakes* are charged only 25 percent. Maybe your buyer will take small flakes instead of powder. There was an extreme case a few years ago, before the Harmonized System was adopted: the trademark on a shipment of blue jeans was held to be ornamental because the "e" in the mark was slanted rather than straight, and that made the duty higher.

If your product is hard to classify and you plan to bring it in through different ports, you may want to get a written ruling of its classification. To do this, you should send a sample to a National Import Specialist at New York Seaport Customs, 6 World Trade Center, New York, NY 10048. You will not get the sample back, but you *will* get a written ruling that you or your broker can show to Customs inspectors at any port in the country.

Customs Procedures

When your goods arrive at a port of entry, the air or steamship line should notify the party named on the documents. Of course you should know, long before that, which ship or plane your goods will be on. You will want to act fast; you have only five working days to pick up the merchandise before it is taken to a Customs warehouse. If that happens, you will have to pay cartage to the warehouse, storage charges, cartage out, and an extra broker's fee.

As stated before, you can clear shipments worth less than $1,250 (except of textiles and apparel) with an Informal Entry form. If the value is over $1,250 or the shipment contains textile or apparel products, and you try to clear it yourself, you will probably be asked to complete a Consumption Entry form and pay the duty (Figure 10.2).

If you travel abroad and bring goods for resale back with you, you can clear them immediately unless they are worth more than $1,250 or include textiles or apparel.

Customs brokers now use a different system, however. A broker will usually complete an *Application for*

CONSUMPTION ENTRY
U.S. CUSTOMS SERVICE

INTERNAL REVENUE COPY

This Space For Census Use Only		This Space For Customs Use Only
BLOCK AND FILE NO.	M.O.T.	ENTRY NO AND DATE
	MANIFEST NO	Form approved. O.M.B. No. 48-R0217.

FOREIGN PORT OF LADING	U.S. PORT OF UNLADING	Dist and Port Code	Port of Entry Name	Term Bond No

Importer of Record (Name and Address)

For Account of (Name and Address)

Importing Vessel (Name) or Carrier	B/L or AWB No	Port of Lading	I T No and Date
Country of Exportation	Date of Exportation	Type and Date of Invoice	I T From (Port)
U.S. Port of Unlading	Date of Importation	Location of Goods—G O No	I T Carrier (Delivering)

MARKS & NUMBERS OF PACKAGES COUNTRY OF ORIGIN OF MERCHANDISE (1)	DESCRIPTION OF MERCHANDISE IN TERMS OF T.S.U.S ANNO, NUMBER AND KIND OF PACKAGES (2)		ENTERED VALUE IN U.S. DOLLARS (3)	T.S.U.S ANNO REPORTING NO (4)	TARIFF OR I R C RATE (5)	DUTY AND I R TAX (6)	
	GROSS WEIGHT IN POUNDS (2a)	NET QUANTITY IN T.S.U.S ANNO UNITS (2b)				Dollars	Cents

MISSING DOCUMENTS

THIS SPACE FOR CUSTOMS USE ONLY

I declare that I am the ☐ nominal consignee and that the actual owner for customs purposes is as shown above, or ☐ consignee or agent of the consignee I further declare that the merchandise ☐ was or ☐ was not obtained in pur

suance of a purchase or agreement to purchase I also include in my declaration all the statements in the declaration on the back of this entry -

DATE

(Signature)

(Address)

☐ Principal
☐ Member of the firm
☐ _____ of the corporation
(Title)
☐ Authorized agent

CUSTOMS FORM 9-12-78 7501

Figure 10.2. Consumption Entry. (Reprinted with permission of the U.S. Customs Service, U.S. Department of Treasury.)

Immediate Delivery and receive your box or boxes. Customs may or may not actually open them. There isn't time to inspect every shipment but they often check those of new importers, those that there is some reason to be suspicious of, and a few at random.

After filing the Application for Immediate Delivery, the broker has 10 working days to file an Entry Summary (Figure 10.3) with the commercial invoice and other documents, and a check for the duty.

In other words, you will have your merchandise before the duty is paid. How does Customs know you will pay the duty? That's one function of the bond that was discussed in Chapter 9.

In some cases, especially when goods are highly perishable, your broker may be able to get them pre-cleared so they will be released from Customs as soon as they arrive in the United States. Customs and some port authorities are developing and testing systems for doing this. In fact, you may want to look for shipping lines, Customs brokers, and ports that are using the Automated Manifest System (AMS) and Automated Broker Interface (ABI).

The final step in the entry process is called *liquidation.* This is when a commodity specialist reviews the entry, within one year, and decides whether the proper duty was paid. When this happens, you will receive a notice that liquidation has taken place. If you feel that Customs has charged too much for duty, you have 90 days from the date of liquidation to file a protest with Customs. If this protest is denied, you have 180 days from the date of the denial in which to file a summons with the U.S. Court of International Trade. This gets you into the big time, and you'll need a big time Customs attorney.

Under current law, there is also a Customs user fee charged on entries of goods other than from Canada, Israel, and the CBI countries. This fee is 0.17 percent (.0017) of "Customs value," with a minimum of $21 and a maximum

DEPARTMENT OF THE TREASURY
UNITED STATES CUSTOMS SERVICE

ENTRY SUMMARY

Form Approved OMB No. 1515-0065

(1) Entry No.	(2) Entry Type Code	3. Entry Summary Date
4. Entry Date	(5) Port Code	
6. Bond No.	7. Bond Type Code	8. Broker/Importer File No.

9. Ultimate Consignee Name and Address	10. Consignee No.	(11) Importer of Record Name and Address	(12) Importer No.
		(13) Exporting Country	14. Export Date
		(15) Country of Origin	16. Missing Documents
	State	(17) I.T. No.	(18) I.T. Date
(19) B/L or AWB No.	20. Mode of Transportation	21. Manufacturer I.D.	22. Reference No.
(23) Importing Carrier	24. Foreign Port of Lading	25. Location of Goods/G.O. No.	
26. U.S. Port of Unlading	(27) Import Date		

(28) Line No.	(29) Description of Merchandise: 30. (A) T.S.U.S.A. No. B. ADA/CVD Case No.	31. (A) Gross Weight B. Manifest Qty.	(32) Net Quantity in T.S.U.S.A. Units	33. (A) Entered Value B. CHGS C. Relationship	34. (A) T.S.U.S.A. Rate B. ADA/CVD Rate (C) I.R.C. Rate D. Visa No.	(35) Duty and I.R. Tax: Dollars	Cents

(36) Declaration of Importer of Record (Owner or Purchaser) or Authorized Agent

I declare that I am the

☐ importer of record and that the actual owner, purchaser, or consignee for customs purposes is as shown above. OR ☐ owner or purchaser or agent thereof.

I further declare that the merchandise

☐ was obtained pursuant to a purchase or agreement to purchase and that the prices set forth in the invoice are true. OR ☐ was not obtained pursuant to a purchase or agreement to purchase and the statements in the invoice as to value or price are true to the best of my knowledge and belief.

I also declare that the statements in the documents herein filed fully disclose to the best of my knowledge and belief the true prices, values, quantities, rebates, drawbacks, fees, commissions, and royalties and are true and correct, and that all goods or services provided to the seller of the merchandise either free or at reduced cost are fully disclosed. I will immediately furnish to the appropriate customs officer any information showing a different state of facts.

Notice required by Paperwork Reduction Act of 1980: This information is needed to ensure that importers/exporters are complying with U.S. customs laws, to allow us to compute and collect the right amount of money, to enforce other agency requirements, and to collect accurate statistical information on imports. Your response is mandatory.

U.S. CUSTOMS USE		TOTALS
A. Liq. Code	B. Ascertained Duty	(37) Duty
	C. Ascertained Tax	(38) Tax
	D. Ascertained Other	(39) Other
	E. Ascertained Total	(40) Total

(41) Signature of Declarant, Title, and Date

PART 1 — RECORD COPY

Customs Form 7501 (030884)

Figure 10.3. Entry Summary. (Reprinted with permission of the U.S. Customs Service, U.S. Department of Treasury.)

of $400 per entry. In some cases there are small fees (no more than $8) charged on informal entries as well. There is also a new $3.00 per entry surcharge if your broker does not use electronic entry procedures.

Quotas on Imports

Most textiles and apparel, and several other products, are subject to U.S. import quotas. They serve to protect domestic industry, raise the prices to U.S. consumers, and allocate production among supplying countries. For example, quotas on ladies blouses from Korea, China, and Hong Kong limit their sales to the United States and so permit several other countries to take part of the market.

Most of the quotas are fixed ceilings on the quantities of an item that can be imported each calendar year from each country. For example, the 1991 quota on men's cotton shirts from Malaysia will be a certain number of dozens. There are also *tariff rate quotas,* which means that the rate of duty increases each year when a certain quantity of an item has cleared U.S. Customs.

Foreign governments need systems for deciding which of their companies will be able to use their quotas in the U.S. market, and, of course, they want to get the highest possible value of exports from the allowable quantities. They use different systems to allocate quotas, including auctioning them in blocks. Holders of quotas are often permitted to sell them to other suppliers who can get higher prices from their American buyers.

U.S. Customs helps many countries enforce their quota arrangements by requiring that import shipments of quota goods be accompanied by visas, issued by the competent authorities in the exporting countries. This means that, if your shipment of men's cotton shirts from Malaysia reaches U.S. Customs and there is no visa among the documents, they cannot be entered. You can apply to the Malaysian Consulate for a visa, but it will not be granted unless the responsible agency in Kuala Lumpor gives its consent.

Classification and Value specialists in Customs' district offices should know the details of quotas on the items they handle, but even they cannot always tell you the annual quota on a specific item from a specific country or how much of the year's quota is still available. They can, however, translate the HS number of your product into a quota category number. Then you can phone the textile group of Customs at 202-377-4212 to find out the quota and the status of its fulfillment. Also, Customs has 24-hour recorded phone messages on the status of quota fulfillment for several countries. Call 202-566-5810 to get the telephone number for the message you need.

Occasionally, a product will be in a special *watched* status. In such a case, you will need a visa to import it, even if it is not actually under quota.

Extra Duties

There are occasionally circumstances in which importers are charged extra duties. For example, if the U.S. government determines that a foreign country is subsidizing its exports and that (for GATT members) imports of the subsidized goods are hurting American producers, a *countervailing duty* can be applied to counteract the subsidies. Also, if the government finds that a country is "dumping" goods on the U.S. market (selling in the U.S. at less than the fair market value in the country of origin), an anti-dumping duty may be charged.

In addition, there are sometimes extra duties or import prohibitions to try to pressure foreign countries into opening their markets to American goods or protecting intellectual property (patents, copyrights, etc.) of American firms.

In 1990, for example, very high duties levied on several Brazilian products had a lot to do with opening Brazil's market to American computer products.

Temporary Entries

If you want to ship goods through the United States without paying duty on them, such as from Mexico to Canada, you can do so with a bond and a special kind of Customs entry. The same applies to goods that are in the country temporarily for repair or to be exhibited in a trade show. Your Customs broker can help you with this kind of Temporary Importation under Bond (TIB).

You can also use a special Customs entry to bring goods into the United States and warehouse them, without paying duty, until you either re-export them or enter them into the commerce of the United States. Only minor processing, such as re-packaging, can be done in a bonded warehouse.

If you care to bring the goods into a *foreign trade zone* — an area under customs control that you can find in major ports and some inland cities—you can do almost any kind of processing. You can, for example, import foreign parts for small engines and combine them with American parts in a foreign trade zone. If you export the engines, you never pay Customs duty on the imported parts. If you sell them in the United States, you can pay duty on the imported parts, or on the finished engines, whichever is lower.

Finally, you can bring goods such as components into the United States under a *drawback* entry. Then if you later re-export them, even if they have been combined with American components to make finished goods, you can "draw back" most of the duty that was paid. You can even draw back duty if the components you export are not the same as the ones you brought in with a drawback entry, as long as they are identical.

There are still other types of customs entries that you can find out about in the book, *Importing into the United States,* prepared by the U.S. Customs Service. Every importer should buy a copy in a U.S. government bookstore or order one from the Superintendent of Documents, U.S. Government Printing Office, Washington, DC 20402.

OTHER FEDERAL REGULATIONS

There are numerous federal laws that affect both domestic and imported goods. The detailed text of each is printed in a massive set of books called the *Code of Federal Regulations,* but importers usually get information about them from the concerned government agencies. The following is a summary of some (though not all) of these laws. Much of the information is from the book just mentioned, *Importing into the United States.*

Food Products

The Federal Food, Drug and Cosmetic Act is the basic legislation governing imports of products that go in or on the body, including both human and animal bodies; the responsible agency is the Department of Health and Human Services of the Food and Drug Administration (FDA), Rockville, Maryland 20857. Each FDA district is the final authority for products entering through ports in its area. You can't get a written ruling in Florida that says your canned strawberries can be imported in Oregon.

Moreover, FDA will not analyze your product before you import it to tell you whether it will pass inspection. You should probably have it analyzed yourself by a private company that is familiar with FDA regulations. Otherwise you will risk bringing in a shipment that cannot enter into the United States. One such company is Werby Labs in Chelsea, Massachusetts, telephone 617-884-4109.

The FDA *will* tell you, however, whether the label on your can, bottle, or package is satisfactory. This is important because there are numerous requirements about information on labels of food products.

In one instance I had a product—instant powdered yams from Nigeria—tested in a specialized laboratory. It met FDA standards, but just barely. If the sample was barely acceptable, there seemed to be a good chance of having substandard items in a large shipment. As far as I know this product was not, and is still not being, imported from Nigeria to the United States.

Food products processed at high temperatures are more likely to meet FDA standards than other food products, provided they are properly handled and packed. There is a category of so-called "low acid" canned foods for which the producer must obtain a special Food Canning Establishment (FCE) number in order to export to the United States.

Meat and Poultry

Fresh and frozen meat, poultry, and related products are allowed only from foreign factories that have been approved to export to the United States. The fear is that meat from diseased animals will be processed and shipped or that conditions in the slaughterhouse will be unsanitary. Even some industrialized Western countries, such as Spain and Argentina, do not sell raw meat to the United States because none of their factories has the necessary certification.

The principal agencies involved with these products are the Food Safety and Quality Service and the Animal and Plant Health Inspection Service, both of the U.S. Department of Agriculture (USDA). For some kinds of poultry, such as quail, you should also consult the Fish and Wildlife Service of the Department of the Interior.

Fruits and Vegetables

Fresh produce imports are limited to specific items from specific countries, upon approval by the Animal and Plant Health Inspection Service of USDA. The reason for this is to control the entry of insect pests that might damage U.S. agriculture. There are also strict limitations on pesticide residues, established by the Environmental Protection Agency (EPA) and enforced by the FDA. Finally, several kinds of produce are subject to "Marketing Orders," related to quality. These are established by the Agricultural Marketing Service, U.S. Department of Agriculture, Washington, DC 20250.

Dairy Products

Many types of cheese are under quota and require import licenses. Contact the Foreign Agricultural Service, USDA, Washington, DC 20250. Milk and cream are regulated by both the Food and Drug Administration and the Department of Agriculture. Milk is under a tariff rate quota which, as you saw earlier in this chapter, means that the duty goes up after a specific quantity is imported each year. Condensed and evaporated milk, cream, and ice cream are under absolute quotas.

Other Food Products

There are quotas on various food products including several species of fish, potatoes, chocolate, sugar, and peanuts. Candy containing more than 0.5 percent alcohol is prohibited entirely.

Unexpected things can happen. A few years ago, American companies found that it was profitable to import food products containing large amounts of sugar, extract the sugar, and sell it. This was possible because the price of sugar in the United States is maintained at several times the world price in order to protect the beet growers in the south and the cane growers in Hawaii. The government responded to this sugar extraction business by temporarily banning imports of a category of miscellaneous food items, some of which did not contain any sugar at all. The measure was put into effect so suddenly that quite a bit of merchandise that had been bought and shipped was illegal by the time it reached the United States.

Textiles and Apparel

Textile and apparel imports are subject to numerous requirements. They must be labeled with the country of origin, fiber content, laundering instructions, and the name or trademark of the producer, importer, or marketing organization. A Registration Number (RN), obtained from the Federal Trade Commission, can be substituted for some of this information. The Federal Trade Commission, Washington, DC 20580, can give you information about requirements of the Textile Fiber Identification Act and the Wool Products Labeling Act.

When the Harmonized System took effect in the United States on January 1, 1990, the soft goods importing community expected massive confusion because of changes in the codes, classifications, and duty rates of so many items. In-depth information was presented in numerous publications and seminars, and the transition was made with very little trouble. One problem is that many fabrics are blends of different materials, such as polyester and cotton. For proper classification, you need to know the relative content, by weight, of each kind of fiber.

You should check also on regulations enforced by the Consumer Products Safety Commission, Washington, DC 20207, especially with regard to flammability of fabrics.

There are several countries in which flame-resistant cloth is not produced and cannot be imported. Be very careful about ordering items such as children's pajamas from such countries.

Alcoholic Beverages

Imports to the United States of beer, wine, and liquor are so highly regulated that you might want to avoid dealing with these products. First, you'll need an Importer's Basic Permit from the Bureau of Alcohol, Tobacco and Firearms, Department of the Treasury, Washington, DC 20226. You will have to fill out forms and pay a fee (technically a tax) of around $500, and you are unlikely to be approved if you have a criminal record or have ever declared bankruptcy. You will also need a wholesaler's permit from the state to which you plan to import. This usually costs more than the Importer's Basic Permit, but is easier to obtain. Unfortunately, you need a different permit for each state in which you plan to sell.

For wine and liquor, the bottles must be in metric sizes and the labels must be approved in advance by the Bureau of Alcohol, Tobacco and Firearms. There are several label requirements, one of which (in several states) is that the alcohol content be printed on the label. In some states, beer labels also need prior approval.

For liquor, you will need to buy federal red strip stamps to place on the bottles. These are evidence that the excise tax has been paid. If you import liquor without the strips, you will have to buy them and paste them on before making deliveries. Alcoholic beverages are also subject to inspection by the Food and Drug Administration.

Motor Vehicles

Two kinds of laws apply to cars, trucks, and motorcycles—safety and environmental cleanliness. Imported vehicles manufactured after December 31, 1967, must conform to safety regulations. For information contact the Office of Enforcement, Motor Vehicle Program, National Highway Traffic Safety Administration, U.S. Department of Transportation, Washington, DC 20590. *All* imported vehicles must meet the requirements of the Clean Air Act. Information about this is available from the Public Information Center, Environmental Protection Agency, Washington, DC 20460.

It used to be fairly easy for an individual to go overseas, buy a new or used car, and import it to the United States. It could be brought up to American standards in the foreign country or in the United States. Now, however, only authorized importers can bring in automobiles. The stated reason for this was to make sure that all imported vehicles met the safety and clean air standards. Of course, there's another reason—to help automobile companies by reducing the number of people who import their own cars.

Contact the Customs district office in your area to find out which firms have been approved to import motor vehicles.

Other Products

Household appliances are subject to consumer products safety, energy efficiency, and energy labeling laws. For information contact the Consumer Products Effectiveness Branch, U.S. Department of Energy, Washington, DC 20585 and the Division of Energy and Product Information, Federal Trade Commission, Washington, DC 20580.

Electronic products that emit radiation must meet standards enforced by the Bureau of Radiological Health, Food and Drug Administration, Rockville, Maryland 20857. For electronic products that broadcast on the airwaves, contact the Federal Communications Commission, Washington, DC 20554.

Plants and plant products must always be inspected at the border, by the Animal and Plant Health Inspection Service of the Department of Agriculture, for potentially destructive insect pests.

Drugs and cosmetics must be safe for human use and are subject to inspection and approval by the Food and Drug Administration. The testing period is long and the standards are strict. One result is that many remedies are much cheaper abroad than in the United States or are simply not available in this country.

Pesticides and toxic substances are regulated by the Office of Pesticides and Toxic Substances, Environmental Protection Agency, Washington, DC 20460. Legislation has recently been introduced in the U.S. Congress to restrict the exportation of pesticides that should not be used on crops that are to be sold in the United States.

Hazardous substances, such as dangerous chemicals, must meet regulations enforced by the Food and Drug Administration and the Consumer Products Safety Commission. Their transportation is closely regulated by the Materials Transportation Bureau, U.S. Department of Transportation, Washington, DC 20590.

STATE AND LOCAL REGULATIONS

Government authority in the United States is fragmented among various jurisdictions. Individual states regulate some products. Toys for children, for example, can't be sold in many areas without being approved by the consumer protection offices of the state governments. With imported toys, it is usually the importer who has to apply for (and pay for) state approval. I once assisted a Chilean company that was making light switches and other simple electrical goods and was planning to export them to the United States. Federal regulations presented no difficulties, but no city or county would buy the products unless they met local standards. We had to begin by contacting Underwriters Laboratories and having both the products and the factory in Chile inspected by UL personnel. Then, even with UL approval, we had to establish that the products met building standards in some of the cities where they were to be sold.

Counties and towns often regulate the thickness of insulation in houses, the color of trash cans, the size of mail boxes, and so on. If you import one-inch high street numbers for houses, and a new county law specifies two-inch numbers, you'll have to find a new supplier or get your existing supplier to retool in a hurry.

How do you find out about these kinds of regulations? First, look carefully at products like yours in stores to see if there is any mark or label on them that you don't understand. If there is, find out what it is and why it is there. Second, ask people in the trade as well as local government authorities.

At the same time, keep your eyes open for new ordinances that are about to be enacted. If your town is debating a dog litter law, there may be a market for leashes and pooper scoopers. If it is about to start a complete trash recycling program, every house will need containers for glass and tin, newspaper, wet garbage, and miscellaneous trash.

REGULATIONS FOR EXPORTERS

A lawyer specializing in international trade could probably list a hundred laws that affect small-scale export operations. I will mention just a few—those that are most likely to be encountered by small-scale exporters. They are the Trading with The Enemy Act, the Business Practices and Records Act, the Anti-Boycott Law, and tax incentives.

Trading with The Enemy Act

This is the law that authorizes most of the U.S. export control regulations. These regulations are to prevent harming the U.S. national interest by exporting products that are in scarce supply at home (very few) or that should be kept in the United States in order to maintain this country's military and industrial positions. In general, the less friendly a country is with the United States the fewer products can be exported under Open General License (OGL). An Open General License is for non-restricted product-destination combinations. It is one that an exporter can give to him/herself, by simply writing G-DEST (General License for this destination) in the box reserved for the license symbol on the Shipper's Export Declaration. Also, the less friendly a country is with the United States the harder it is to get "validated" licenses for products that require them.

The first step in complying with export control legislation is to find your product on the Commodity Control List (CCL) at a U.S. Department of Commerce field office. Also you can find the list in the book, *U.S. Export Administration Regulations,* available from the Superintendent of Documents, U.S. Government Printing Office, Washington, DC 20402, telephone 202-783-3238. When you find your product on this list, you will see a four-digit Export Commodity Control Number (ECCN). You will also see a letter, from A to M (not all letters from A to M are used). This letter indicates the country groups for which your product requires a validated license.

Next, you most look at the Country List, which also is available at USDC field offices. For example, the letter G after your ECCN on the commodity control list means that your product needs a validated license for S and Z countries. From the Country List you can tell if your destination is an S or Z country. If it is, you need to get a rather complicated form and submit it to the Department of Commerce for approval of your export shipment.

Applications for export licenses are supposed to be approved within two weeks, unless they have to be reviewed also by the Department of Defense. Then it can take much longer. Sometimes requests even go to Congress, as when Saudi Arabia places a major order for military equipment with an American firm.

There are some special types of export licenses, and there are often requirements that applications be accompanied by special statements or certificates. You may have to state on your bill of lading or airway bill that the product cannot be diverted to a third country without authorization from the U.S. government, and your buyer may have to provide a written statement that the product will not be diverted. Every shipment that requires a validated license, no matter what its value or destination, also requires a shippers Export Declaration.

Assistance with export licensing is available from a few private firms including MK Technology-Deltac, in Washington, DC, telephone (202) 463-0904.

If you want to find out what is happening to your application for a license, call Stela. Her complete name is System for Tracking Export License Applications, and her telephone number is 202-377-2752.

With the opening of Eastern Europe, the export license categories are under nearly constant review. Many of us hope that, in the near future, the licensing process will be simplified and licensing itself will become less important.

Business Practices and Records Act

This replaced the Anti-Foreign Corrupt Practices Act, which was commonly known as the "anti-bribery law." The intent is to enhance America's image by reducing bribery by American firms abroad. The primary means of enforcement is by the recordkeeping requirements that are built into the act.

Essentially, this law makes it illegal for U.S. exporters to bribe foreign officials to do something that is not one of their normal functions. Of course the definitions of "bribe," "foreign official," and other terms are critical. It is legal to give a small payment to a foreign Customs inspector to get your shipment cleared expeditiously. The small payment would not be considered a bribe, the Customs inspector would not be considered a foreign official, and clearing your shipment expeditiously is one of his normal functions. It is *not* legal to give the brother of the Minister of Health several thousand dollars to bring about the purchase of your line of antibiotics. If your foreign sales agent makes a bribe and you didn't know about it, you can still be held accountable if the Justice Department believes that you *should* have known about it.

Most recent U.S. government administrations, however, have realized that not being able to offer bribes puts U.S. firms at a competitive disadvantage with regard to firms of other countries. Therefore, the law has not been enforced very diligently. Still, there have been major convictions with regard to selling aircraft to The Netherlands, petroleum equipment to Mexico, and so on.

Anti-Boycott Legislation

Talk about a law that has teeth in it!—the fines on this one can be high enough to really hurt! This legislation was designed to counter the Arab boycott of Israel, but it applies to any boycott that the U.S. government does not support.

You may, for example, be asked by a buyer in Syria to certify that your goods are not of Israeli origin, were not made by an Israeli-owned company, and will not be shipped on Israeli vessels. If you make such a statement, you will be in violation of U.S. law. You can usually make a positive statement, such as certifying that the goods *are* a product of the United States.

If you receive a boycott request, it should be reported to the U.S. Department of Commerce in Washington, DC. Your USDC field office or a specialized attorney can advise you as to what you can and cannot do without getting into trouble. If you receive a letter of credit that contains boycott provisions, your bank will probably refuse to handle it.

DISCs and FISCs

I will end this chapter on a happy note, with a few words about tax incentives known as DISCs and FISCs. The former is a Domestic International Sales Corporation, while the latter is a Foreign Sales Corporation. Both are legal devices to reduce the tax burden on U.S. exporters.

The DISC law allowed U.S. exporters to channel their exports through shell corporations, on their own premises if they wished, and to postpone payment of income tax on part of the export profits. When the GATT ruled that this was a subsidy, the rules of DISCs were changed to make them less attractive and FISCs were created.

A FISC must be a separate corporation, which is set up offshore in an approved country and which has personnel to handle export paperwork. Export transactions (not actual merchandise) are routed through the FISC, and income taxes on a portion of the profits are waived. Your company alone may be too small to own its own FISC, but the law allows trade groups and associations to set up FISCs that serve all their members. If you become a substantial exporter, these tax incentives will definitely be worth looking into.

11

Sources of Information and Assistance

Throughout the text of this book I've named a number of information sources, but much remains to be said. Every day the work of importing and exporting brings new questions and new challenges. Just when you learn about C&F it gets changed to CFR, and just when you learn about assignable letters of credit someone wants you to pay him with a *transferable* LC. Your need to obtain correct information, quickly and inexpensively, is practically limitless.

This chapter will give you some of the sources of information. It discusses books, magazines, newspapers and electronic databases, government organizations, private companies, and world trade clubs and associations. The material in this chapter cannot be exhaustive, but it *can* save you time and money.

IN PRINT AND ON LINE

There are literally hundreds of printed and electronic information sources. A number of them are mentioned in this book, and following is a discussion of a few that are especially important.

Books

For introductory books, it's hard to beat the ones that are available from the U.S. Department of Commerce and the Small Business Administration. Both have offices in major U.S. cities. Just call and they'll send information about their publications. You may also want to contact Braddock Communications Inc., in Alexandria, Virginia, for *The World is Your Market,* from AT&T, and *International Direct Marketing Guide,* from the U.S. Postal Service. The telephone number is 703-549-6500. Any good library or bookstore will have a variety of books on international trade. One particularly useful book is *The Do's and Taboos of International Trade,* by Roger Axtell, published by John Wiley & Sons, Inc., 605 Third Avenue, New York, NY 10158, telephone 212-850-6000. Steer clear of those that make the business sound like an easy way to get rich quickly.

A company named OSBDCN, at 99 West 10th Avenue, Eugene, OR 97401-3017, publishes a book named, *Your International Business Plan.* The telephone number is 503-726-2250.

Another book that can be very useful to importers is called *How to Conquer the U.S. Market.* It was published in 1990 by Routledge of London, and authored by myself. The Routledge telephone number in New York City is 212-244-3336. Exporters may want to read a copy of *Going International,* by Copeland and Griggs. It was published in New York by New American Library in New York, telephone 212-366-2000.

If you are importing and want to find foreign suppliers, find a good library that has the *Kompass* directory series. It will give you many names to contact.

For help in segmenting your market, take a look at the Rand McNally *Commercial Atlas & Marketing Guide.* The 1990 edition was priced at $295, but contains maps and extensive information on buying power and purchasing patterns by zip code areas and by counties. There is also a more detailed *Zip Code Atlas and Market Planner* for $475. Both books are sold by Rand McNally, P.O. Box 1697, Skokie, IL 60076-9871, telephone 800-627-2897, Operator 450. They are available in many libraries.

For selling to retail stores, I've already mentioned publications from The Salesman's Guide and similar companies. There is no easier way to find prospective clients and the names of their buyers.

If you plan to sell directly to industrial firms, try the directories published by Manufacturers' News, Inc., 4 East Huron Street, Chicago, IL 60611. For example, a detailed listing of more than 2,400 manufacturers in the state of Arkansas costs $62. Information given includes the companies' sizes and names and addresses of executives.

And, to do your own public relations or help your P.R. person, look at *Bacon's Publicity Checker* in your library. You should get to know this book because it can be a lot cheaper to obtain publicity than to use paid advertising.

Exporters will find many books on export marketing, and perhaps the best place to start is to look at college textbooks. Many colleges and universities have good libraries that are open for limited use by the public. I suggest that, of the many excellent authors, you look for a book written by Vernon Terpstra or Mary Hilger. If you like your reading a bit heavier on the theory side, find something by Franklin Root. If you would like a little levity after reading Root, try to find either a copy of a little book called *Big Business Blunders*, which shows how even giant companies can make foolish mistakes overseas, or Roger Axtell's *Do's and Taboos Around the World*, which was mentioned earlier in this section.

Regarding trade procedures, I've strongly recommended *Importing Into the United States* by the U.S. Customs Service. You may also want to get the *Guide to Incoterms,*

Commercial Agency: A Guide to Drawing Up Contracts, and A Guide to Drafting International Distributorship Agreements (more pamphlets than books) from the ICC Publishing Corporation, 156 5th Avenue, Suite 819, New York, NY 10010, telephone 212-206-1150.

To learn the basics of legal procedures in foreign countries, try Foreign Business Practices, from the U.S. Government Printing Office. It may save you from a serious faux pas.

Magazines

As with books, there are many magazines to choose from. Importers from the Caribbean islands and Central America should take out free subscriptions to the LA/C Business Bulletin from USDC/ITA, LA/C Center H3203, Washington, DC 20230. Exporters should probably read Business America, a serial publication of the U.S. Department of Commerce. As of this writing it costs $49.00 per year, and gives quite a bit of information that will help you select potential markets and promote your merchandise.

I also recommend Global Executive, free from the North American Publishing Company in Philadelphia, 401 North Broad Street, Philadelphia, PA 19108, and a fairly new one, International Business. You can buy a subscription for $59.97 a year from American International Publishing Co., 401 Theodore Fremd Avenue, Rye, NY 10580, telephone 800-274-8187. Note that prices may change by the time this book gets into your hands. There's an even newer journal, Overseas Business, that is free if the publisher judges you qualified. Contact Overseas Business at P.O. Box 3726, Escondido, CA 92025-9938, telephone 800-334-8152 (in California 800-255-3302). Finally, you'll find good ideas in Wisconsin International Trade from the Wisconsin Department of Development, P.O. Box 7970, Madison, WI 53707, telefax 608-266-5551.

Beyond these, you should definitely subscribe to the major trade magazines that discuss the kinds of products you deal with. If you are exporting and your market countries have appropriate trade magazines, subscribe to those too. Your local library will have the *Standard Periodicals Index* and perhaps an international periodicals directory called *Ulrich's*.

Many books and magazines can be purchased from U.S. International Marketing Co., Inc., 17057 Bellflower Blvd., Bellflower, CA 90706, telephone 213-925-2918. This is the same company that sells the "Import-Export Business Starter Kit."

Croner Publications also sells a number of books and magazines. It's located at 34 Jericho Turnpike, Westbury, NY 11753, telephone 516-333-9085. You may even want to buy the *World Trade Plan* from The Mellinger Company, 6100 Variel Avenue, Woodland Hills, CA 91376, telephone 818-884-4400. Call for information, but don't buy right away. You may get a lower price offer via a second or third mailing.

Newspapers

In the business of trade, you should read a good newspaper like *The New York Times* or the *Los Angeles Times*. *The Journal of Commerce* is a superb newspaper of trade and transportation, and I've already mentioned *Export Channel* as a source of information on products and suppliers. Also, if you're trading with Latin America you should take a look at *International Business Chronicle.* It is an excellent little newspaper from a company by the same name at 4770 Biscayne Blvd., Ph-G, Miami, FL 33238-2012, telephone 800-783-4685.

Electronic Databases

For those of you who have computers with modems, there are several on-line sources of useful information. I've already mentioned "Network" and "International Business Network" as means of posting, and finding, buy and sell notices. There are also on-line services from the U.S. Department of Commerce, the Journal of Commerce Publishing Company, Dialog, publishers of steamship rates, and other firms. Many of these, however, are either too time consuming or too expensive for new importers and exporters to use.

Let me suggest, to importers, that you look into the SICE information service operated by the Organization of American States (OAS) in Washington, DC, for exporters in Latin American countries. It has recently been opened to subscribers in the United States. As of this writing a deposit of $2,500 is required, but there is some talk of reducing or eliminating this charge.

SICE includes several databases so that it can provide users with U.S. foreign trade statistics, names and addresses of importers, customs duties, relevant parts of the *Code of Federal Regulations,* and other information. For more information write to Mr. Bernardo Gluch at the OAS, 1889 F Street NW, Washington, DC 20006.

GOVERNMENT ORGANIZATIONS

Whatever impression you may have of government services, if you want to export, the government really *is* here to help you. The biggest helper is the U.S. Department of Commerce, but assistance is available also from other U.S. government agencies and also from state or local governments.

Unfortunately, government doesn't particularly care for you if you want to import. Customs and other regulatory agencies will tell you their rules, and volunteer advisors (usually retired) who are connected with the Small Business Administration are sometimes helpful. Other than these, you will have to look to private firms for assistance.

U.S. Department of Commerce.   The main number of the USDC in the nation's capital is 202-377-2000. At this number friendly (but overworked) operators can connect you to sources of information about the USDC services. If that doesn't work, try the U.S. & Foreign Commercial Service at 202-377-5777. Your local field office of the USDC International Trade Administration can provide the same information.

The Commerce Department has desk officers assigned to every country and industry officers for industries that are important in the United States. It also publishes *Foreign Economic Trends* for most countries and numerous market research reports. "Market Share Reports" will help you identify potential target markets, and the "Comparison Shopping Service" will help you decide whether to enter particular markets. This one is rather expensive, however, at about $1,000 per country.

The USDC's Trade Opportunities Service will help you find potential buyers in any country. The "Agent/ Distributor Services" serves to identify likely agents and distributors, and the "World Trader Data Reports" will assist you in making export credit decisions. For any additional services, call your local USDC field office and ask for an informational brochure.

Small Business Administration.   For years the SBA talked about its assistance to exporters, but there really wasn't much available. Now, however, it offers publications, seminars, some counseling, and sometimes financing. Perhaps its most important service is the Export Information Service (XIS) data reports on major markets for American products. Why not call your nearest SBA office and ask what they have to offer?

Other Federal Agencies.   If you plan to export agricultural products, the U.S. Department of Agriculture has numerous services including trade statistics, buyer identification, and financing (through the Commodity Credit Corporation). It even encourages the exportation of selected commodities by replacing part of what you send abroad, from surplus stocks in the United States.

The best way to begin learning about USDA services is probably to call "Ag Export Connections" at 202-447-7103. Alternatively, you can write the Foreign Agricultural Service, U.S. Department of Agriculture, Room 4647 South Building, Washington, DC 20250-1000, and ask for an "AgExport Connections" information kit.

The Agency for International Development, of the U.S. Department of State, finances projects abroad that often involve procurement of supplies and equipment from U.S. sources. Look into this if you want to, but the regulations and the competition are both ferocious.

The U.S. Export Import Bank and its affiliate, the Foreign Credit Insurance Association, can help with financing and insuring export transactions. They have small business programs, but small business for EXIMBANK is a little larger than it is for you and me. Still, if you're interested, call 202-566-8990 for information.

If you decide to place your life's savings in productive assets in a foreign country, you may get some help from the Overseas Private Investment Corporation (OPIC). Their telephone number is 202-454-7128.

A few other services are available from federal government dependencies, such as standards in foreign countries, from the National Technical Information Service. The ones listed, however, offer close to 100 percent of the available assistance.

State and Local Governments. State governments have all plunged into export promotion, although not always with high effectiveness. Appendix B to this book, "Trade

Contacts," contains the names and telephone numbers of the appropriate entities in each state.

It is common for state governments to hold seminars, provide export opportunities, and organize selling missions to foreign countries. Your state can send information on what it can do to help you. If for some reason the state you live in doesn't offer much in the way of services to exporters, try a different state. Just have a friend who lives there call and ask for the information you need.

California has pioneered in an interesting concept—a specialized bank to finance exports from that state. In several other states, there is talk of following California's good example.

Even some county and city governments are in the business of assisting exporters. A few are mentioned in the Trade Contacts list.

PRIVATE COMPANIES

Import and export operations can't be done in a vacuum. You will need help from service firms such as banks, freight forwarders, customs brokers, air and steamship lines, insurance companies, and perhaps accountants and lawyers. You can get limited amounts of free help from some of these firms in your start-up phase. If you grow to be an important customer of any service firm, the help you can get will increase exponentially.

Both importers and exporters can get advice on methods of payment from international bankers, on transportation from airlines and steamship lines, and on packing and insurance from insurance brokers and underwriters. Importers can get free ideas about purchasing from foreign countries' trade promotion officials, on documentation from customs brokers, and on marketing from advertising and public relations firms. Exporters can, without paying, speak with American trade associations about sources of supply and with foreign freight forwarders about export procedures.

There are numerous attorneys who specialize in international trade. Their assistance can be invaluable in matters of supply agreements, copyright protection, taxation, and so on. They don't come cheap, but you have to compare the cost with the expected benefit. A legal agreement for which your lawyer charges a thousand dollars may prevent you from losing commissions worth many times that amount.

There are also numerous colleges, universities, and other organizations that offer courses and seminars in international trade. I've recently received a list of what appear to be very useful courses from Coastline Community College in Costa Mesa, Newport Beach, and Fountain Valley, California. I was in on the beginning of the MBA in International Trade program at Laredo State University in Laredo, Texas, and it has become an excellent program. The World Trade Education Center of Cleveland State University, Ohio, has become a leader in training in that part of the country. In New York City, Pace University, New York University, and the Fashion Institute of Technology all have excellent courses in international trade, and there are many others.

You should also know about the world trade centers. A world trade center is essentially a building, whose owners try to rent space to companies that are involved in international trade. There is usually a world trade club for firms and individuals who wish to hold membership, and services of training and/or information about importing and exporting.

Since the World Trade Center was formed in New York about 20 years ago, this concept has spread throughout the country and the world. The World Trade Institute, in the

World Trade Center in New York, organizes more than 100 courses and seminars every year. If you are in or near a large city, it probably has a world trade center. Look for it in your phone directory, ask at the USDC field office, or call the city department of economic development for information.

It is also common to find courses and seminars organized by the American Management Association, headquartered in New York City, telephone 212-795-5400, UNZ and Company, in Jersey City, NJ, telephone 201-795-5400, international banks, port authorities, and other organizations. You can find out about them by watching your local business newspaper. In some areas the USDC field offices publish small newsletters, free of charge, that list coming events of interest to exporters.

Some of the port authorities in the United States also have foreign offices, arrange appointments in their areas for foreign buyers, organize trade missions of U.S. exporters, host exhibits of foreign products, and sponsor U.S. exhibits overseas. Massport, in Boston, is a good example.

You can also receive some assistance from consulting firms. There are few that deal in the area of import/export procedures, but several that offer help with marketing in the United States and abroad. Almost none will help you "on spec," or for a percentage of your sales or profits. They want cash for their services. In general, the larger the firm, the less interested it is in accepting small jobs or accounts.

Importers can find plenty of local marketing consultants in the telephone directory. Exporters will sometimes find them advertising in specialized magazines or shaking hands at meetings of international trade clubs and associations (the next kind of organization to be discussed). Before hiring consultants, make sure there is a written document that says exactly what they will do for you, by when, and in what form you will receive the information. Don't pay the final bill until you are satisfied with both the oral and the written reports.

CLUBS AND ASSOCIATIONS

I encourage joining world trade clubs and associations, or at least attending their meetings. Why is this? Because you can meet people involved in all aspects of international trade and pick their brains for the price of a lunch or dinner. Often there are speakers or panelists on important topics, but the main benefit is that which has come to be known as "networking."

Most areas in which foreign trade is important have world trade clubs, whose members are mainly large exporting companies, and import/export associations, whose members are mainly companies and individuals in the traffic functions—packing, forwarding, insurance, shipping, customs brokerage, and so on. You can identify clubs in your area from the trade contacts list at the end of this book.

Following are a few miscellaneous sources of information that may prove useful to you. The Sutton Family, 11565 Ridgewood Circle North, Seminole, FL 34642 are the self-proclaimed gurus on flea marketing. They sell directories, research reports, and related information. The International Business Diplomacy faculty of Georgetown University offers free market research, done by students. While they would prefer to deal with established firms that can pay out-of-pocket costs and act promptly on the information, you may have a small project that will interest them. For more information, call Professor Nelson Joyner at 202-687-5854. There may be a university near you that offers a similar service. The Small Business Foundation of America offers free consulting on exporting to small companies. The telephone number is 800-243-7232, and in Massachusetts 800-244-7232. A company called International Strategies offers a similar service, but only in Massachusetts. Its telephone number is (800) USA-EXPORT.

Finally, a company called Witgang Far East Ltd. has written to offer initial market research in the Far East as well as agency and representation services. The standard, quoted price is $2,000, for "a product-specific analysis of market potential, offering a base from which a company can decide whether to pursue the Asian market." Witgang Far East Ltd. is at 4 Oxford Road, Howloon Tong, Hong Kong, fax 852-338-4604. I've never dealt with them so cannot vouch for their honesty or ability.

12

Trade with the New Europe

Europe is in an exciting phase of rapid transition, bringing both an abundance of obstacles and even greater opportunities. Let's look at the continent and see how it may relate to small-scale import and export businesses.

EUROPE—A DESCRIPTION

Please forgive me if Europe is different by the time you read this book; right now it is changing every day.

As of this writing, the European Economic Community (EEC) (technically one of three European communities), includes 12 countries with a combined land area of 2,250,000 square miles (much smaller than the United States) and a population of 324 million people (compared to the U.S.'s 260 million). The EEC's imports are about equal to those of the United States, while its exports are about 50 percent higher. These figures do not include trade among the EEC countries themselves.

The EEC member countries are Germany (reunited at midnight on October 2, 1990), France, Spain, the United Kingdom, Italy, Ireland, Portugal, Holland, Greece, Denmark, and Belgium/Luxembourg. Several other countries have applied and/or are considering applying for membership, but their applications will not be considered until 1993. According to the Treaty of Rome, any democratic European country with a market economy is eligible to join the Community.

The EEC cooperates closely with EFTA, the European Free Trade Association, whose members are Austria, Finland, Iceland, Norway, Sweden, and Switzerland.

EEC countries are beginning to become much more economically involved with the countries of Eastern Europe and Russia. Their economic union, the Council for Mutual Economic Assistance (CMEA or COMECON), has collapsed and each country is seeking its own deals with former friends and enemies. The political entities involved are Albania, Bulgaria, Czechoslovakia, Hungary, Poland, Rumania, and Yugoslavia. We might also add the Union of Soviet Socialist Republics including the Baltic republics of Estonia, Latvia, and Lithuania.

The population figures are impressive: 324 million in the EEC countries, 32 million in EFTA countries, 139 million in the countries of Eastern Europe, and 292 million in the Soviet Union. This gives a total market of 787 million people, more than double the population of the United States.

There are, however, several problems that restrict trade with the United States. Some of these are described in the next two sections.

IMPORTING FROM EUROPE

Western and Northern Europe are generally developed areas with internal production of virtually everything they need. These countries each have particular strengths as far as trade is concerned—Italy is known for its great designers, Spain and Portugal for low costs, Sweden, Germany, and Switzerland for excellent quality, and so on. A myriad of small and large firms now export to the United States, and neither recent nor future events are likely to change this situation.

A good source of information on European products is the *Made in Europe* group of magazines, mentioned in Chapter 4 and in the Index of this book. "Trade Channel" newspaper, European trade magazines, "Network," and other sources will also give you leads on whom to buy from. Generally, transportation to the United States is excellent and payments move easily. Customs duties on products from all of the western and northern European countries are levied at the Most Favored Nation rates, in the "General" column of the Harmonized Tariff Schedule.

Eastern Europe, however, is quite a different story. In general there are few exportable products, and most are of poor quality. Also, the business community has little experience exporting to the United States and knows little about concepts such as consumer behavior or market segmentation. Most readers of this book will not be able to name a single company in Eastern Europe, although some are quite large: Polimemt and Polichim in Bulgaria (chemicals), Skoda and ZTS in Czechoslovakia (cars and heavy machinery), Huta Katowice and Lenin Steel in Poland (steel), Tissa Chemicals and Ikarus (buses) in Hungary, Electronica (electric and electronic equipment) and Danubiana (rubber, plastics, and chemicals) in Rumania, Avto Vaz and GAZ (cars and trucks) in the Soviet Union. Most of these firms are not yet able to hold their own with exporters from Japan or other leading industrialized countries, particularly in the competitive U.S. market.

Transportation from Eastern Europe to the United States is improving. Payment is still a problem, as most of the countries still have rules designed to make sure the hard currency from exports goes into the government's account. Import duties are undergoing changes. As of this writing, some countries pay Column 2 (very high) duties, others are classified as Most Favored Nations (normal duties), and others are beneficiaries of the Generalized System of Preferences (no duties on many products). There are various proposals in Congress to liberalize rules on imports from selected countries.

Sources of information, for would-be U.S. importers from Eastern Europe, are few and far between. As good a place as any to start is with the commercial counselors of the embassies in Washington, DC. Albania has no commercial representation in the United States. The telephone number of the Embassy of Bulgaria is 387-7969. The commercial office of Czechoslovakia is at 363-6307, while that of Hungary is at 387-3191. The Polish Embassy has number 234-3800. Rumania has a commercial agency at 232-4749, and Yugoslavia is at number 462-6566. The USSR has a trade representatives office with telephone numbers 232-2917, 232-5988, and 234-7170. There is also a Latvian Legation at 726-8213 and a Lithuanian Legation at 234-5860. (All are in the 202 area.)

EXPORTING TO EUROPE

Europe as a whole has high per capita income and purchasing power. There are, however, still important regional differences in demand for products, distribution systems, laws on advertising, prices, and other aspects of marketing.

A magazine called *Overseas Business,* using data from the World Bank and CartaGen DemoGraphics, presents the area in six clusters of geographical areas, as follows:

- Cluster 1, Northeastern Europe: UK and Ireland. Population 60 million; age profile average for the EC. Average per capita income: $11,450. English language.

- Cluster 2, Central Europe: Central and Northern France, Southern Belgium, Central Germany, and Luxembourg. Population 55 million. Low proportion of middle-aged persons and high proportion of elderly. Average income: $15,470. Common languages: French and German.

- Cluster 3, Southwestern Europe: Spain and Portugal. Population 50 million; population younger than the EC average. Average income: $6,530. Common languages: Spanish and Portuguese.

- Cluster 4, Central Europe: Southern Germany, Northern Italy, Southeastern France, and Austria. Population 71 million. High proportion of middle-aged persons. Average income: $16,740. Common languages: German, French, and Italian.

- Cluster 5, Southeastern Europe: Greece and Southern Italy. Population 31 million, population younger than the EC average. Average income: $7,610. Common languages: Greek and Italian.

- Cluster 6, Northern Europe: Denmark, Northern Germany, the Netherlands, Northern Belgium, Switzerland, Iceland, Sweden, Norway, and Finland. Population 58 million, high proportion of middle-aged persons. Average income: $19,420. Main languages: Scandinavian languages, French, Italian, and German.

These clusters are different market segments, to be approached in different ways. Note that East Germany is not included in any cluster because it was part of Eastern Europe until October, 1990.

The same magazine also gives selected data on the countries of Eastern Europe. Population ranges from 1.6 million, in Estonia, to 38 million in Poland. Per capita Gross National Product ranges from $930, in Albania, to $10,130 in Czechoslovakia and $12,500 in East Germany. The languages are different in each country, and the cultures are a reflection of the languages. Marketing in these lands will be a challenge that many American firms will accept, and at which many hopefully will succeed.

For U.S. exporters the main benefit of European unity in 1992 will be the harmonization of standards, which will allow the same product to be accepted in all of the 12 countries. There is a plan to prepare and enact 279 new sets of regulations as part of the unification program. These will relate to many kinds of products and services as well as to government procurement, taxation, the behavior of companies, veterinary and phytosanitary controls, and the movement of commerce, capital, and persons within the economic community.

Transportation to Western and Northern Europe is readily available, and payment mechanisms function well. There is, however, a rather complicated schedule of import tariffs on which the United States is given most-favored nation treatment but no special preferences. There are preferences for most developing countries, and trade within the community is free of duty.

The recent decision by Britain to link its currency to the European Currency Unit (ECU), has made possible the creation of a single monetary unit for the Community. For several years the ECU has been used for certain purposes such as recording international trade statistics. Gradually now, European importers and exporters seem likely to begin insisting on making and receiving payment in ECUs. This will be a more stable currency than the U.S. Dollar and so may replace the dollar as the preferred currency in international trade.

Access to the European market for U.S. exporters, especially of agricultural products and services, will be influenced by the outcome of the long "Uruguay Round" of GATT negotiations. These negotiations were suspended without agreement in December, 1990, but were renewed in March, 1991. They must be successful for trade to move as it should among the United States, the EEC, and other world areas.

Transportation and payment with Eastern Europe are much more difficult, and customs duties are constantly changing and all but impossible to predict. When you're ready to start selling, check on duties and other regulations with sources mentioned in this book including the country desk officers of the U.S. Department of Commerce.

Finally, I should mention in this chapter on Europe the continuing rise of Asia. Its share of world income, and therefore of world imports, is predicted to rise enormously in the next 50 years. As important as Europe is and will be in the future, Asia will almost certainly pass it as a market for U.S. products. This suggests that you set your long export sights on targets such as South Korea, Taiwan, and Singapore.

SOURCES OF INFORMATION ON EUROPE

U.S. Department of Commerce (USDC). In a recent article in *Business America* magazine, the USDC describes the following services for exporters to the European Community:

Counseling

Business facilitation services

Trade opportunity reporting

Commercial news USA

World traders data reports

Agent distributor service

Comparison shopping service

Trade missions

Matchmaker events

Catalog/video exhibitions

Trade fair certification

Trade dispute assistance.

It also offers a Single Internal Market Information Service (SIMIS), at telephone number (202) 377-5276. Information on European standards can be obtained from the American National Standards Institute, at (212) 642-4900, and from the National Center for Standards Certification at (301) 975-4040.

The current telephone numbers of the country desk officers for Western Europe are as follows (all area 202):

Belgium and Luxembourg, 377-5401

Denmark, 377-3254

France, 377-8008

Germany, 377-2434

Greece, 377-3945

Ireland, 377-4104

Italy, 377-2177

Netherlands, 377-5401

Portugal, 377-3945

Spain, 377-4508

United Kingdom, 377-3748.

There are also industry experts assigned to the 1992 program. Names may change, but hopefully the telephone numbers will stay the same for at least a few years. They are as follows:

Textiles and apparel, Michael Hutchinson, 377-2043

Service industries, Fred Elliot, 377-3734

Information technology, instrumentation and electronics, Myles Denny-Brown, 377-4466

Chemicals, construction industry products, and basic industries, Maryanne Smith, 377-0614

Autos and consumer goods, Bruce Miller, 377-2762

Construction projects and industrial machinery, Kay Thompson, 377-2474

Aerospace, Marci Kenney, 377-8228

Office of industrial trade, 377-3733.

There is also a USDC Eastern Europe Business Information Center at (202) 377-2645. The telefax number is (202) 377-4473. To start learning about exporting to the USSR, call (202) 377-4655.

Other Recommended Information Sources. The European Communities Commission has information centers in the United States and depositories for publications in several major libraries. To get a list of EC publications, and/or to find the location of the information facility nearest you, call the Commission in the District of Colombia at (202) 862-9555. At the same time ask about an excellent magazine called *Europe,* which sells for only $14.95 per year.

UNIPUB, in Lanham, Maryland, has many useful publications on Europe. For information about these call UNIPUB at (800) 274-4888. Export marketing lists and other information can be purchased form Interdata at 1480 Grove Street in Healdsburg, CA 95448. The telephone number is (707) 433-3900. This is the company that publishes the International Directory of Importers series, of which one volume covers Europe. Also there is a Europe/USSR Center established at KPMG Peat Marwick, 767 Fifth Avenue, New York, NY 10153, telephone (212) 909-5000.

You can call (800) 866-8275 for a free sample of the "Euro-American Letter," and you may want to get information about "ABC Europe Production-Europex" from the Western Hemisphere Publishing Corporation at (916) 823-3532. There is also a *European Directory of Marketing*

Information Sources available from Gale Research Company, Book Tower, Detroit, MI 48226, telephone (313) 961-2242. The cost is approaching $200.

The Trans Alliance Group, at telephone number (800) 624-1992, offers several kinds of information and consultation on doing business in Europe. Prices vary with the size of the client firm.

The main source of statistical information on Europe is Eurostat. For a list of their publications write the Eurostat Information Office at L-2920 Luxembourg, Belgium. The telephone number is 4301-4567.

There is also an excellent book, called *Selling to the Allies,* by the U.S. Department of Defense. It is available from the Superintendent of Documents, U.S. Government Printing Office.

There are many other useful sources of information, including commercial attachés and chambers of commerce of European countries in the United States. Also, seminars and conferences on Europe are being held throughout the United States.

In sum, then, there are many trade opportunities with the European continent. The opportunities with the more advanced countries are generally easier and more visible, but they will also be easier and more visible to your competitors. Trade with Eastern Europe will take time to develop. If you're in this business for the long haul, it may be wise to look for opportunities there.

In general, business people in Europe are not as interested in small-scale U.S. importers and exporters as are their counterparts in other parts of the world. Still, many small firms trade successfully with Europe and many more will do so. If you have some particular advantage in one or more of the European countries, look it over well. A pot of silver may be waiting for you, beyond the Atlantic Ocean.

Appendixes

Appendix A

Outline for a Business Plan

Note: While I've used the sample of a small apparel importer in Minneapolis for this outline, you can easily adapt it for preparing a business plan for any import or export business.

I. Executive Summary
   A. The Company and Its Products
   B. Market Potential and Marketing
   C. Competitive Advantages
   D. Summary of Financial Projections

II. General Company Description
   A. Ownership
   B. Objectives
   C. Type of Operations
   D. Office and Equipment

III. The Company's Products
   A. The Product Line(s)
   B. Trademarks and Packaging
   C. Customer Benefits of the Products
   D. Product Sources/Resources
   E. Product Testing

IV. Marketing
   A. The Target Market(s)
   B. Competition
   C. Environmental Influences

D. Marketing Strategy
E. Market Research

V. Operations

A. Product Sourcing and Ordering
B. International Transportation and Insurance
C. Payment for Merchandise
D. Customs Clearance and Duties
E. Quotas
F. Warehousing
G. Legal Considerations

VI. Management and Organization

A. The Owner/Manager
B. Employees
C. Investors and Advisors
D. Strategy and Policies

VII. Structure and Capitalization

A. Type of Business Entity
B. Capital Requirements
C. Likely Sources of Capital

VIII. Finances

A. Schedule of Start-Up Costs
B. Projected Income and Expense Statements (3 years)
C. Projected Cash Flow Statements (3 years)
D. Projected Balance Sheets (3 years)

Appendixes

A. Sources of Information
B. Procedures for Making Estimates

Annexes:

A. State of Minnesota Corporation Division Fee Schedule and Certificate
B. Application for Minnesota Tax Identification Number
C. Book—*Guide to Doing Business in Minnesota*
D. Application for a Registered Identification Number
E. List of manufacturers representatives handling apparel in the upper Midwest
F. List of apparel manufacturers in India

Appendix B

Trade Contacts*

Alabama

Alabama Development Office
Fred Braswell, Dir.
State Capitol
Montgomery, Ala. 36130
(205) 263-0048

Alabama Intl. Trade Center
University of Alabama
Nisa Miranda, Dir.
P.O. Box 870396
University, Ala. 35487-0396
(205) 348-7621

Alabama State Docks
John Dutton, Dir.
P.O. Box 1588
Mobile, Ala. 36633
(205) 690-6112

Alabama World Trade Assn.
Dr. Robert Lager, Exec. Secr.
Ste. 131, 250 N. Water St.
Mobile, Ala. 36602
(205) 433-3174

Birmingham Area Chamber of
Commerce
Don Medley
P.O. Box 10127
Birmingham, Ala. 35202
(205) 323-5461

Center for Intl. Trade &
Commerce
Dr. Robert Lager, Dir.
Ste. 131, 250 N. Water St.
Mobile, Ala. 36602
(205) 433-1151

North Alabama Intl. Trade Assn
Peggy Barnard, Dir.
Madison County Commission
7th Floor, Madison County
Courthouse
Huntsville, Ala. 35801
(205) 532-3570

U.S. Dept. of Commerce (ITA)
Tad Lidikay, Deputy Dir.
Room 302, 2015 2nd Ave. N.
Birmingham, Ala. 35203
(205) 731-1331

Alaska

State of Alaska
Dept. of Commerce & Econ.
Dev.
Larry Merculieff, Commissioner
P.O. Box D
Juneau, Alaska 99811
(907) 465-2500

State of Alaska
Governor's Office of Intl. Trade
Bob Poe, Dir.
3601 C St., Ste. 798
Anchorage, Alaska 99503
(907) 561-5585

Alaska State Chamber of
Commerce
George Krusz, Pres.
310 Second St.
Juneau, Alaska 99801
(907) 586-2323

Anchorage Chamber of
Commerce
Horace Hunt, Pres.
437 E St., Ste. 300
Anchorage, Alaska 99501
(907) 272-2401

Fairbanks Chamber of Commerce
Larry Kelly, Pres.
709 Second Ave.
Fairbanks, Alaska 99701
(907) 452-1105

U.S. Department of Commerce
(ITA)
Charles F. Becker, Dir.
222 West 7th Ave., Box 32
Anchorage, Alaska 99513-5041
(907) 271-5041

University of Alaska
Alaska Center for Intl. Business
Dr. John Choon Kim, Exec. Dir.
4201 Tudor Centre Dr., Ste. 120
Anchorage, Alaska 99508
(907) 561-2322

World Trade Center Alaska
Carolyn DePalatis, Dir.
4201 Tudor Centre Dr., Ste. 300
Anchorage, Alaska 99508
(907) 561-1615

Arizona

Amer. Graduate School of Intl.
Management
William Kane, Dir. of Intercom
Thunderbird Campus
Glendale, Ariz. 85306
(602) 978-7115

Arizona Dept. of Commerce
Donald Cline, Exec. Dir.
3800 N. Central
Phoenix, Ariz. 85012
(602) 280-1300

Ariz. District Export Council
Barbara M. Barrett, Chairwoman
4617 E. Ocotillo Rd.
Paradise Valley, Ariz. 85253
(602) 840-7439

Ariz.-Mexico Commission
David Jankofski
1700 W. Washington
State Office Tower
Phoenix, Ariz. 85007
(602) 542-1345

Ariz. World Trade Assn.
Vince Zamis, Pres.
c/o Phoenix Chamber of
Commerce
34 W. Monroe
Phoenix, Ariz. 85003
(602) 254-5521

*Reprinted with permission of the U.S. Department of Commerce from
Business America, July 16, 1990.

Consular Corps of Arizona
Skipper Ross, Liaison Attache
8331 E. Rose Lane
Scottsdale, Ariz. 85253
(602) 947-6011

Sunbelt World Trade Assn.
Robert Bean
P.O. Box 42995
Tucson, Ariz. 85733
(602) 885-7866

U.S.Dept. of Commerce (ITA)
Donald W. Fry, Dir.
3412 Federal Bldg.
230 N. 1st Ave.
Phoenix, Ariz. 85025
(602) 379-3285

Arkansas

Ark. Assn. of Planning & Dev.
District
Charles Cummings, Pres.
P.O. Box 187
Lonoke, Ark. 72086
(501) 676-2721

Ark. District Export Council
Vernon Markham, III, Chairman
Savers Building, Ste. 811
Capitol at Spring St.
Little Rock, Ark. 72201
(501) 378-5794

Ark. Industrial Dev. Commission
Maria Haley, Mkting. Dir.
#1 State Capitol Mall
Little Rock, Ark. 72201
(501) 371-7678

Ark. Intl. Center
Dr. Harold Vaughn
University of Arkansas at Little
Rock
33rd and University
Little Rock, Ark. 72204
(501) 569-3782

Ark. State Chamber of
Commerce
Brent Stephenson
P.O. Box 3645
Little Rock, Ark. 72203-3645
(501) 374-9225

Little Rock Chamber of
Commerce
Paul Harvel, Dir.
#1 Spring St.
Little Rock, Ark. 72201
(501) 374-4871

World Trade Club
D. Joseph O'Brien, Pres.
1100 TCBY Tower
425 W. Capitol
Little Rock, Ark. 72201
(501) 688-8229

World Trade Club of Northeast
Ark.
Dr. John Kaminarides, Dir.
Office of Business Research
P.O. Box 970
State University, Ark. 72467
(501) 972-3823

U.S. Dept. of Commerce (ITA)
Lon Hardin, Dir.
Savers Bldg., Ste. 811
Capitol at Spring St.
Little Rock, Ark. 72201
(501) 378-5794

California

British-American Chamber of
Commerce
Peter Gardiner, Pres.
Stewart Hume, Exec. Dir.
41 Sutter St., Ste. 303
San Francisco, Calif. 94104
(415) 296-8645

Calif. Assn. of Port Authorities
Philip H. Schott, Exec. Secy.
1510-14th St.
Sacramento, Calif. 95814
(916) 446-6339

Calif. Chamber of Commerce
Susanne Stirling, Dir. of Intl.
Trade Dept.
1201 K St., 12th Floor
P.O. Box 1736
Sacramento, Calif. 95812-1736
(916) 444-6670

Calif. Council for Intl. Trade
Martina H. Johnson, Exec. Dir.
700 Montgomery St., Ste. 305
San Francisco, Calif. 94111
(415) 788-4127

Calif. Export Finance Office
J.H. Dethero, Reg. Manager
World Trade Center, Box 250-S
San Francisco, Calif. 94111
(415) 556-5868

Calif. Export Finance Office
107 S. Broadway, Ste. 8039
Los Angeles, Calif. 90012
(213) 620-2433

Calif. State Dept. of Commerce
Kenneth L. Gibson, Dir.
1121 L. St., Ste. 600
Sacramento, Calif. 95814
(916) 322-1394

Calif. State World Trade
Commission
Gregory Mignano, Exec. Dir.
1121 L St., Ste. 310
Sacramento, Calif. 95814
(916) 324-5511

Coordination Council for North
American Affairs on Taiwan
Enti Liu, Director General
555 Montgomery St., Ste. 501
San Francisco, Calif. 94111
(415) 362-7680

Coordination Council for North
American Affairs, Cultural
Division (Taiwan)
Ding Yih Liu, Dir.
530 Bush St., Ste. 401
San Francisco, Calif. 94108
(415) 398-4979

Econ. Dev. Corp.
County of Los Angeles
Reg Bottger, Pres.
221 S. Figueroa St., Ste. 100
Los Angeles, Calif. 90112
(213) 625-7752

Export Managers Assn. of Calif.
Dan Dahlo-Johnson, Chairman
14549 Victory Blvd., Ste. 5
Van Nuys, Calif. 91411
(818) 782-3350

Foreign Trade Assn. of S. Calif.
Jay K. Winter, Exec. Secy.
900 Wilshire Blvd., Ste. 1434
Los Angeles, Calif. 90017
(213) 672-0634

French-American Chamber of
Commerce
Cyril Yansouni, Pres.
Jean Ward Jacote, Exec. Dir.
425 Bush St., Ste. 401
San Francisco, Calif. 94108
(415) 398-2449

German-American Chamber of
Commerce of the Pacific Coast,
Inc.
T.H. Heinrichs, Pres.
Adam J. Heldenreich, Mging.
Dir.
465 California St., Ste. 910
San Francisco, Calif. 94104
(415) 392-2262

Inland Pacific World Trade
Committee
Dale King, Dir.
1035 W. Bonnie Brae
Ontario, Calif. 91762
(714) 984-3680

Intl. Business Assn. of S. Calif.
Long Beach Chamber of
Commerce
Corky Gill, V.P.
One World Trade Center, Ste.
350
Long Beach, Calif. 90831-0350
(213) 436-1251

L.A. Chamber of Commerce
Corinne Muratt, Manager
404 Bixel St.
Los Angeles, Calif. 90017
(213) 629-0602

Greater L.A. World Trade Center
Assn.
Merry A. Tuten, Exec. Dir.
One World Trade Center, Ste.
295
Long Beach, Calif. 90831-0295
(213) 495-7070

Hong Kong Econ. and Trade
Office
Peter Johnson, Director
180 Sutter St., 4th Fl.
San Francisco, Calif. 94104
(415) 397-2215

JETRO San Francisco
Makoto Ochida, Dir. Gen.
360 Post St., Ste. 501
San Francisco, Calif. 94108
(415) 392-1333

Marine Exchange of the San
Francisco Bay Region
Robert H. Langner, Exec. Dir.
303 World Trade Center
San Francisco, Calif. 94111
(415) 982-7788

New Zealand-American Assn.
John E. Ritchie, Pres.
POB 2888
San Francisco, Calif. 94126

Northern Calif. District Export
Council
J.H. Dethero, Chairman
450 Golden Gate Ave.
Box 36013
San Francisco, Calif. 94102
(415) 556-5870

Oakland Chamber of Commerce
Donald I. Barber, Pres. and CEO
475-14th St.
Oakland, Calif. 94612
(415) 874-4800

Oakland World Trade Assn.
Sharon Vonderau, Bd. of Dir.
475-14th St.
Oakland, Calif. 94612-1900
(415) 388-8829

Orange County Intl. Marketing
Assn.
Dr. Irene Lange, Dept. Chairman
Cal State Fullerton
Dept. of Marketing
Fullerton, Calif. 92634
(714) 773-2223

Pacific Indonesian Chamber of
Commerce
Eugene Mihaly, Pres.
Jeremy Potash, Exec. Dir.
1946 Embarcadero, Ste. 200
Oakland, Calif. 94606
(415) 536-1967

Pan American Society of San
Francisco
Carlos E. Monge, Exec. Dir.
312 Sutter St., Ste. 604
San Francisco, Calif. 94108
(415) 788-4764

San Diego Chamber of
Commerce
110 West "C" St., Ste. 1600
San Diego, Calif. 92101
(619) 232-0124

County of San Diego
Intl. Trade Commission
1600 Pacific Highway, Room
375
(Mail Station A-227)
San Diego, Calif. 92101

San Diego District Export
Council
6363 Greenwich Drive, Ste. 145
San Diego, Calif. 92122
(619) 557-5395

San Diego Unified Port District
3165 Pacific Highway
San Diego, Calif. 92112
(619) 291-3900

San Diego World Trade Assn.
6363 Greenwich Dr., Ste. 140
San Diego, Calif. 92122
(619) 453-4605

San Francisco Custom Brokers &
Freight Forwarders Assn.
Robert H. Langner, Exec. Dir.
303 World Trade Center
San Francisco, Calif. 94111
(415) 982-7788

San Francisco Intl. Managers
Assn.
Herbert H. Heberling, Pres.
P.O. Box 2425
Custom House
San Francisco, Calif. 94126
(415) 461-3286

San Francisco Intl. Trade Council
Jolene Munoz, Pres.
465 California St., 9th Flr.
San Francisco, Calif. 94104
(415) 392-4511

San Francisco World Trade
Assn., San Francisco Chamber of
Commerce
Harry Orbelian, Sr. V.P.
465 California St., 9th Flr.
San Francisco, Calif. 94104
(415) 392-4511, ext. 801

San Mateo County Econ. Dev.
Assn.—World Trade Council
Henry "Bud" Bostwick, Jr.,
Exec. V.P.
840 Malcolm Rd., Ste. 100
Burlingame, Calif. 94010
(415) 692-7632

Santa Clara Valley World Trade
Assn.
Tzitza Bozinovich, Pres.
P.O. Box 4180
Santa Clara, Calif. 95054
(408) 986-1406

S. Calif. District Export Council
Shirley Frahm, Chairman
11000 Wilshire Blvd., Rm. 9200
Los Angeles, Calif. 90024
(213) 575-7115

Southwestern College
Small Business & Intl. Trade
Center
7101 Siempre Viva Rd., Ste. 200
Otay Mesa, Calif. 92073
(619) 661-1135

U.S.-Arab Chamber of
Commerce (Pacific)
J.S. Patterson, Pres.
D.J. Asfour, Exec. Dir.
One Hallidie Plaza, Ste. 504
San Francisco, Calif. 94102
(415) 398-9200

U.S. Dept. of Commerce (ITA)
Sherwin Chen, Act. Dir.
11000 Wilshire Blvd., Rm. 9200
Los Angeles, Calif. 90024
(213) 575-7203

U.S. Dept. of Commerce (ITA)
Richard Powell, Dir.
6363 Greenwich Dr., Ste. 145
San Diego, Calif. 92122
(619) 557-5395

U.S. Dept. of Commerce (ITA)
Betty D. Neuhart, Reg.
Managing Dir.-Western Region
450 Golden Gate Ave.
Box 36013
San Francisco, Calif. 94102
(415) 556-5868

U.S. Dept. of Commerce (ITA)
Jesse Campos, Intl. Trade
Specialist
116-A W. 4th St., Ste. 1
Santa Ana, Calif. 92701
(714) 836-2461

U.S. Small Business
Administration
880 Front St., Rm. 4529
San Diego, Calif. 92188
(619) 557-7272

U.S. Small Business
Administration
Laurance M. Pier, Reg. Intl.
Trade Officer
450 Golden Gate Ave.
Box 36044
San Francisco, Calif. 94102
(415) 556-4724

World Trade Center Assn. of
Orange County
Susan T. Lentz, Exec. Dir.
One Park Plaza, Ste. 150
Irvine, Calif. 92714
(714) 724-9822

Colorado

Colo. Assn. of Commerce and
Industry
George Dibble, Pres. and CEO
1776 Lincoln St., Ste. 1200
Denver, Colo. 80203
(303) 831-7411

Colo. Intl. Trade Office
Morgan Smith, Dir.
1625 Broadway, Ste. 680
Denver, Colo. 80202
(303) 892-3850

Denver Chamber of Commerce
Richard D. Fleming, Pres. &
CEO
1600 Sherman St.
Denver, Colo. 80203
(303) 894-8500

Intl. Business Assn. of the
Rockies
Jan Sandhouse Hurst, Pres.
10200 W. 44th Ave., Ste. 304
Wheat Ridge, Colo. 80033
(303) 422-7905

Rocky Mt. World Trade Center
Assn.
John J. Reardon, Pres.
World Trade Center
1625 Broadway, Ste. 680
Denver, Colo. 80202
(303) 592-5760

U.S. Dept. of Commerce (ITA)
James W. Manis, District Dir.
World Trade Center
1625 Broadway, Ste. 680
Denver, Colo. 80202
(303) 844-3246

U.S. Small Business Admin.
Dennis Chrisbaum, Reg. Intl.
Trade Officer
999 18th Street, Ste. 701
Denver, Colo. 80202
(303) 294-7872

Connecticut

Conn. Business & Industry Assn.
370 Asylum St.
Hartford, Conn. 06103-2022
(203) 547-1661

Conn. Dept. Econ. Devel.
Intl. Division
Matthew J. Broder, Dir.
865 Brook St.
Rocky Hill, Conn. 06067-3405
(203) 258-4256

Conn. District Export Council
David E. Moore, Chairman
450 Main St., Room 610B
Hartford, Conn. 06103

Conn. Foreign Trade Assn.
Robert S. Adamsky, Pres.
611 Access Rd.
Stratford, Conn. 06497
(203) 336-7323

Conn. Intl. Trade Assn.
Florence A. Millette, Pres.
P.O. Box 317
Windsor Locks, Conn. 06096
(203) 272-9175

Conn. Small Business Devel.
Center
John Patrick O'Connor,
State Dir.
Room 422, U-41SB
368 Fairfield Rd.
Storrs, Conn. 06268
(203) 486-4135

Greater Hartford Chamber of
Commerce
Timothy Moynihan, Pres.
250 Constitution Plaza
Hartford, Conn. 06103
(203) 525-4451

Greater New Haven Chamber of
Commerce
Mathew Nemerson, Pres.
195 Church St.
New Haven, Conn. 06510
(203) 787-6735

Middlesex County Chamber of
Commerce
Larry McHugh, Pres.
393 Main St.
Middletown, Conn. 06457
(203) 347-6924

Southwestern Area Chamber of
Commerce and Industry Assn. of
Conn., Inc.
Christopher Bruhl, Pres.
One Landmark Square
Stamford, Conn. 06901
(203) 359-3220

U.S. Dept. of Commerce (ITA)
Eric B. Outwater, RMD
450 Main St., Room 610B
Hartford, Conn. 06103
(203) 240-3530

U.S. Small Business Admin.
Michael P. McHale, Dir.
330 Main St.
Hartford, Conn. 06106
(203) 240-4670

Westconn Intl. Trade Assn. Inc.
Victor M. Madeira, Pres.
P.O. Box 3063
Stamford, Conn. 06905
(203) 468-2863

Delaware

Delaware Dept. of Agriculture
Robert Smallwood, Export
Specialist
2320 S. DuPont Highway
Dover, Del. 19901
(302) 736-4811

Delaware Dev. Office
Business Dev. Office
Donal Sullivan, Dir.
P.O. Box 1401
Dover, Del. 19903
(302) 736-4271

Delaware-Eastern Pa. District
Export Council
Paul J. Roessel, Vice Chair
475 Allendale Rd., Ste. 202
King of Prussia, Pa. 19406
(215) 962-4980

U.S. Department of Commerce
(ITA)
Robert Kistler, Dir.
475 Allendale Rd., Ste. 202
King of Prussia, Pa. 19406
(215) 962-4980

World Trade Center Institute
(Del.)
Michael Rice, Dir.
DuPont Bldg., Ste. 1022
Wilmington, Del. 19899
(302) 656-7905

District of Columbia

D.C. Office of Intl. Business
Diane Paige
1250 I St.
Ste. 1003
Washington, D.C. 20005
(202) 727-1576

U.S. Dept. of Commerce (ITA)
Branch Office
Stephen B. Hall, Trade Specialist
Room 1066, Hoover Bldg.
Washington, D.C. 20230
(202) 377-3181

Greater Washington Board of
Trade
Allan Gesser
1129 20th St. N.W.
Washington, D.C. 20036
(202) 857-5900

World Trade Center, Washington
Richard Anderson
1101 King St.
Alexandria, Va. 22314
(703) 684-6622

Florida

Beacon Council
Intl. Business Development
George Von Gries, Exec. V.P.
One World Trade Plaza
Ste. 2400
80 S.W. 8th St.
Miami, Fla. 33130
(305) 536-8000

Coral Gables Chamber of
Commerce
Intl. Trade Committee
Len Pagano, Pres.
50 Aragon St.
Coral Gables, Fla. 33134
(305) 446-1657

District Export Council
Charles McKay, Chairman
c/o U.S. Department of
Commerce
51 S.W. First Ave., Room 224
Miami, Fla. 33130
(305) 536-5267

Florida Bar
International Section
George R. Harper, Chairman
650 Apalachee Parkway
Tallahassee, Fla. 32399-2300
(904) 561-5600

Florida Council of Intl. Dev.
J. Lamar Merk, Exec. Dir.
2701 LeJeune Rd., Ste. 330
Coral Gables, Fla. 33134
(305) 448-4035

Florida Customs Brokers &
Forwarders Assn.
Barbie Reilly, Exec. V.P.
P.O. Box 522022
Miami, Fla. 33152
(305) 871-7177

Florida Delegation, Southeast
U.S./Japan Assn.
J. Lamar Merk, Exec. Dir.
2701 LeJeune Rd., Ste. 330
Coral Gables, Fla. 33134
(305) 448-4035

Florida Dept. of Commerce
Bureau of Intl. Trade and Dev.
Tom Slattery, Chief
331 Collins Building
Tallahassee, Fla. 32399-2000
(904) 488-6124

Florida Department of Commerce
Office for Latin American Trade
Manny Mencia, Chief
2701 LeJeune Rd., Ste. 330
Coral Gables, Fla. 33134
(305) 446-8106

Florida Exporters & Importers
Assn.
Harry Diamond, Pres.
One World Trade Plaza, Ste.
1800
80 S.W. 8th St.
Miami, Fla. 33130
(305) 579-0094

Florida Intl. Agricultural Trade
Council
Leroy Baldwin, Pres.
Mayo Building, Room 412
Tallahassee, Fla. 32399-0800
(904) 488-4366

Florida Intl. Bankers Assn.
Charlotte Gallogly, Exec. Dir.
One World Trade Plaza, Ste.
1800
80 S.W. 8th St.
Miami, Fla. 33130
(305) 579-0064

Florida/Korea Economic
Cooperation Committee
J. Lamar Meck, Exec. Dir.
2701 LeJeune Rd., Ste. 330
Coral Gables, Fla. 33134
(305) 448-4035

Florida Ports Council
Paul deMariano, Pres.
2701 Ponce de Leon Blvd.
Ste. 203
Coral Gables, Fla. 33134
(305) 446-7297

Jacksonville Chamber of
Commerce
Intl. Dev. Dept.
Rebecca Harrington, Dir.
P.O. Box 329
Jacksonville, Fla. 32201
(904) 353-0300

Jacksonville Customs Brokers &
Forwarders Assn.
Fred Whelan, Pres.
P.O. Box 3342
Jacksonville, Fla. 32206
(904) 356-9646

Greater Miami Chamber of
Commerce
Intl. Econ. Development
Gilbert Lee Sandler, Vice
Chairman
Omni Complex
1601 Biscayne Blvd.
Miami, Fla. 33132
(305) 350-7700

Miami Foreign Trade Assn.
Kenneth English, Exec. Dir.
2501 N.W. 72nd Ave..
Miami, Fla. 33122
(305) 592-4893

Greater Orlando Chamber of
Commerce
Intl. Business
Margie Varney, Coord.
P.O. Box 1234
Orlando, Fla. 32802
(407) 425-1234

Orlando World Trade Assn.
Hal Sumral, Coord.
c/o Greater Orlando Chamber of
Commerce
P.O. Box 1234
Orlando, Fla. 32802
(407) 425-1234

Polk Intl. Trade Assoc.
Waneta Curtis, Coord.
600 N. Broadway St., Ste. 300
P.O. Box 1839
Bartow, Fla. 33830
(813) 534-6066

Tampa Bay Intl. Trade Council
Cliff Topping, Exec. Dir.
P.O. Box 420
Tampa, Fla. 33601
(813) 228-7777

U.S. Department of Commerce
(ITA)
Ivan Cosimi, Dir.
51 S.W. First Ave., Room 224
Miami, Fla. 33130
(305) 536-5267

World Trade Center Miami
Ken Claussen, Pres.
One World Trade Plaza, Ste.
1800
80 S.W. 8th St.
Miami, Fla. 33130
(305) 579-0064

World Trade Council of N.W.
Florida
Gordon Lawless, Pres.
P.O. Box 1972
Pensacola, Fla. 32589-1972
(904) 444-1222

Georgia

Business Council of Georgia
Gene Dyson, Pres..
233 Peachtree St.
Ste. 200
Atlanta, Ga. 30303
(404) 223-2264

Georgia Dept. of Agriculture
Thomas T. Irvin, Commissioner
Capitol Square
328 Agriculture Building
Atlanta, Ga. 30334
(404) 656-3740

Georgia Dept. of Industry, Trade
and Tourism
Randy Cardoza, Commissioner
285 Peachtree Center Ave.
Stes. 1000 & 1100
P.O. Box 1776
Atlanta, Ga. 30303
(404) 656-3556

Georgia Ports Authority
George J. Nichols, Exec. Dir.
P.O. Box 2406
Savannah, Ga. 31412
(912) 964-1721

U.S. Dept. of Commerce (ITA)
George T. Norton, Jr., Dir.
Plaza Square N.
4360 Chamblee-Dunwoody Rd.
Ste. 310
Atlanta, Ga. 30341

U.S. Dept. of Commerce (ITA)
James W. McIntire, Dir.
120 Barnard St.
Savannah, Ga. 31401
(912) 944-4204

Hawaii

Chamber of Commerce of Hawaii
Robert B. Robinson, Pres.
735 Bishop St.
Honolulu, Hawaii 96813
(808) 522-8800

Economic Development Corp. of
Honolulu
Frederick A. Sexton, Pres.
1001 Bishop St., Ste. 735
Honolulu, Hawaii 96813
(808) 545-4533

Foreign Trade Zone No. 9
Homer A. Maxey, Administrator
521 Ala Moana Blvd., Pier 2
Honolulu, Hawaii 96813
(808) 548-5435

State of Hawaii
Dept. of Bus. and Econ. Dev.
Trade and Ind. Dev. Branch
Dennis Ling, Chief
P.O. Box 2359
Honolulu, Hawaii 96804
(808) 548-7719

Pacific Basin Dev. Council
Jerry B. Norris, Ex. Dir.
567 S. King St., Ste. 325
Honolulu, Hawaii 96813
(808) 523-9325

U.S. Dept. of Commerce (ITA)
George Dolan, Director
300 Ala Moana Blvd.
Box 50026
Honolulu, Hawaii 96817
(808) 541-1782

Idaho

District Export Council
Mark Samson, Chairman
Idaho Wheat Commission
1109 Main St., Ste. 310
Boise, Idaho 83702
(208) 334-2353

Division of Intl. Business
David P. Christensen,
Administrator
Idaho Dept. of Commerce
700 W. State St.
Boise, Idaho 83720
(208) 334-2470

Intl. Trade Committee
Shirl C. Boyce, Manager
Boise Area Chamber of
Commerce
P.O. Box 2368
Boise, Idaho 83701
(208) 334-5515

U.S. Dept. of Commerce (ITA)
Stephen B. Thompson, Sr., Intl.
Trade Specialist
700 W. State St., 2nd Floor
Boise, Idaho 83720
(208) 334-3857

Illinois

Automotive Exporters Club of
Chicago
Mrs. Martha Herrera, V.P.
3205 S. Shields Ave.
Chicago, Ill. 60616
(312) 567-6500
Toll Free (1-800) 666-1552

Carnets
U.S. Council for Intl. Business
Susan Underwood
1930 Thoreau Dr., Ste. 101
Schaumburg, Ill. 60173
(708) 490-9696

Central Illinois Coord.
Committee for Intl. Trade
J. Terry Iversen
205 Arcade Bldg.
725 Wright St.
Champaign, Ill. 61820
(217) 333-1465

Chicago Assn. of Commerce &
Industry
Robert Lahey, Dir.
World Trade Div.
200 N. LaSalle
Chicago, Ill. 60603
(312) 580-6900

Chicago Convention and Tourism
Bureau, Inc.
Gerald Roper, Pres.
McCormick Place-on-the-Lake
Chicago, Ill. 60616
(312) 567-8500

Chicago Council on Foreign
Relations
John E. Rielly, Pres.
116 S. Michigan Ave., 10th Fl.
Chicago, Ill. 60603
(312) 726-3860

Chicago Midwest Credit
Management Assn.
Liza Blanding, Credit Reporting
Mgr.
315 South N.W., Hwy.
Park Ridge, Ill. 60068
(708) 696-3000

Customs Brokers and Foreign
Freight Forwarders Assn. of
Chicago, Inc.
Len Lesiak, Pres.
P.O. Box 66584/AMP O'Hare
Chicago, Ill. 60666
(708) 678-5400

Econ. Dev. Commission
Mary Tittman, Intl. Business
Consultant
1503 Merchandise Mart
Chicago, Ill. 60654
(312) 744-9550

Foreign Credit Insurance Assn.
Richard A. Klein, Reg. Mgr.
20 N. Clark St., Ste. 910
Chicago, Ill. 60602
(312) 641-1915

Ill. Ambassadors
233 S. Wacker Drive
633 Sears Tower
Chicago, Ill. 60606
(312) 715-0734

Ill. Dept. of Commerce and
Community Affairs
Dan Rutherford, Mgr.
Intl. Business Div.
310 S. Michigan Ave.,
Ste. 1000
Chicago, Ill. 60604
(312) 793-7164

Ill. District Export Council
George Wilcox, Chairman
55 E. Monroe, Rm. 1406
Chicago, Ill. 60603
(312) 353-4450

Ill. Export Council
Robert H. Newtson, Dir.
321 N. Clark St., Ste. 550
Chicago, Ill. 60610
(312) 793-1WTC

Ill. Export Dev. Authority
Joseph P. Hannon, Exec. Dir.
321 N. Clark St., Ste. 550
Chicago, Ill. 60610
(312) 793-4982

Ill. Intl. Port District
Anthony G. Ianello, Exec. Dir.
3600 E. 95th St.
95th St. at Lake Front
Chicago, Ill. 60617
(312) 646-4400

Ill. Manufacturers' Assn.
Jack Roadman, V.P. Admin./
Secy.
175 W. Jackson Blvd., Ste. 1321
Chicago, Ill. 60604
(312) 372-7373

Ill. State Bar Assn.
75 E. Wacker Dr., Ste. 2100
Chicago, Ill. 60601
(312) 726-8775

Ill. Quad City Chamber of
Commerce
John Verona, Exec. Mgr.
622 19th St.
Moline, Ill. 61265
(309) 762-3661

Institute for Intl. Education
Robert Houston, Dir.
401 N. Wabash Ave., Ste. 722
Chicago, Ill. 60611
(312) 644-1400

Intl. Air Cargo Assn. of Chicago
P.O. Box 66235/AMF O'Hare
Chicago, Ill. 60666
(312) 782-8122

Intl. Trade Assn. of Greater
Chicago
Gilberto Mundaca, Pres.
P.O. Box 454
Elk Grove Village, Ill.
60009-0454
(708) 980-4109

Intl. Trade Club of Chicago
Scott Dunbar, Pres.
203 N. Wabash, Ste. 1102
Chicago, Ill. 60601
(312) 368-9197

Intl. Visitors Center
James Morrissy, Dir.
520 N. Michigan Ave., Ste. 522
Chicago, Ill. 60611
(312) 645-1836

Library of Intl. Relations
77 S. Wacker Dr.
Chicago, Ill. 60605
(312) 567-5234

Mid-America Intl. Agri-Trade
Council (MIATCO)
Drayton Mayers, Exec. Dir.
820 Davis St.
Evanston, Ill. 60201
(708) 866-7300

U.S. Dept. of Commerce (ITA)
LoRee P. Silloway, Dir.
55 E. Monroe, Ste. 1406
Chicago, Ill. 60603
(312) 353-4450

U.S. Dept. of Commerce (ITA)
Branch Office
c/o Rockford Area Chamber of
Commerce
P.O. Box 1747
Rockford, Ill. 81110-0247
(815) 987-8123 or 8128

U.S. Dept of Commerce (ITA)
Branch Office
c/o W.R. Harper College
Roselle and Algonquin Rd.
Palatine, Ill. 60067
(312) 397-2000, ext. 2532

U.S. Great Lakes Shipping Assn.
Vera Paktor, Exec. Dir
3434 E. 95th St.
Chicago, Ill. 60617
(312) 978-0342

U.S. Small Business Admin.
District Export Develop/SCORE
John L. Smith, District Dir.
219 S. Dearborn St., Ste. 437
Chicago, Ill. 60604
(312) 353-4528

World Trade Council of Northern
Ill.
Thomas Bailey, Pres.
515 N. Court
Rockford, Ill. 61103
(815) 987-8100

Indiana

Forum for Intl. Professional
Services
Attn: President
One N. Capitol, Ste. 200
Indianapolis, Ind. 46204
(317) 264-3100

Greater Ft. Wayne Chamber of
Commerce
Jan A. Mills, Dir., World Trade
826 Ewing St.
Ft. Wayne, Ind. 46802
(219) 424-1435

Indiana-Asean Council, Inc.
David W.B. Anderson, Exec.
Dir.
One American Square
Box 82017
Indianapolis, Ind. 46282
(317) 685-1341

Indiana Chamber of Commerce
Christine S. Huston, Manager
Econ. and Business Dev.
One N. Capitol, Ste. 200
Indianapolis, Ind. 46204-2248
(317) 264-6892

Indiana Dept. of Commerce
Dir. of Intl. Trade
Business Dev. Div.
One N. Capitol, Ste. 700
Indianapolis, Ind. 46204-2288
(317) 232-3527

Michiana World Trade Club
Michael Bruno, Pres.
P.O. Box 1715-A
South Bend, Ind. 46634
(219) 289-7323

Tri State World Trade Council
Bryan Williams, Pres.
Old Post Office Place
100 N.W. 2nd St., Ste. 202
Evansville, Ind. 47708
(812) 425-8147

U.S. Dept. of Commerce (ITA)
Andrew W. Thress, Dir.
One N. Capitol, Ste. 520
Indianapolis, Ind. 46204-2227
(317) 226-6214

World Trade Club of Indiana,
Inc.
One N. Capitol, Ste. 200
Indianapolis, Ind. 46204-2248
(317) 264-6892

Iowa

Cedar Falls Chamber of
Commerce
Northeast Iowa Intl. Trade
Council
10 Main St.
P.O. Box 367
Cedar Falls, Iowa 50613
(319) 266-3593

Cedar Rapids Area Chamber of
Commerce
Intl. Trade Office
424 1st Ave., N.E. 52401
P.O. Box 4860
Cedar Rapids, Iowa 52407

Greater Des Moines Chamber of
Commerce
300 Saddlery Bldg.
309 Court Ave.
Des Moines, Iowa 50309
(515) 286-4950

Iowa Dept. of Agriculture
Intl. Mkting. Div.
Wallace Bldg.
Des Moines, Iowa 50319
(515) 281-6190

Iowa Dept. of Econ. Dev.
Intl. Mkting. Div.
200 E. Grand Ave.
Des Moines,.Iowa 50309
(515) 281-3251

Iowa Intl. Trade Center
312-8th St.
Des Moines, Iowa 50309
(515) 246-6013

Midwest Agribusiness Trade and
Information Center (MATRIC)
312-8th St., Ste. 240
Des Moines, Iowa 50309
(515) 246-6027

Sioux City Chamber of
Commerce
Siouxland Intl. Trade Council
101 Pierce St.
Sioux City, Iowa 51101
(712) 255-7903

U.S. Dept. of Commerce (ITA)
Branch Office
Harvey Timberlake, Trade
Specialist
424 1st Ave. N.E.
Cedar Rapids, Iowa 52401
(319) 362-8418

U.S. Dept. of Commerce (ITA)
John H. Steuber, Jr., Dir.
210 Walnut St., Room 817
Des Moines, Iowa 50309
(515) 284-4222

U.S. Small Business Admin.
210 Walnut St., Room 749
Des Moines, Iowa 50309
(515) 284-4522

U.S. Small Business Admin.
373 Collins Rd. N.E.
Cedar Rapids, Iowa 52402
(319) 393-8630

Kansas

Mid-America World Trade Center
Elliott Wimberly, Pres.
301 N. Main St.
Epic Center-Ste. 1810
Wichita, Kans. 67202
(316) 291-8475

Kansas Dept. of Commerce
Trade Development Div.
Harry J. Salisbury, Dir.
400 SW 8th St., Ste. 500
Topeka, Kans. 66603
(913) 296-4027

Sedgwick County Foreign Trade
Zone #161
Ms. Louanna Honeycutt
525 N. Main St.
Wichita, Kans. 67203
(316) 383-7575

U.S. Dept. of Commerce (ITA)
Wichita Branch Office
George D. Lavid, Trade Spec.
River Park Place, Ste. 580
727 N. Waco
Wichita, Kans. 67203
(316) 269-6160

U.S. Small Business
Administration
Eugene F. Keady, Chief, Finance
Div.
110 E. Waterman
Wichita, Kans. 67202
(316) 269-6273

Wichita Area Chamber of
Commerce
Tim Witsman, Pres.
350 W. Douglas
Wichita, Kans. 67202
(316) 265-7771

World Trade Council of Wichita
Dr. Dharma deSilva, Chairperson
Barton School of Business
Campus Box 88
Wichita State Univ.
Wichita, Kans. 67208
(316) 689-3176

Kentucky

Bluegrass Area Dev. District
Kathy Figlestahler, Secy.
3220 Nicholasville Rd.
Lexington, Ky. 40503
(606) 272-6656

Kentuckiana World Commerce
Council
Marsha J. Adkins, Bus. Mgr.
Secy.
P.O. Box 58456
Louisville, Ky. 40258
(502) 583-5551

Ky. Cabinet for Econ. Dev.
Michael Hayes, Dir.
Office of Intl. Mkting.
Capital Plaza Tower
Frankfort, Ky. 40601
(502) 564-2170

Ky. District Export Council
James Hansen, Vice Chairman
First Nat. Bank of Louisville
P.O. Box 3600
Louisville, Ky. 40233
(502) 581-4228

Louisville/Jefferson County
Office of Econ. Dev.
Howard Gudell, Exec. Dir.
200 Brown & Williamson Tower
401 S. Fourth Street
Louisville, Ky. 40202
(502) 625-3051

Northern Kentucky Intl. Trade
Assn.
Morag Adlon, Secy.
7505 Sussex Drive
Florence, Ky. 41042
(606) 283-1885

U.S. Dept. of Commerce (ITA)
Don R. Henderson, Dir.
Courthouse Building
601 W. Broadway, Room 636B
Louisville, Ky. 40202
(502) 582-5066

Louisiana

Chamber of Commerce/New
Orleans and River Region
David Batzel, Pres.
301 Camp St.
New Orleans, La. 70130
(504) 527-6900

La. Dept. of Econ. Devel.
William Jackson, Dir.
Office of Intl. Trade, Finance
and Devel.
P.O. Box 94185
Baton Rouge, La. 70804-9185
(504) 342-5362

Port of New Orleans
J. Ron Brinson, Executive Port
Dir. and Gen. Mgr.
P.O. Box 60046
New Orleans, La. 70160
(504) 528-3259

U.S. Dept. of Commerce (ITA)
Paul Guidry, Dir.
432 World Trade Center
2 Canal St.
New Orleans, La. 70130
(504) 589-6546

World Trade Center of New
Orleans
Eugene Schreiber, Mging Dir.
Executive Offices, Ste. 2900
2 Canal St.
New Orleans, La. 70130
(504) 529-1601

World Trade Club of Greater
New Orleans
Rose Mary PeDotti, Exec. Secy.
1132 World Trade Center
2 Canal St.
New Orleans, La. 70130
(504) 525-7201

Maine

Greater Bangor Chamber of
Commerce
Elizabeth S. Stowell, Exec. Dir.
519 Main St.
P.O. Box 1443
Bangor, Maine 04401
(207) 947-0307

Biddeford-Saco Chamber of
Commerce and Industry
James E. Chandler, Jr., Exec.
Dir.
170 Main Street
Biddeford, Maine 04005
(207) 282-1567

Caribou Chamber of Commerce
Kristine C. Blancq, Exec. Dir.
111 High St.
P.O. Box 357
Caribou, Maine 04736
(207) 498-6156

Lewiston-Auburn Area Chamber
of Commerce
James R. Saunders, Pres.
179 Lisbon St.
Lewiston, Maine 04240
(207) 783-2249

Maine Chamber of Commerce &
Industry
John S. Dexter, Jr., Pres.
126 Sewall St.
Augusta, Maine 04330
(207) 623-4568

Maine State Dev. Office
Lynn Wachtel, Commisioner
State House, Station 59
Augusta, Maine 04333
(207) 289-2656

Oxford Hills Area Dev. Corp.
Denise N. Paquette, Exec. Dir.
174 Main St.
Norway, Maine 04268
(207) 743-2425

Greater Portland Chamber of
Commerce
William N. Nugent, Pres.
142 Free St.
Portland, Maine 04101
(207) 772-2811

U.S. Dept. of Commerce (ITA)
Branch Office
Stephen M. Nyulaszi, Trade
Spec.
77 Sewall St.
Augusta, Maine 04330
(207) 622-8249

Maryland

Greater Baltimore Committee,
Inc.
Robert Keller, Dir.
Ste. 900, 2 Hopkins Plaza
Baltimore, Md. 21201
(301) 727-2820

Baltimore Econ. Dev. Corp.
David Gillece, Pres.
36 S. Charles St., Ste. 2400
Baltimore, Md. 21201
(301) 837-9305

Baltimore/Washington Common
Market
Washington/Baltimore Regional
Assn.
Robert T. Grow, Deputy Dir.
Suite 202
1129 20th St. N.W.
Washington, D.C. 20036
(202) 861-0400

Md. Chamber of Commerce
Christopher Costello—V.P.
Marketing
275 West St., Ste. 400
Annapolis, Md. 21401-3480
(301) 269-0642

Md. Dept. of Econ. and
Community Dev.
J. Randall Evans, Secy.
45 Calvert St.
Annapolis, Md. 21401
(301) 269-3176

Md. Econ. Growth Associates,
Inc. (MEGA)
Jane M. Shaab, Dir. of Nat.
Marketing
Legg Mason Tower, Ste. 2220
111 S. Calvert St.
Baltimore, Md. 21202
(301) 724-0447

Md. Industrial Dev. Financing
Auth. (MIDFA)
Dept. of Econ. Employment Dev.
Marie Torres, Commercial Loan
Officer
World Trade Center
401 E. Pratt St.
Baltimore, Md. 21202
(301) 689-4264

Md. Manufacturing Assn.
Catonsville Community College
800 South Rolling Rd.
Catonsville, Md. 21228
(301) 455-4392

Md. Office of Intl. Trade
(MOIT)
Harold Zassenhaus, Exec. Dir.
7th Floor, World Trade Center
401 E. Pratt St.
Baltimore, Md. 21202
(301) 333-4295

Md. Small Business
Dev. Center
John P. Paris
123 W. 24th St.
Baltimore, Md. 21210
(301) 889-5772

Md. Port Administration
Brendan O'Malley, Exec. Dir.
World Trade Center
401 E. Pratt St.
Baltimore, Md. 21202-3041
(301) 333-4500

U.S. Chamber of Commerce
1615 H St. N.W.
Washington, D.C. 20062
(202) 463-5486

U.S. Dept. of Commerce (ITA)
David Earle, Dir.
Room 415, U.S. Customhouse
40 S. Gay St.
Baltimore, Md. 21202
(301) 962-3560

U.S. Small Business
Administration
Suite 453
10 N. Calvert St.
Baltimore, Md. 21202
(301) 962-2054

Massachusetts

Associated Industries of Mass.
John Gould, Pres.
441 Stuart St., 5th Fl.
Boston, Mass. 02116
(617) 262-1180

Greater Boston Chamber of
Commerce
James L. Sullivan, Pres.
Federal Reserve Plaza
600 Atlantic Ave., 13th Fl.
Boston, Mass. 02210-2200
(617) 227-4500

Central Berkshire Chamber of
Commerce
G.C. Dodd, Pres.
Berkshire Common
Pittsfield, Mass. 01201
(413) 499-4000

Greater Chicopee Chamber of
Commerce
John S. Frykenberg, Pres.
93 Church St.
Chicopee, Mass. 01020
(413) 594-2101

Econ. Dev. and Industrial Corp.
of Boston
Marilyn Swartz Lloyd, Dir.
38 Chauncy St.
Boston, Mass. 02111
(617) 725-3342

Fall River Area Chamber of
Commerce
Mark C.W. Montigny, Pres.
200 Pocasset St.
P.O. Box 1871
Fall River, Mass. 02722
(508) 676-8266

Intl. Business Center of New
England, Inc.
Albert H. Thomann, Pres.
World Trade Center Boston, Ste.
323
Boston, Mass. 02210
(617) 439-5280

Lawrence Chamber of Commerce
Laurence R. Smith, Exec. V.P.
264 Essex Street
Lawrence, Mass. 01840
(508) 686-9404

Mass Office of Intl. Trade
Gwen Pritchard, Exec. Dir.
100 Cambridge St., Ste. 902
Boston, Mass. 02202
(617) 367-1830

Mass. Office of Business Dev.
Alden Raine, Secy.
100 Cambridge St.—13th Fl.
Boston, Mass. 02202
(617) 727-8380

Metro South Camber of
Commerce
Mark Eagan, Pres.
60 School St.
Brockton, Mass. 02401
(508) 586-0500

Metrowest Chamber of
Commerce
A. Theodore Welte, Pres.
1617 Worcester Road, Ste. 201
Framingham, Mass. 01701
(508) 879-5600

Lynn Area Chamber of
Commerce
Raymond P. McGuiggin, Exec.
V.P.
170 Union St.
Lynn, Mass. 01901
(617) 592-2900

New England Council, Inc.
Nicholas Koskores, Pres.
581 Boylston St., 7th Fl.
Boston, Mass. 02116
(617) 437-0304

North Central Mass. Chamber of
Commerce
David L. McKeehan, Pres.
80 Erdman Way
Leominster, Mass. 01453
(508) 343-6487

Northern Berkshire Chamber of
Commerce
Thomas R. King, Exec. V.P.
69 Main St.
North Adams, Mass. 02147
(413) 663-3735

Smaller Business Assn. of New
England, Inc.
Lewis A. Shattuck, Pres.
69 Hickory Drive
Waltham, Mass. 02254
(617) 890-9070

Greater Springfield Chamber of
Commerce
James L. Shriver, Pres.
600 Bay State W. Plaza
1500 Main St., Ste. 600
Springfield, Mass. 01115
(413) 734-5671

Tri-Community Chamber of
Commerce
Richardson K. Prouty, Jr., Exec.
Dir.
11 Main St.
Southbridge, Mass. 01550
(508) 764-3283

U.S. Dept. of Commerce (ITA)
Francis J. O'Connor, Dir.
World Trade Center, Ste. 307
Boston, Mass. 02210
(617) 565-8563

Watertown Chamber of
Commerce
Robert Leonard, Pres.
75 Main St.
Watertown, Mass. 02172
(617) 926-1017

Worcester Area Chamber of
Commerce
William J. Short, Jr., Pres.
33 Waldo St.
Worcester, Mass. 01608
(508) 753-2924

Michigan

Ann Arbor Council for Intl.
Business
Ed Fadden, Chairman
207 E. Washington St.
Ann Arbor, Mich. 48104
(313) 662-0550

BC/CAL/KAL Inland Port Auth.
of South Central Mich. Dev.
Corp.
4950 W. Dickman Road
Battle Creek, Mich. 49015
(616) 962-7530

Greater Detroit Chamber of
Commerce
Frank E. Smith, Pres.
600 W. Lafayette Blvd.
Detroit, Mich. 48226
(313) 964-4000

Detroit Customhouse Brokers &
Foreign Freight Forwarders Assn.
c/o Intl. Customs Consultants,
Inc.
3874 Penobscot Building
Detroit, Mich. 48226
(313) 964-2190

Detroit/Wayne County Port Auth.
James H. Kellow, Exec. Dir.
174 S. Clark St.
Detroit, Mich. 48209
(313) 841-6700

Greater Grand Rapids Chamber
of Commerce
Birgit Klohs, Exec. Dir.
17 Fountain St. NW
Grand Rapids, Mich. 49503
(616) 771-0300

Great Lakes Trade Adjustment
Assistance Center
Marian Krzyzowski, Prog. Dir.
School of Bus. Admin.
Univ. of Michigan
2901 Baxter Rd.
Ann Arbor, Mich. 48226
(313) 763-4085

KITCO
Bill Lewis, Chairman
P.O. Box 1169
Kalamazoo, Mich. 49007
(616) 381-4000

Mich. Dept. of Agriculture
D. Gregory Main, Dir.
Manufacturing Dev.
P.O. Box 30017
Lansing, Mich. 48909
(517) 373-1054

Mich. Dept. of Commerce
Director
World Trade Services Div.
P.O. Box 30225
Lansing, Mich. 48909
(517) 373-0601

Mich. District Export Council
Edward A. Massura, Chairman
1140 McNamara Bldg.
Detroit, Mich. 48226
(313) 226-3650

Mich. Manufacturers Assn.
John G. Thodis, Pres.
124 E. Kalamazoo
Lansing, Mich. 48933
(517) 372-5900

Mich. Small Business Dev.
Center
Norman Schlafmann, Dir.
2727 Second Ave.
Detroit, Mich. 48021
(313) 577-4848

Mich. State Chamber of
Commerce
Philip G. Guyeskey, Mgr.
Small Business Programs
600 S. Walnut
Lansing, Mich. 48933
(517) 371-2100

Mich. State University
S. Tamer Cavusgil, Dir.
205 Intl. Center
East Lansing, Mich. 48824-1035
(517) 353-4336

Muskegon Econ. Growth
Alliance (MEGA)
349 W. Webster
Muskegon, Mich. 49440
(616) 722-3751

Operation Action U.P.
Richard T. Dunnebacke, Exec.
Dir.
100 Portage St.
Houghton, Mich. 49931
(906) 482-3210

Twin Cities Area Chamber of
Commerce
Edward J. Conrad, Exec. V.P
185 E. Main St.
P.O. Box 1208
Benton Harbor, Mich. 49023
(616) 925-0044

U.S. Customs
William L. Morandini, Dir.
2nd Floor, McNamara Bldg.
Detroit, Mich. 48226
(313) 226-3177

U.S. Dept. of Commerce (ITA)
Don Schilke, Dir.
1140 McNamara Bldg.
477 Michigan Ave.
Detroit, Mich. 48226
(313) 226-3650

U.S. Dept. of Commerce (ITA)
Tom Maguire, Intl. Trade
Specialist
300 Monroe NW, Room 406A
Grand Rapids, Mich. 49503
(616) 456-2411

U.S. Small Bus. Admin.
Raymond L. Harshman, Dir.
515 McNamara Bldg.
Detroit, Mich. 48226
(313) 226-7240

W. Mich. World Trade Assn.
Steve Nobel, Acting Pres.
17 Fountain St. NW
Grand Rapids, Mich. 49503
(616) 771-0319

World Trade Center
Townsend Lathrup, Ste. 1510
150 W. Jefferson Ave.
Detroit, Mich. 48226
(313) 965-6500

World Trade Club of the Gr.
Detroit Chamber of Commerce
Cynthia McMahon, Exec. V.P.
600 W. Lafayette Blvd.
Detroit, Mich. 48226
(313) 964-4000

Minnesota

Minn. Export Finance Authority
M. Noor Doja, Exec. Dir.
1000 World Trade Center
30 E. 7th St.
St. Paul, Minn. 55101
(612) 297-4658

Minn. Trade Office
P. Richard Bohr, Exec. Dir.
1000 World Trade Center
30 E. 7th St.
St. Paul, Minn. 55101
(612) 297-4227

Minn. World Trade Assn.
Nancy Frost Perkins, Bus. Mgr.
P.O. Box 24069
Apple Valley, Minn. 55124
(612) 431-1289

Minn. World Trade Center
Corporation
Richard Nolan, Pres.
400 Minn. World Trade Center
30 E. 7th St.
St. Paul, Minn. 55101
(612) 297-1580

Seaway Port Authority of Duluth
Sam Browman, Mkting. Dir.
P.O. Box 16877
Duluth, Minn. 55816-0877
(218) 727-8525

U.S. Dept. of Commerce (ITA)
Ronald E. Kramer, Dir.
108 Federal Building
110 S. 4th St.
Minneapolis, Minn. 55401
(612) 348-1638

Mississippi

Greenville Port Commission
Edward Thompson, Port Dir.
P.O. Box 446
Greenville, Miss. 38702
(601) 335-2683

International Trade Club of
Miss., Inc.
Peter Gilderson, Pres.
P.O. Box 16353
Jackson, Miss. 39236
(601) 949-0245

Jackson County Port Authority
Paul D. Pella, Port Dir.
P.O. Box 70
Pascagoula, Miss. 39568
(601) 762-4041

Miss. Dept. of Econ. &
Community Dev.
Elizabeth Cleveland, Export
Office
P.O. Box 849
Jackson, Miss. 39205
(601) 359-3552

Miss. State Port Authority
William Edwards, Port Dir.
P.O. Box 40
Gulfport, Miss. 39502
(601) 865-4300

U.S. Dept. of Commerce (ITA)
Mark E. Spinney, Dir.
300 Woodrow Wilson Blvd.,
#328
Jackson, Miss. 39213
(601) 965-4388

Missouri

Intl. Trade Club of Greater
Kansas City
Anita Williams, Exec. Secy.
920 Main St., Ste. 600
Kansas City, Mo. 64105
(816) 221-1460

Missouri Dept. of Agriculture
Intl. Marketing Div.
James Foster, Dir.
P.O. Box 630
Jefferson City, Mo. 65102
(314) 751-5611

Missouri Dept. of Commerce
Intl. Business Office
Robert Black, Dir.
P.O. Box 118
Jefferson City, Mo. 65102
(314) 751-4855

Missouri District Export Council
Richard A. Murray, Chairman
7911 Forsyth Blvd., Ste. 610
St. Louis, Mo. 63105
(314) 425-3305

U.S. Dept. of Commerce (ITA)
John Kupfer, Dir.
601 E. 12th St.
Kansas City, Mo. 64106
(816) 426-3142

U.S. Dept. of Commerce (ITA)
Sandra C. Gerley, Dep. Dir.
7911 Forsyth Blvd., Ste. 610
St. Louis, Mo. 63105
(314) 425-3302

World Trade Club of St. Louis,
Inc.
Ralph Percival, Pres.
412 S. Clay Ave.
St. Louis, Mo. 63122
(314) 965-9940

Montana

Mont. Dept. of Agriculture
Moe Wosepka
Capital Station
Helena, Mont. 59621
(406) 444-2402

Mont. Dept. of Commerce
Business Dev. Div.
John Maloney
1424-9th Ave.
Helena, Mont. 59620
(406) 444-3923

U.S. Dept. of Commerce (ITA)
Boise Branch Office
Stephen B. Thompson
700 W. St., 2nd Floor
Boise, Idaho 83720
(208) 334-3857

Nebraska

Midwest Intl. Trade Assn.
P.O. Box 37402
Omaha, Neb. 68137
(402) 333-6572

Nebraska Dept. of Econ. Devel
Susan Rouch, Intl. Trade
Specialist
301 Centennial Mall S.
Lincoln, Neb. 68509
(402) 471-3111

Omaha Chamber of Commerce
Toby Churchill, Intl. Affairs
1301 Harney St.
Omaha, Neb. 68102
(402) 346-5000

U.S. Dept. of Commerce (ITA)
George H. Payne, Dir.
11133 "O" St.
Omaha, Neb. 68137
(402) 221-3664

U.S. Small Business Admin.
Jerry Kleber, Intl. Trade
Specialist
11145 Mill Valley Rd.
Omaha, Neb. 68154
(402) 221-3607

Nevada

Commission on Econ. Dev.
Jim Spoo, Exec. Dir.
Capitol Complex
Carson City, Nev. 89710
(702) 687-4325

Econ. Dev. Auth. of W. Nev.
Kenneth Lynn, Exec. Dir.
5190 Neil Rd., #11
Reno, Nev. 89502
(702) 829-3700

Las Vegas Chamber of
Commerce
Mark Smith, Pres.
2301 E. Sahara St.
Las Vegas, Nev. 89104
(702) 457-8450

Latin Chamber of Commerce
Otto Merida, Exec. Dir.
P.O. Box 7534
Las Vegas, Nev. 89125-2534
(702) 385-7367

Nevada Devel. Auth.
Dennis Stein, Pres./CEO
3900 Paradise Rd., #155
Las Vegas, Nev. 89109
(702) 791-0000

Nev. District Export Council
Kevin Day, Chairman
P.O. Box 11007
Reno, Nev. 89520
(702) 784-3844

Nev. World Trade Council
Larry Struve, Pres.
P.O. Box 2882
Carson City, Nev. 89702
(702) 687-4250

Greater Reno/Sparks Chamber of
Commerce
Ron Watson, Exec. V.P.
405 Marsh Ave.
Reno, Nev. 89509
(702) 786-3030

U.S. Dept. of Commerce (ITA)
J. Jerry Jeremy, Dir.
1755 E. Plumb Lane, #152
Reno, Nev. 89502
(702) 784-5203

New Hampshire

Greater Manchester Chamber of
Commerce
Thomas H. Schwieger, Pres.
889 Elm St.
Manchester, N.H. 03101
(603) 625-5753

(State of) New Hampshire
Dept. of Resources and Econ.
Dev.
George C. Jones, Commissioner
P.O. Box 856
Concord, N.H. 03301
(603) 271-2341

N.H. Assn. of Commerce and
Industry
Michael J. Valuk, Exec. Secy.
1 Tara Blvd., Ste. 211
Nashua, N.H. 03062
(603) 891-2471

Greater Portsmouth Chamber of
Commerce
Ms. Kerry Hadley, Pres.
500 Market St.
Box 239
Portsmouth, N.H. 03801
(603) 436-1118

U.S. Dept. of Commerce (ITA)
Francis J. O'Connor, Dir.
World Trade Center, Ste. 306
Boston, Mass. 02210
(617) 565-8563

New Jersey

Center for Intl. Business
Education (CIBE)
Charles A. Nanry
James H. Levin Bldg.
Kilmer Campus, Rutgers Univ.
P.O. Box 5062
New Brunswick, N.J.
08903-5062
(201) 932-5639

Delaware River Port Auth.
Ray Heinzelman, Dir.
World Trade Div.
Bridge Plaza
Camden, N.J. 08101
(609) 963-6420

Intl. Round Table
Bergen County Community
College
Lynda Icochea, Prof.
400 Paramus Rd.
Paramus, N.J. 07652
(201) 477-7167

(Metro) Newark Chamber of
Commerce
Eric J. Vicioso
V.P. Intl. Trade and
Transportation
40 Clinton St.
Newark, N.J. 07102-3795

N.J. Business and Industry Assn.
Joseph A. Gonzalez, Exec. V.P.
102 W. State St.
Trenton, N.J. 08608
(609) 393-7707

(State of) N.J. Div. of Intl. Trade
Philip Ferzen, Dir.
744 Broad St., Rm. 1709
Newark, N.J. 07102
(201) 466-8499

N.J./N.Y. Port Auth.
Herb Ouida, Project Dir.
One World Trade Center, 63-S
New York, N.Y. 10048
(212) 466-8499

N.J. Small Business Dev. Center
Richard K. Meisenbacher, Dir.,
Intl. Trade
Rutgers, State Univ. Grad.
School of Management
180 University Ave.
Newark, N.J. 07102
(201) 648-5950

Princeton Chamber of Commerce
Intl. Business Dev. Council
100-300 Village Blvd.
Princeton Forrestal Village
Princeton, N.J. 08540
(609) 520-1776

U.S. Dept. of Commerce (ITA)
Thomas J. Murray, Dir.
3131 Princeton Pike
Bldg. 6, Ste. 100
Trenton, N.J. 08648
(609) 989-2100

New Mexico

(State of) New Mexico
Economic Dev. and Tourism
Dept.
Trade Division
1100 St. Francis Dr., Joseph M.
Montoya Bldg.
Santa Fe, N.M. 87503
(505) 827-0307

New Mexico Dept. of Agriculture
Intl. Marketing Program
Box 30005, Dept. 5600
New Mexico State Univ. Campus
Las Cruces, N.M. 88003
(505) 646-4929

New Mexico Intl. Trade Council
c/o SW Intl. Technology and
Trading Co., Ltd.
4300 Silver, S.E.
Albuquerque, N.M. 87108
(505) 821-2318

New Mexico Small Business
Dev. Center
P.O. Box 4187
Santa Fe, N.M. 87502-4187
(505) 438-1362

New Mexico Trade Fdn.
c/o Econ. Dev. and Tourism
Dept.
1100 St. Francis Dr., Joseph M.
Montoya Bldg.
Santa Fe, N.M. 87503
(505) 827-0264

U.S. Dept. of Commerce (ITA)
Branch Office
c/o Small Business
Administration
625 Silver, S.W., 3rd Floor
Albuquerque, N.M. 87102
(505) 766-2070

U.S. Dept. of Commerce (ITA)
Branch Office
c/o Econ. Dev. and Tourism
Dept.
1100 St. Francis Dr., Joseph
Montoya Bldg.
Santa Fe, N.M. 87503
(505) 988-6261

U.S. Small Business
Administration
625 Silver, S.W., 3rd Fl.
Albuquerque, N.M. 87102
(505) 766-1879

New York

Greater Buffalo Chamber of
Commerce
Randall J. Brown, V.P. Bus.
Develop./Govt. Relations
107 Delaware Ave.
Buffalo, N.Y. 14202
(716) 852-7100

Buffalo World Trade Assn.
Lydia Shapiro, Exec. Secy.
P.O. Box 591
Williamsville, N.Y. 14221
(716) 631-5602

Canada-U.S. Trade Center
James E. McConnell, Dir.
Dept. of Geography
Fronczak Hall
Buffalo, N.Y. 14260
(716) 636-2299

Foreign Credit Insurance Assn.
Terry Dolan, Mgr.
Sharyn H. Hess, Asst. V.P.
40 Rector St., 11th Floor
New York, N.Y. 10006
(212) 306-5000

Intl. Executives Assn., Inc.
Ed Flanagan, Exec. Dir.
13 E. 37th St., 8th Fl.
New York, N.Y. 10016
(212) 683-9755

Long Island Assn. Inc.
James La Rocca, Pres.
80 Hauppaugo Rd.
Commack, N.Y. 11725
(516) 499-4400

Mohawk Valley World Trade
Council
Johann Skaly, Pres.
P.O. Box 4126
Utica, N.Y. 13504
(800) 848-8483

Nat. Assn. of Credit Mgrs.
(NACM)
Finance Credit Intl.
Business (FCIB)
Paul Mignini, Exec. V.P. of
NACM
Raymond Schweitzer V.P. of
FCIB
520 8th Ave.
New York, N.Y. 10018
(212) 947-5368

Nat. Assn. of Credit Manageme
(NACM)—Upstate New York
Gerald J. Weidner, Exec. V.P.
250 Delaware Ave., Ste. 4
Buffalo, N.Y. 14202
(716) 854-7018

Nat. Customs Brokers &
Forwarders Assn. of America,
Inc.
John Hammon, Exec. V.P.
One World Trade Center, Rm.
1153
New York, N.Y. 10048
(212) 432-0050

N.Y. Chamber of Commerce &
Industry
Ronald Shelt, Pres.
200 Madison Ave.
New York, N.Y. 10016
(212) 561-2028

N.Y. State Dept. of Commerce
Dept. of Econ. Dev.
1515 Broadway
New York, N.Y. 10036
(212) 827-6100

Overseas Automotive Club, Inc.
Secretary
P.O. Box 1638
300 Sylvan Ave.
Englewood Cliffs, N.J. 07632
(201) 894-6810

Port Auth. of N.Y. and N.J.
Trade Devel. Office
Thomas J. Leatham, Gen. Mgr.
Rm. 64E
One World Trade Center
New York, N.Y. 10048
(212) 466-8333

Greater Rochester Metro
Chamber of Commerce
World Trade Dept.
Charles M. Goodwin, V.P.
Intl. Trade & Transportation
55 St. Paul St.
Rochester, N.Y. 14604
(716) 454-2220

Southern Tier World Commerce
Assn.
Robert Turrisini, Pres.
c/o School of Management
SUNY Binghamton
P.O. Box 60000
Binghamton, N.Y. 13902-6000
(607) 777-2342

Greater Syracuse Chamber of
Commerce
Intl. Trade Council
Joseph D. Russo, V.P. for Gov't.
Rel.
100 E. Onondaga St.
Syracuse, N.Y. 13202
(315) 470-1343

Tappan Zee Intl. Trade Assn.
Pamela Hurst, Pres.
One Blue Hill Plaza
Pearl River, N.Y. 10965
(914) 735-7040

U.S. Council for Intl. Business
1212 Ave. of the Americas
New York, N.Y. 10036
(212) 354-4480

U.S. Dept. of Commerce (ITA)
George Buchanan, Dir.
1312 Fed. Bldg.
Buffalo, N.Y. 14202
(716) 846-4101

U.S. Dept. of Commerce (ITA)
Joel Barkan, Dir.
26 Federal Plaza, Rm. 3718
New York, N.Y. 10278
(212) 264-0634

U.S. Dept. of Commerce (ITA)
William Freirt, Branch Mgr.
111 E. Ave., Ste. 220
Rochester, N.Y. 14604
(716) 263-6480

U.S. Small Bus. Admin.
Sidney Zieler of Harold
Demerest, Counselors on Exports
26 Fed. Plaza, Rm. 3130
New York, N.Y. 10278
(212) 264-4507

U.S. Small Bus. Admin.
Robert Mergle, Mgmt. Assistance
Officer
100 S. Clinton St.
Syracuse, N.Y. 13260
(315) 423-5383

Westchester County Assn. Inc.
World Trade Club of Westchester
Richard Chaab, Dir. of Prog.
Operations
235 Mamaroneck Ave.
White Plains, N.Y. 10605
(914) 948-6444

Western N.Y. Intl. Trade Council
Roberta A. Dayer, Exec. Director
P.O. Box 1271
Buffalo, N.Y. 14240
(716) 852-7160

World Commerce Assn. of
Central N.Y.
Joe Russo, V.P. for Govt. Rel.
100 E. Onandaga St.
Syracuse, N.Y. 13202
(315) 470-1343

World Trade Institute
Blair Nare, Dir.
One World Trade Center
New York, N.Y. 10048
(212) 466-4044

North Carolina

N.C. Dept. of Agriculture
Wayne Miller
P.O. Box 27647
Raleigh, N.C. 27611
(919) 733-7912

N.C. Dept. of Econ. and
Community Dev., Intl. Division
Richard (Dick) Quinlan, Dir.
430 N. Salisbury St.
Raleigh, N.C. 27611
(919) 733-7193

N.C. District Export Council
Herbert L. Pocklington
Pres., Hatteras Intl.
P.O. Box 2690
High Point, N.C. 27261
(919) 889-6621

N.C. State University Intl. Trade
Center
Tom Brown, Dir.
P.O. Box 7401
Raleigh, N.C. 27695-7401
(919) 737-3793

N.C. World Trade Assn.
Ms. Janice Faulkner, Dir.
Reg. Dev. Institute
E. Carolina University
Willis Bldg.
Corner First & Reade St.
Greenville, N.C. 27858
(919) 757-6650

Research Triangle World Trade
Center
Ruth D. Turner, Managing Dir.
1007 Slater Road, Ste. 200
Morrisville, N.C. 27560
(919) 941-5120

U.S. Dept. of Commerce (ITA)
Samuel P. Troy
Reg. Managing Dir.
P.O. Box 1950
Greensboro, N.C. 27402
(919) 333-5345

North Dakota

Fargo Chamber of Commerce
John C. Campbell, Pres.
321 N. 4th St.
Fargo, N.D. 58108
(701) 237-5678

N.D. Econ. Devel. Commission
Jack Minton, Intl. Consultant
Liberty Memorial Bldg.
State Capital Grounds
Bismarck, N.D. 58505
(701) 224-2810

U.S. Dept. of Commerce (ITA)
George H. Payne, Dir.
11133 "O" St.
Omaha, Neb. 68137
(402) 221-3664

U.S. Small Business Admin.
John Cosgriff, Intl. Trade
Specialist
P.O. Fed. Bldg., Box 3086
Fargo, N.D. 58108
(701) 239-5131

Ohio

Akron Reg. Dev. Board
Intl. Business and Trade Assn.
Walter R. Johnson, Intl. Trade
Specialist
One Cascade Plaza, Ste. 800
Akron, Ohio 44308
(216) 379-3157

Greater Cincinnati Chamber of
Commerce
Neil Hensley, Dir. of Intl.
Mkting.
300 Carew Tower
441 Vine St.
Cincinnati, Ohio 45202
(513) 579-3170

Cincinnati Council on World
Affairs
William C. Messner, Pres.
Tri-State Building, Ste. #300
432 Walnut St.
Cincinnati, Ohio 45202
(513) 621-2320

Port of Cleveland
Anthony F. Fugaro, Dir.
Cleveland-Cuyahoga County Port
Auth.
101 Erieside Ave.
Cleveland, Ohio 44114-1095
(216) 241-8004

Cleveland Council on World
Affairs
Henry Precht, Pres.
539 Hanna Bldg.
1422 Euclid Ave.
Cleveland, Ohio 44115
(216) 781-3730

Cleveland World Trade Assn.
Richard N. Kirby, Dir., Intl.
Trade & Business Dev.
690 Huntington Bldg.
Cleveland, Ohio 44115
(216) 621-3300

Columbus Area Chamber of
Commerce
Intl. Trade Dev. Office
Kathy Walsh, Intl. Coordinator
37 N. High St.
Columbus, Ohio 43215
(614) 221-1321

Columbus Council on World
Affairs
Carol Garner, Exec. Dir.
Two Nationwide Plaza
280 N. High St.
Columbus, Ohio 43215
(614) 249-8450

Dayton Council on World Affairs
Judith Baker, Exec. Dir.
Wright Brothers Branch
P.O. Box 9190
Dayton, Ohio 45409
(513) 229-2319

Miami Valley Intl. Trade Assn.
Barry Block, Pres.
P.O. Box 291945
Dayton, Ohio 45429
(513) 439-9465

N. Central Ohio Intl. Trade Club
Chris Clarke, Pres.
c/o Warren Rupp, Inc.
P.O. Box 1568
Mansfield, Ohio 44901
(419) 524-8388

N. Ohio District Export Council
Sven A. Langmack, Chairman
Ste. 600
668 Euclid Ave.
Cleveland, Ohio 44114
(216) 522-4750

Ohio Dept. of Agriculture
Steven B. Maurer, Dir.
Ohio Dept. Bldg., Room 607
65 S. Front St.
Columbus, Ohio 43215
(614) 466-2732

Ohio Dept. of Dev.
Intl. Trade Division
Dan Waterman, Dep. Dir.
77 S. High St., 29th Floor
Columbus, Ohio 43215
(614) 466-5017

Ohio Foreign Commerce Assn.,
Inc.
c/o Raymond W. Luzar, Secy.
21010 Center Ridge Rd., Ste.
702
Rocky River, Ohio 44116
(216) 333-6069

S. Ohio District Export Council
Robert C. Eisenach, Chairman
9504 Fed. Office Bldg.
550 Main St.
Cincinnati, Ohio 45202
(513) 684-2944

Toledo Area Intl. Trade Assn.
Wynn Spurgeon, Pres.
218 Huron St.
Toledo, Ohio 43604
(419) 243-8191

Port of Toledo
Norman A. Fox, Dir. of Trade
Dev.
Toledo-Lucas County Port Auth.
One Maritime Plaza
Toledo, Ohio 43604-1866
(419) 243-8251

U.S. Customs Service
Robert Moore, Port Dir.
Room 116, Dayton Intl. Airport
Vandalia, Ohio 45377
(513) 225-2877

U.S. Customs Service
John F. Nelson, Dir.
55 Erieview Plaza
Cleveland, Ohio 44114
(216) 522-4284

U.S. Customs Service
Hilton B. Duckworth, Port Dir.
8511 Fed. Office Bldg.
550 Main St.
Cincinnati, Ohio 45202
(513) 684-3682

U.S. Customs Service
Robert Hill, Port Dir.
4600 17th Ave., Room 221
Columbus, Ohio 43219
(614) 469-6670

U.S. Department of Commerce
(ITA)
Gordon B. Thomas, Reg.
Managing Dir.
Great Lakes Region IV
9504 Fed. Office Bldg.
550 Main St.
Cincinnati, Ohio 45202
(513) 684-2944

U.S. Dept. of Commerce (ITA)
Toby Zettler, Dir.
Ste. 600
668 Euclid Ave.
Cleveland, Ohio 44114
(216) 522-4750

U.S. Small Business
Administration
Elmar Koeberer, District Dir.
317 AJC Fed. Bldg.
1240 E. 9th St.
Cleveland, Ohio 44199
(216) 522-4194

Youngstown Area Chamber of
Commerce
World Trade Committee
John Camp, Pres.
200 Wick Bldg.
Youngstown, Ohio 44503-1474
(216) 744-2131

Oklahoma

Center for Intl. Trade Dev.
Chris Wyatt, Exec. Dir.
Oklahoma State University
109 Cordell N.
Stillwater, Okla. 74078
(405) 744-7693

Foreign Zone #53
Bob James
Tulsa Port of Catoosa
5555 Bird Creek Ave.
Catoosa, Okla. 74015
(918) 266-5830

Foreign Trade Zone #106
Carolyn Lyon
Foreign Trade Zone
Administrator
City of Oklahoma City
Planning and Econ. Dev.
300 S.W. 7th St.
Oklahoma City, Okla. 73109
(405) 297-2583

Metro. Tulsa Chamber of
Commerce
Mickey Thompson, V.P.
Econ. Dev. Division
616 S. Boston Ave.
Tulsa, Okla. 74119
(918) 585-1201

Muskogee City-County Port
Authority
Foreign Trade Zone #164
Scott Robinson
Route 6, Port 50
Muskogee, Okla. 74401
(918) 682-7886

Oklahoma City Intl. Trade Assn.
Larry Cotter, Pres.
P.O. Box 1936
Oklahoma City, Okla. 73101
(405) 478-3530

Oklahoma Dept. of Agriculture
Anna Belle Wiedemann, Dir.
Market Dev. Division
2800 Lincoln Blvd.
Oklahoma City, Okla. 73105
(405) 521-3864

Oklahoma Dept. of Commerce
Gary H. Miller, Dir.
6601 Broadway Extension
Oklahoma City, Okla. 73116
(405) 841-5217

Oklahoma District Export
Council
Warren L. Jensen, Chairman
6601 Broadway Extension
Oklahoma City, Okla. 73116
(405) 231-5302

Oklahoma State Chamber of
Commerce
Kenneth E. Moore, Exec. Dir.
4020 Lincoln Blvd.
Oklahoma City, Okla. 73105
(405) 424-4003

Small Business Development
Center
Carl R. Echols
6420 S.E. 15th
Midwest City, Okla. 73110
(405) 841-5224

Tulsa International Council
616 S. Boston Ave.
Tulsa, Okla. 74119
(918) 584-4685

Tulsa Port of Catoosa
Robert W. Portiss, Dir.
5350 Cimarron Road
Catoosa, Okla. 74015
(918) 266-2291

Tulsa World Trade Assn.
616 S. Boston Ave.
Tulsa, Okla. 74119
(918) 585-1201, Ext. 234

U.S. Dept. of Commerce (ITA)
Ronald L. Wilson, Dir.
6601 Broadway Extension
Oklahoma City, Okla. 73116
(405) 231-5302

Oregon

Central Oregon Intl. Trade
Council
Paul Lonnquist
2600 NW College Way
Bend, Ore. 97701

Intl. Trade Institute
Gil Latz
One World Trade Center
121 SW Salmon, Ste. 230
Portland, Ore. 97204
(503) 725-3246

Mid Willamette Valley Council
of Governments
Ray Teasley
105 High St., S.E.
Salem, Ore. 96301

Oregon Dept. of Agriculture
Richard Fritz
One World Trade Center
121 SW Salmon, Ste. 240
Portland, Ore. 97204
(503) 229-6734

Oregon District Export Council
Frank Dausz
One World Trade Center
121 SW Salmon, Ste. 242
Portland, Ore. 97204
(503) 228-6501

Oregon Econ. Devel. Dept., Intl.
Trade Division
Glenn Ford
One World Trade Center
121 SW Salmon, Ste. 300
Portland, Ore. 97204
(503) 229-5625

Oregon Trade & Marketing
Center, Inc.
Ryan Malarkey
One World Trade Center
121 SW Salmon, Ste. 200
Portland, Ore. 97204
(503) 274-7475

Pacific Northwest Intl. Trade
Assn.
Virginia Hopkirk
200 SW Market, Ste. 190
Portland, Ore. 97201
(503) 228-4361

Portland Chamber of Commerce
Donald McClave
221 NW 2nd Ave.
Portland, Ore. 97209
(503) 228-9411

Small Business Intl. Trade
Program
John Otis
One World Trade Center
121 SW Salmon, Ste. 210
Portland, Ore. 97204
(503) 274-7482

Southern Oregon Intl. Trade
Council
290 NE "C" St.
Grants Pass, Ore. 97526

U.S. Dept. of Commerce (ITA)
Richard M. Lenahan, Dir.
One World Trade Center
121 SW Salmon, Ste. 242
Portland, Ore. 97204
(503) 326-3001

Western Wood Products Assn.
H.A. Roberts
522 SW 5th Ave.
Portland, Ore. 97204
(503) 224-3930

Willamette Intl. Trade Center
Arly Knight
Room 209
1059 Willamette
Eugene, Ore. 97401
(503) 686-0195

World Trade Center Portland
Charles Allcock
One World Trade Center
121 SW Salmon, Ste. 250
Portland, Ore. 97204
(503) 464-8888

Pennsylvania

Airport Area Chamber of
Commerce
Eileen Muha
986 Brodhead Rd.
Moon Township
Coraopolis, Pa. 15106
(412) 264-6270

American Soc. of Intl.
Executives, Inc.
Anthony M. Swartz, Pres.
18 Sentry Parkway, Ste. One
Blue Bell, Pa. 19422
(215) 540-2295

Berks County Chamber of
Commerce
P.O. Box 1698, 645 Penn St.
Reading, Pa. 19603
(215) 376-6766

Del. County Chamber of
Commerce
Jack Holefelder, Pres.
602 E. Baltimore Pike
Media, Pa. 19063
(215) 565-3677

Media, Pa. 19063
(215) 565-3677

Del.-Eastern Pa. District Export
Council
Robert P. Replogle, Vice Chair
475 Allendale Rd., Ste. 202
King of Prussia, Pa. 19406
(215) 962-4980

Del. River Port Auth.
World Trade Division
Dr. Raymond Heinzelmann, Dir.
Bridge Plaza
Camden, N.J. 08101
(215) 925-8780, ext. 2264

Econ. Dev. Council of NE Pa.
Howard J. Grossman, Exec. Dir.
1151 Oak St.
Pittston, Pa. 18640
(717) 655-5581

Erie-Western Pa. Port Auth.
Larry Morosky, Exec. Dir.
17 W. Dobbins Landing
Erie, Pa. 16507-1424
(814) 455-7557

Foreign Trade Zone #33
Regional Industrial Dev. Corp.
Frank Brook Robinson, Pres.
1220 Frick Bldg.
Pittsburgh, Pa. 15219
(412) 471-3939

Greater Willow Grove Chamber
of Commerce
603 N. Easton Rd.
P.O. Box 100
Willow Grove, Pa. 19090
(215) 657-2227

Intl. Business Forum
Sally Bullard, Exec. Dir.
1520 Locust St.
Philadelphia, Pa. 19102
(215) 732-3250

Intl. Trade Committee
Erie Excellence Council
Don Hosford, Chairman
928 West 19th St.
Erie, Pa. 16502
(814) 455-6533

Intl. Trade Executives Club of
Pittsburgh
John McCartney, Exec. Secy.
2002 Federal Bldg.
1000 Liberty Ave.
Pittsburgh, Pa. 15222
(412) 644-2850

Lancaster Chamber of Commerce
and Industry
Jerry L. Moll, Pres.
Southern Market Center
100 S. Queen St.
P.O. Box 1558
Lancaster, Pa. 17603-1558
(717) 397-3531

Lehigh Univ. Small Business
Dev. Center
Intl. Trade Dev. Program
Dr. Mehdi Hojjat, Coordinator
310 Broadway
Bethlehem, Pa. 18015
(215) 758-4630

Montgomery County Dept. of
Commerce
Dwight A. Dundore, Dir.
#3 Stony Creek Office Center
151 W. Marshall Road
Norristown, Pa. 19401
(215) 278-5950

North Central Pa. Regional
Planning & Dev. Commission
Chris Perneski
P.O. Box 488
651 Montmorenci Ave.
Ridgeway, Pa. 15853
(814) 772-6901 or (814)
773-3162

Northern Tier Reg. Planning and
Dev. Commission
Philip D. Koos, Jr., Exec. Dir.
507 Main St.
Towanda, Pa. 18848
(717) 265-9103

NW Pa. Reg. Planning & Dev.
Commission
Janet Anderson
614 11th St.
Franklin, Pa. 16323
[Erie] (814) 871-7322; [Franklin]
(814) 437-3024

Pa. Dept. of Agriculture
Bureau of Markets
Ronald Gaskill, Dir.
2301 N. Cameron St.
Harrisburg, Pa. 17110
(717) 783-3181

Pa. Dept. of Commerce
Office of Intl. Dev.
Paul Haugland, Bureau of Intl.
Trade
433 Forum Bldg.
Harrisburg, Pa. 17120
(717) 787-7190

Pa. Dept. of Commerce
Bureau of Intl. Dev.
Terrence Foley, Dir.
433 Forum Bldg.
Harrisburg, Pa. 17120
(717) 783-5107

Pa. State Univ. Small Business
Dev. Center
Export Development Program of
South Central Pa.
Thomas N. Sherburne, Dir.
Middletown, Pa. 17057
(717) 948-6069

Greater Philadelphia Chamber of
Commerce
Charles Pizzi, Pres.
1346 Chestnut St., Ste. 800
Philadelphia, Pa. 19107
(215) 545-1234

Philadelphia Industrial Dev.
Corp.
William Hankowsky, Pres.
123 So. Broad St., 22nd Floor
Philadelphia, Pa. 19109
(215) 875-3508

Pittsburgh Council for Intl.
Visitors
Marion Hook Exec. Dir.
Rm. 263, Thackeray Hall
139 University Place
Pittsburgh, Pa. 15260
(412) 624-7800

Greater Pittsburgh World Trade
Assn.
Michael Campbell
Greater Pittsburgh Chamber of
Commerce
3 Gateway Center
14th Floor
Pittsburgh, Pa. 15222
(412) 392-4500

SEDA-Council of Governments
Dennis E. Robinson, Exec. Dir.
Timberhaven Rd #1
Lewisburg, Pa. 17838
(717) 524-4491

Small Business Dev. Center
Clarion Univ. of Pa.
Malinda Wray, Asst. Dir.
Dana Still Bldg.
Clarion, Pa. 16214
(814) 226-2060

Small Business Dev. Center
Duquense Univ.
Robert Logan/Emma Easteppe
Rockwell Hall, Room 10
Concourse
600 Forbes Ave.
Pittsburgh, Pa. 15282
(412) 434-6233

Small Business Dev. Center
Indiana Univ. of Pa.
Dr. Robert Boldin, Dir.
202 McElhaney Hall
Indiana, Pa. 15705
(412) 357-2929

Small Business Dev. Center
St. Francis College
Joyce Remillard
Loretto, Pa. 15940
(814) 472-3200

Small Business Dev. Center
St. Vincent College
John A. Fabean, Dir.
Latrobe, Pa. 15650
(412) 537-4572

Small Business Dev. Center
Univ. of Pittsburgh
Clarence F. Curry, Dir.
343 Mervis Hall
Pittsburgh, Pa. 15260
(412) 648-1544

Southern Alleghenies
Commission
Andrea Hewitt
541 58th St.
Altoona, Pa. 16602
(814) 949-6500

SW Pa. Econ. Dev. District
Jang Kim
12300 Perry Highway
Wexford, Pa. 15090
(412) 935-6122

U.S. Customs Service
William Booth, Port Director of
Customs
822 Federal Bldg.
1000 Liberty Ave.
Pittsburgh, Pa. 15222
(412) 644-3589

U.S. Dept. of Commerce (ITA)
Erie Associate Office
John Lancia, Intl. Trade
Specialist
3537 W. 12th St.
Erie, Pa. 16505
(814) 459-3335

U.S. Dept. of Commerce (ITA)
Robert Kistler, Dir.
475 Allendale Rd. Ste. 202
King of Prussia, Pa. 19406
(215) 962-4980

U.S. Dept. of Commerce (ITA)
John McCartney, Dir.
2002 Federal Bldg.
1000 Liberty Ave.
Pittsburgh, Pa. 15222
(412) 644-2850

U.S. Small Business Admin.
William T. Gennetti, Dist. Dir.
475 Allendale Rd., Ste. 201
King of Prussia, Pa. 19406
(215) 962-3815

U.S. Small Business Admin.
Stephen R. Drozda, Export
Assistance
Fifth Floor
960 Penn Ave.
Pittsburgh, Pa. 15222
(412) 644-5438

Univ. of Scranton Small Business
Dev. Center
Elaine Tweety, Dir.
415 N. Washington Ave.
Scranton, Pa. 18510
(717) 961-7588

Western Pa. District Export
Council
F.J. Sarknas, Chairman
1000 Liberty Ave.
Pittsburgh, Pa. 15222
(412) 644-2850

Wharton Export Network
Hans H.B. Koehler, Dir.
Wharton School
Univ. of Pennsylvania
3733 Spruce St., 413 Vance Hall
Philadelphia, Pa. 19104
(215) 898-4187

Wilkes College Small Business
Dev. Center
Edward Sieminski, Dir.
Hollenbeck Hall
192 S. Franklin St.
Wilkes Barre, Pa. 18766

Women's Intl. Trade Assn.
Ronnie Barlow, Pres.
P.O. Box 40004
Philadelphia, Pa. 19106
(215) 922-6610

World Trade Assn. of
Philadelphia
George Mohr, Dir.
P.O. Box 58640
Philadelphia, Pa. 19102
(215) 988-0711

Puerto Rico

District Export Council
Lucas Valdivieso, Chairman
Diversified Farming Complex
Firm Delivery
Ponce, P.R. 00731
(809) 836-1818

P.R. Chamber of Commerce
Rafael Rivera, Exec. Dir.
P.O. Box 3789
San Juan, P.R. 00904
(809) 721-6060

P.R. Department of Commerce
Jorge Santiago, Secy.
P.O. Box 4275
San Juan, P.R. 00905
(809) 721-3290

P.R. Econ. Devel. Admin.
Alfredo Salazar, Administrator
GPO Box 2350
San Juan, P.R. 00936
(809) 758-4747

P.R. Manufacturers Assn.
Hector Jimenez, Exec. Dir.
P.O. Box 2410
Hato Rey, P.R. 00919
(809) 759-9445

P.R. Products Assn.
Juan Rivera Bigas, Exec. Dir.
GPO Box 3631
San Juan, P.R. 00936
(809) 753-8484

U.S. Dept. of Commerce (ITA)
Enrique Vilella, Dir.
Rm. G-55, Federal Building
Hato Rey, P.R. 00918
(809) 766-5555

Rhode Island

Greater Providence Chamber of
Commerce
James G. Hogan, Pres.
30 Exchange Terrace
Providence, R.I. 02903
(501) 521-5000

R.I. Dept. of Econ. Dev.
Arthur Markos, Dir. of Mkting
7 Jackson Walkway
Providence, R.I. 02903
(401) 277-2601

U.S. Dept. of Commerce (ITA)
Branch Office
Raimond Meerbach, Trade Spe
7 Jackson Walkway
Providence, R.I. 02903
(401) 528-5104

South Carolina

Charleston-Trident Chamber of
Commerce
Virginia Norvell, V.P., Intl.
Dept.
P.O. Box 975
Charleston, S.C. 29402
(803) 577-2510

Greater Columbia Chamber of
Commerce
Mike Eade, Sen. Dir., Econ.
Dev.
P.O. Box 1360
Columbia, S.C. 29202
(803) 733-1110

Greater Greenville Chamber of
Commerce
Sean Griffin
P.O. Box 10048
Greenville, S.C. 29603
(803) 242-1050

Jobs-Economic Dev. Authority
Charles Kerekes, Export Trade
Program Mgr.
1201 Main St., Ste. 1750
Columbia, S.C. 29201
(803) 737-0079

Low Country Intl. Trade Assn.
James Tobias, Pres.
P.O. Box 159
Charleston, S.C. 29402
(803) 724-3566

Midlands Intl. Trade Assn.
Donnie Turbeville
101 Trade Zone Drive
Ste. 1A
West Columbia, S.C.
29169-3911
(803) 822-5039

Pee Dee Intl. Trade Assn.
(Florence)
Everette Hendrick, Pres.
P.O. Box 25
Darlington, S.C. 29532
(803) 393-4341

Small Business Dev. Center
Judy Sidlow
College of Business
Univ. of South Carolina
Columbia, S.C. 29208
(803) 777-5118

S.C. Dist. Export Council
George Freire, Chairman
1835 Assembly St., Ste. 172
Columbia, S.C. 29201
(803) 765-5345

S.C. State Dev. Board
Will Lacey, Mgr., Intl. Business
Div.
P.O. Box 927
Columbia, S.C. 29202
(803) 737-0400

S.C. State Ports Authority
Craig Lund, Nat. Sales Mgr.
P.O. Box 817
Charleston, S.C. 29402
(803) 577-8100

Western S.C. Intl. Trade Assn.
Bettie Belenchia, Pres.
P.O. Box 2081
Greenville, S.C. 29602-2081
(803) 574-4400

U.S. Dept. of Commerce (ITA)
Ed. Rojas, Dir.
1835 Assembly St., Ste. 172
Columbia, S.C. 29201
(803) 765-5345

South Dakota

Rapid City Area Chamber of
Commerce
John Schmit, Pres.
P.O. Box 747
Rapid City, S.D. 57709
(605) 343-1744

Sioux Falls Chamber of
Commerce
Evan Nolte, V.P.
315 S. Phillips St.
Sioux Falls, S.D. 57101
(605) 336-1620

S.D. Governor's Office of Econ.
Dev., Export & Mktg. Div.
David Brotzman, Dir.
Capitol Lake Plaza
Pierre, S.D. 57501
(605) 773-5032

U.S. Dept. of Commerce (ITA)
Harvey Roffman, Trade
Specialist
11133 "O" St.
Omaha, Neb. 68137
(402) 221-3664

U.S. Small Business Admin.
E. Duane Harder, Deputy
Director
101 S. Main Ave.
Sioux Falls, S.D. 57102
(605) 336-2980, ext. 231

Tennessee

E. Tenn. Intl. Commerce Council
P.O. Box 2688
Knoxville, Tenn. 37901

Memphis Area Chamber of
Commerce
John Threadgill, Intl. Dev. Mgr.
P.O. Box 224
Memphis, Tenn. 38101
(901) 575-3500

Memphis World Trade Club
Phil Johnson, Pres.
P.O. Box 3577
Memphis, Tenn. 38173
(901) 678-2500

Middle Tenn. World Trade Club
P.O. Box 100574
Nashville, Tenn. 37210-0574

Mid-South Exporters' Roundtable
P.O. Box 3521
Memphis, Tenn. 38173
(901) 320-2210

Tenn. Dept. of Agriculture
Joe Gaines, Dir. of Mkting.
Ellington Agricultural Center
P.O. Box 40627, Melrose Sta.
Nashville, Tenn. 37204
(615) 360-0160

Tenn. District Export Office
Jim Thomas, Acting Chairman
Pen Trading Co.
P.O. Box 2128
Brentwood, Tenn. 37027
(615) 371-7350

Tenn. Export Office
Ms. Leigh Wieland, Dir.
320 6th Ave. N.
7th Floor
Nashville, Tenn. 37219-5308
(615) 741-5870

World Trade Club of
Chattanooga
1001 Market St.
Chattanooga, Tenn. 37402

U.S. Dept. of Commerce (ITA)
Ree Russell, Intl. Trade
Specialist
22 N. Front St., Ste. 200
Memphis, Tenn. 38103
(901) 544-4137

U.S. Dept. of Commerce (ITA)
Jim Charlet, Dir.
Ste. 1114
404 James Robertson Pkwy.
Nashville, Tenn. 37129-1505
(615) 736-5161

Texas

Austin Foreign Trade Council
Jim Ghedi
P.O. Box 4533
Austin, Tex. 78765
(512) 928-3706

Austin World Affairs Council
Wendy Brennan
P.O. Box 1967
Austin, Tex. 78767
(512) 469-0158

Port of Beaumont
Bill Masters, Dir.
P.O. Drawer 2297
Beaumont, Tex. 77704
(409) 835-5367

Brownsville Econ. Dev. Council
Michael R. Hale, Exec. Dir.
1600 E. Elizabeth
Brownsville, Tex. 78520
(512) 541-1183

Brownsville Minority Business
Development Center
Hernan I. Orellana, Dir.
2100 Boca Chica Tower, Suite
301
Brownsville, Tex. 78521-2265
(512) 546-3400

Brownsville Navigation District
C. James Kruse, Gen. Mgr. and
Port Dir.
Brownsville, Navigation District
P.O. Box 3070
Brownsville, Tex. 78523-3070
(512) 542-4341

Cameron County Private Industry
Council
Wanda Garza, Exec. Dir.
285 Kings Hwy.
Brownsville, Tex. 78521
(512) 542-4351

Center for Govt. Contracts
Glen Harris, Dir.
1400 Woodlock Forest Dr., Ste.
500
The Woodlands, Tex. 77380
(713) 367-5777

Port of Corpus Christi Auth.
Harold Plomarity, Exec. Dir.
P.O. Box 1541
Corpus Christi, Tex. 78403
(512) 882-5633

Corpus Christi Area Econ. Dev.
Corp.
Gary Bushell, Pres.
1201 N. Shoreline, P.O. Box 640
Corpus Christi, Tex. 78403-0640
(512) 883-5571

Port of Corpus Christi Foreign
Trade Zone
Thomas S. Moore, Manager
P.O. Box 1541
Corpus Christi, Tex. 78403
(512) 882-5633

Corpus Christi Small Business
Development Center
Robert Berragan, Dir.
P.O. Box 640
Corpus Christi, Tex. 78403
(512) 883-5571

Council for S. Texas Econ.
Progress (COSTEP)
William Davis, Pres.
1701 W. Business Hwy. 83
Texas Commerce Bank, Ste. 600
McAllen, Tex. 78501
(512) 682-1201

City of Dallas
Office of Intl. Affairs
Amb. (Ret.) James R.
Bullington, Dir.
City Hall, 5EN
1500 Marilla
Dallas, Tex. 75201
(214) 670-3319

Dallas Council on World Affairs
Gen. Willard Latham, Exec. Dir.
P.O. Box 58232
Dallas, Tex. 75258
(214) 748-5663

Dallas/Fort Worth Airport Board
Dave Rystrom, Manager, Trade
Development/FTZ
P.O. Box DFW
DFW Airport, Tex. 75261
(214) 574-3079

Dallas Partnership
Greater Dallas Chamber of
Commerce
Amy Chang, Dir., Intl. Bus.
Dev.
1201 Elm St., Ste. 2000
Dallas, Tex. 75270
(214) 746-6739

Foreign Credit Insurance Assn.
Pat Crilly, Mgr.
600 Travis, Ste. 2860
Houston, Tex. 77002
(713) 227-0987

Port of Houston Authority
James Pugh, Exec. Dir.
1519 Capitol Ave.
Houston, Tex. 77001
(713) 226-2100

Greater Houston Partnership
Edward A. Monto, Pres. and
CEQ
World Trade Division
1100 Milam, 25th Floor
Houston, Tex. 77002
(713) 658-2408

Intl. Small Business Dev. Center
Beth Huddleston, Dir.
P.O. Box 58299
Dallas, Tex. 75258
(214) 653-1777

Intl. Trade Assn. of Dallas/Fort
Worth
President
P.O. Box 58009
Dallas, Tex. 75258
(214) 748-3777

Intl. Trade Resource Center
Scott Grant, Pres.
Ste. 150, 2050 Stemmons
Freeway
Dallas, Tex. 75258
(214) 653-1113

McAllen Foreign Trade Zone
Mike Allen, Pres.
Joyce Dean, V.P. of Operations
6401 S. 33rd St.
McAllen, Tex. 78503
(512) 682-4306

McAllen Minority Business
Development Center
Arturo Palacios, Project Dir.
1701 W. Business Hwy. 83, Ste.
1023
McAllen, Tex. 78501
(512) 687-5224

N. Harris County College Small
Business Dev. Center
Raymond Laughter, Dir.
20000 Kingwood Dr.
Kingwood, Tex. 77339
(713) 359-1624

N. Texas District Export Council
Jack Horner, Chairman
c/o Bell Helicopter Textron
P.O. Box 482
Forth Worth, Tex. 76101
(817) 280-3622

Port of Port Arthur
Ben Goldstein, Dir.
Box 1428
Port Arthur, Tex. 77640
(409) 983-2011

(Greater) San Antonio Chamber
of Commerce
Intl. Trade Center
P.O. Box 1628
San Antonio, Tex. 78296
(512) 229-2113

San Antonio World Trade Center
Conrad True
118 Broadway, Ste. 600
San Antonio, Tex. 78205
(512) 225-5877

S. Plains Assn. of Governments
(SPAG)
Jerry Casstevens, Exec. Dir.
P.O. Box 3730
Lubbock, Tex. 79452
(806) 762-8721

S. Texas District Export Council
Mark Joye, Chairman
515 Rusk, Rm. 2625
Houston, Tex. 77002
(713) 228-0500

Tex. Dept. of Agriculture
Paul Lewis, Dir. of Intl. Affairs
Export Services Div.
P.O. Box 12847, Capitol Sta.
Austin, Tex. 78711
(512) 463-7624

Texas Dept of Commerce
Office of Intl. Trade
P.O. Box 12728, Capitol Sta.
816 Congress
Austin, Tex. 78711
(512) 472-5059
*The Department maintains export
assistance centers in a number of
Texas cities.*

Texas Dept. of Commerce
Export Finance
Ed Sosa, Dir.
P.O. Box 12728, Capital Sta.
816 Congress
Austin, Tex. 78711
(512) 320-9662
*The export finance division has
marketing representatives in 10
Texas cities.*

U.S. Chamber of Commerce
Harry L. Cowan, Reg. Manager
4835 LBJ Freeway, Ste. 750
Dallas, Tex. 75244
(214) 387-0404

U.S. Customs Service
David Greenleaf, District Dir.
P.O. Box 61050
DFW Airport, Tex. 75261
(214) 574-2170

U.S. Dept. of Commerce (ITA)
Austin Branch
P.O. Box 12728
816 Congress
Austin, Tex. 78701
(512) 482-5939

U.S. Dept. of Commerce (ITA)
C. Carmon Stiles, Dir.
1100 Commerce St., Rm. 7A5
Dallas, Tex. 75242
(214) 767-0542

U.S. Dept. of Commerce (ITA)
James D. Cook, Dir.
515 Rusk St., Rm. 2625
Houston, Tex. 77002
(713) 229-2578

U.S. Small Business
Administration
Gayle Goodloe, Jr., Branch Mgr.
400 Mann, Room 403
Government Plaza Bldg.
Corpus Christi, Tex. 78401
(512) 888-3301

U.S. Small Business
Administration
Miguel A. Cavazos, Jr., District
Dir.
Harlingen District Office
222 E. Van Buren St., Ste. 500
Harlingen, Tex. 78550
(512) 427-8533

Utah

Cache County Chamber of
Commerce
Executive Director
160 N. Main St.
Logan, Utah 84321-4541
(801) 752-2162

Cedar City Chamber of
Commerce
Executive Director
P.O. Box 220
Cedar City, Utah 84720
(801) 586-4022

St. George Chamber of
Commerce
Executive Director
97 E. 100 N.
St. George, Utah 84770
(801) 628-1658

Salt Lake Intermountain Port
Authority
Larry Bernaski, Export Assist.
Spec.
2110 State St., S2100
Salt Lake City, Utah 84190-3710
(801) 468-3246

U.S. Dept. of Commerce (ITA)
Stephen P. Smoot, Dir.
Room 105
324 S. State St.
Salt Lake City, Utah 84111
(801) 524-5116

Utah Dept. of Community &
Econ. Devel.
Andrew Johnson, Director, Intl.
Devel.
Ste. 200
324 S. State St.
Salt Lake City, Utah 84111
(801) 538-8737

U.S. Small Business
Administration
Steve Price, Intl. Trade Officer
2237 Federal Building
125 S. State St.
Salt Lake City, Utah 84138
(801) 524-6831

Utah Valley Economic Devel.
Assn.
Richard M. Bradford, Exec. Dir.
100 East Center St., Ste. 2500
Provo, Utah 84606
(801) 370-8100

World Trade Assn. of Utah
P.O. Box 53522
Salt Lake City, Utah 84116

Vermont

Lake Champlain Regional
Chamber of Commerce
A. Wayne Roberts, Pres.
209 Battery St.
P.O. Box 453
Burlington, Vt. 05402
(802) 863-3489

(State of) Vermont Agency of
Dev. and Community Affairs
Ron Mackinnon, Commissioner
Pavillion Office Bldg.
109 State St.
Montpelier, Vt. 05602
(802) 828-3221

U.S. Dept. of Commerce (ITA)
Francis J. O'Connor, Dir.
World Trade Center, Ste. 307
Boston, Mass. 02210
(617) 565-8563

Virginia

Fairfax County Chamber of
Commerce
Judith Forehand, Pres.
8391 Old Courthouse Rd., Ste.
#300
Vienna, Va. 22182
(703) 749-0400

Hampton Roads Maritime Assn.
Jack W. Mace, Exec. V.P.
P.O. Box 3487
Norfolk, Va. 23514
(804) 622-3487

Institute for Econ.
Competitiveness
J. Roger McCauley, Dir.
Radford University
Radford, Va. 23142
(703) 831-5000

Intl. Trade Assn. of N. Virginia
James K. Alford, Pres.
P.O. Box 2982
Reston, Va. 22090
(703) 860-8795

Intl. Trade Assn. of W. Virginia
Hugh M. Henderson, Pres.
P.O. Box 936
Lexington, Va. 24450
(703) 463-1095

Jefferson Intl. Business Club
Gibboney Huske
269 Monroe Hall
University of Virginia
Charlottesville, Va. 22903
(804) 924-4568

Norfolk Airport Authority
Robert A. Barringer, Mgr., Air
Cargo Dev.
Norfolk International Airport
Norfolk, Va. 23518
(804) 857-3351

Piedmont World Trade Council
John M. Peniche, Pres.
P.O. Box 1374
Lynchburg, Va. 24505
(804) 528-7511

Richmond Export-Import Club
Sandra Hensley, Pres.
P.O. Box 12135
Richmond, Va. 23241
(804) 853-0900

U.S. Dept. of Commerce (ITA)
Philip Ouzts, Dir.
8010 Federal Bldg.
400 N. 8th St.
Richmond, Va. 23240
(804) 771-2246

Va. Chamber of Commerce
Edwin C. Luther, III, Exec. V.P.
9 S. Fifth St.
Richmond, Va. 23219
(804) 644-1607

Va. Dept. of Agriculture &
Consumer Affairs
S. Mason Carbaugh, Comm.
1100 Bank St., Rm. 710
Richmond, Va. 23219
(804) 786-3501

Va. Dept. of World Trade
Richard J. Davis, Exec. Dir.
6000 World Trade Center
Norfolk, Va. 23510
(804) 683-2849

Va. District Export Council
Philip H. Anns, Chairman
P.O. Box 10190
Richmond, Va. 23240
(804) 771-2246

Va. Port Authority
J. Robert Bray, Exec. Dir.
6000 World Trade Center
Norfolk, Va. 23510
(804) 683-8000

Washington

Commencement Bay Intl. Trade
Council
Tacoma-Pierce County Chamber
of Commerce
Gary Brackett, Business Trade
Mgr.
P.O. Box 1933
Tacoma, Wash. 98401
(206) 627-2175

Cowlitz Economic Dev. Council
John Thompson
1338 Commerce Ave., Ste. 211
Longview, Wash. 98632

Export Assistance Center of
Wash.
Ken Keach, Pres.
2001 Sixth Ave., Ste. 1700
Seattle, Wash. 98121
(206) 464-7123

IMPACT (Agricultural
Marketing)
Washington State Univ.
Dr. A. Desmond O'Rourke, Dir.
Hulbert Hall, Room 104
Wash. St. University
Pullman, Wash. 99164-6214
(509) 335-6653

Inland N.W. World Trade
Council
Attn: Kristin Koehler
P.O. Box 1124
Spokane, Wash. 99210
(509) 456-3243

International Business Center
Bellevue Community College
ASR Building
13555 Bel-Red Road, Ste. 208B
Bellevue, Wash. 98005
(206) 562-6154

International Trade Institute
North Seattle Community College
Janis Parsley, Dir.
9600 College Way N.
Seattle, Wash. 98103
(206) 527-3732

National Marine Fisheries Service
Fisheries Development Div.
Linda Chaves, Dept. Chief
7600 Sand Point Way N.E.
Bin C15700
Seattle, Wash. 98115
(206) 526-6117

N.W. Trade Adjustment
Assistance Center
Ronald Horst, Dir.
900 Fourth Ave., Ste. 2430
Seattle, Wash. 98164
(206) 622-2730

Pacific Northwest/Caribbean
Basin Trade Assn.
Robert Sanders, Dir.
5120 W. Third Ave.
Kennewick, Wash. 99336
(509) 783-3337

Seattle Chamber of Commerce
Trade and Transportation Div.
Janet Bumgarner, Acting Mgr.
600 University St., Ste. 1200
Seattle, Wash. 98101
(206) 389-7269

Spokane Chamber of Commerce
Cary Hegreberg, Trade Div.
P.O. Box 2147
Spokane, Wash. 99210
(509) 624-1393

Tri-Ports Export Services
Susan Nelson, Dir.
One Clover Island
Kennewick, Wash. 99336
(509) 586-1188

U.S. Dept. of Commerce (ITA)
C. Franklin Foster, Dir.
3131 Elliott Ave., Ste. 290
Seattle, Wash. 98121
(206) 442-5615

U.S. Dept. of Commerce
(ITA)—Spokane Branch
Bill Schrage, Trade Specialist
P.O. Box 2170
Spokane, Wash. 99210
(509) 353-2922

Greater Vancouver Chamber of
Commerce
Donna Cantonwide
404 E. 15th St.
Vancouver, Wash. 98663
(206) 694-2588

Wash. Council on Intl. Trade
Robert Kapp, Pres.
2615 Fourth Ave., Ste. 350
Seattle, Wash. 98121
(206) 443-3826

Washington Public Ports Assn.
Don White, Exec. Dir.
P.O. Box 1518
Olympia, Wash. 98507
(206) 943-0760

Wash. State Dept. of Trade and
Econ. Dev.
Paul Isaki, Dir.
2001 Sixth Ave.
26th Floor
Seattle, Wash. 98121
(206) 464-7076

World Affairs Council
Jeffrey Demetrescu, Dir.
515 Madison St., Ste. 501
Seattle, Wash. 98104
(206) 682-6986

Wash. State Intl. Trade Fair
Steve Hatch, Pres.
999 Third Ave., Ste. 1020
Seattle, Wash. 98104
(206) 682-6900

World Trade Ctr. of Tacoma
Nancy Peregrine, Dir.
3600 Port of Tacoma Road
Tacoma, Wash. 98424
(206) 383-9474

World Trade Club of Seattle
Margaret Oliver, Sec.
P.O. Box 21488
Seattle, Wash. 98111
(206) 624-9586

West Virginia

Appalachian Export Center for
Hardwoods
West Virginia University
Dr. Ramsey Smith, Dir.
P.O. Box 6061
Morgantown, W. Va. 26506-6061
(304) 293-7577

Governor's Office of Community
and Ind. Dev.
Stephen Spence, Dir.,
Intl. Division
Room 531, Building #6
1900 Washington St. E.
Charleston, W. Va. 25305
(304) 348-2001

Institute for Intl. Trade Dev.
Harold Porter, Dir.
Exporter's Assistance Program
1050 Fourth Ave.
Huntington, W. Va. 25755-2131
(304) 696-2451

U.S. Dept. of Commerce (ITA)
Roger L. Fortner, Dir.
P.O. Box 26
Charleston, W. Va. 25321
(304) 347-5123

W. Va. Chamber of Commerce
John Hurd, Pres.
P.O. Box 2789
Charleston, W. Va. 25330
(304) 342-1115

W. Va. Export Council
Sam Silverstein, Chairman
P.O. Box 26
Charleston, W. Va. 25321
(304) 343-3726

W. Va. Manufacturers Assn.
Pat Gallagher, Pres.
405 Capitol St.
Charleston, W. Va. 25301
(304) 342-2123

Wisconsin

Foreign Trade Zone of Wis. Ltd.
Vincent Boever, Pres.
1925 E. Kelly Lane
Cudahy, Wis. 53110
(414) 764-2111

Milwaukee Assn. of Commerce
John Duncan, Pres.
756 N. Milwaukee St.
Milwaukee, Wis. 53202
(414) 273-3000

Milwaukee World Trade Assn.
Peter Beitzel, Exec. Dir.
756 N. Milwaukee St.
Milwaukee, Wis. 53202
(414) 273-3000

Port of Milwaukee
Kenneth Szallai, Municipal Port
Dir.
500 N. Harbor Dr.
Milwaukee, Wis. 53202
(414) 278-3511

Small Business Dev. Center
Bill Pinkovitz
432 N. Lake St.
Madison, Wis. 53706
(608) 263-7766

U.S. Dept. of Commerce (ITA)
Thos. A. Knapp, Acting Dir.
517 E. Wisconsin Ave., Ste. 606
Milwaukee, Wis. 53202
(414) 297-3473

Wis. Dept. of Development
Ralph Graner, Dir.
P.O. Box 7970
123 W. Washington Ave.
Madison, Wis. 53707
(608) 266-1767

Wis. World Trade Center
John DeVane, Exec. Dir.
Pfister Hotel
424 E. Wisconsin Ave.
Milwaukee, Wis. 53202
(414) 274-3840

Wyoming

U.S. Dept. of Commerce (ITA)
James W. Manis, Dir.
World Trade Center
1625 Broadway, Ste. 680
Denver, Colo. 80202
(303) 844-3246

State of Wyoming
Office of the Governor
George Rex, Acting Intl. Trade
Dir.
Capitol Building
Cheyenne, Wyo. 82002
(307) 777-6412

Appendix **C**

International Trade Administration/US&FCS District Offices†

ALABAMA
*Birmingham—Rm. 302, 2015 2nd Ave. North, Berry Bldg., 35203, (205) 731-1331

ALASKA
Anchorage—222 West 7th Ave., P.O. Box 32, 99513, (907) 271-5041

ARIZONA
Phoenix—Federal Bldg. & U.S. Courthouse, 230 North 1st Ave., Rm. 3412, 85025, (602) 379-3285

ARKANSAS
Little Rock—Suite 811, Savers Fed. Bldg., 320 W. Capitol Ave., 72201, (501) 378-5794

CALIFORNIA
Los Angeles—Rm. 9200, 11000 Wilshire Blvd., 90024, (213) 209-7104

Santa Ana—116-A W. 4th St., Suite #1, 92701, (714) 836-2461

San Diego—6363 Greenwich Dr., Suite 145, 92122, (619) 557-5395

*San Francisco—Fed. Bldg., Box 36013, 450 Golden Gate Ave., 94102, (415) 556-5860

COLORADO
*Denver—680 World Trade Center, 1625 Broadway, 80202, (303) 844-3246

CONNECTICUT
*Hartford—Rm. 610-B, Fed. Office Bldg., 450 Main St., 06103, (203) 240-3530

DELAWARE
Serviced by Philadelphia District Office

DISTRICT OF COLUMBIA
•Washington, D.C.—(Baltimore, Md. District) Rm. 1066 HCHB, Department of Commerce, 14th St. & Constitution Ave., N.W. 20230, (202) 377-3181

FLORIDA
Miami—Suite 224, Fed. Bldg., 51 S.W. First Ave., 33130, (305) 536-5267

•Clearwater—128 North Osceola Ave. 34615, (813) 461-0011

•Jacksonville—3100 University Blvd. South, Suite 200A, 32216, (904) 791-2796

*Orlando—College of Business Administration, CEBA II, Rm. 346, University of Central Florida, 32802, (407) 648-1608

•Tallahassee—Collins Bldg., Rm. 401, 107 W. Gaines St., 32304, (904) 488-6469

GEORGIA
Atlanta—Suite 504, 1365 Peachtree St., N.E., 30309, (404) 347-7000

Savannah—120 Barnard St., A-107, 31401, (912) 944-4204

HAWAII
Honolulu—4106 Fed. Bldg., P.O. Box 50026, 300 Ala Moana Blvd., 96850, (808) 541-1782

IDAHO
•Boise (Portland, Ore. District)—Hall of Mirrors Bldg., 700 W. State St., 2nd fl, Boise, Idaho 83720, (208) 334-3857

* Denotes regional office with supervisory regional responsibilities.

• Denotes trade specialist at a branch office.

† Reprinted with permission of the U.S. Department of Commerce from *Business America,* July 16, 1990.

ILLINOIS
Chicago—Rm. 1406 Mid Continental Plaza Bldg., 55 East Monroe St., 60603, (312) 353-4450
•Palatine—W.R. Harper College, Algonquin & Roselle Rd., 60067, (312) 397-3000, x2532
•Rockford—515 North Court St., P.O. Box 1747, 61110-0247, (815) 987-8123

INDIANA
Indianapolis—One North Capitol Ave., Suite 520, 46204, (317) 226-6214

IOWA
Des Moines—817 Fed. Bldg., 210 Walnut St., 50309, (515) 284-4222

KANSAS
•Wichita—(Kansas City, Missouri District) 7591 River Park Pl., Suite 580, 727 North Waco, 67203, (316) 269-6160

KENTUCKY
Louisville—Rm. 636B, Gene Snyder Courthouse and Customhouse Bldg., 601 W. Broadway, 40202, (502) 582-5066

LOUISIANA
New Orleans—432 World Trade Center, No. 2 Canal St., 70130, (504) 589-6546

MAINE
•Augusta—(Boston, Massachusetts District) 77 Sewall St., 04330, (207) 622-8249

MARYLAND
Baltimore—413 U.S. Customhouse, 40 South Gay and Lombard Sts., 21202, (301) 962-3560

MASSACHUSETTS
Boston—World Trade Center, Suite 307 Commonwealth Pier Area, 02210, (617) 565-8563

MICHIGAN
Detroit—1140 McNamara Bldg., 477 Michigan Ave., 48226, (313) 226-3650
•Grand Rapids—300 Monroe N.W., Rm. 409, 49503, (616) 456-2411

MINNESOTA
Minneapolis—108 Fed. Bldg., 110 S. 4th St., 55401, (612) 348-1638

MISSISSIPPI
Jackson—328 Jackson Mall Office Center, 300 Woodrow Wilson Blvd., 39213, (601) 965-4388

MISSOURI
*St. Louis—7911 Forsyth Blvd., Suite 610, 63105, (314) 425-3302
Kansas City—Rm. 635, 601 East 12th St., 64106, (816) 426-3141

MONTANA
Serviced by Boise, Idaho District Office

NEBRASKA
Omaha—11133 ''O'' St., 68137, (402) 221-3664

NEVADA
Reno—1755 E. Plumb Ln., #152, 89502, (702) 785-5203

NEW HAMPSHIRE
Serviced by Boston District Office

NEW JERSEY
Trenton—3131 Princeton Pike Bldg., #6, Suite 100, 08648, (609) 989-2100

NEW MEXICO
Albuquerque (Dallas, Tex District)—625 Silver SW., 3rd Fl., 87102, (214) 767-0542
Santa Fe (Dallas, Tex District)—c/o Economic Develop. and Tourism Dept., 1100 St. Francis Drive, 87503, (505) 827-0264

NEW YORK
Buffalo—1312 Fed. Bldg., 111 West Huron St., 14202, (716) 846-4191
•Rochester—111 East Ave., Suite 220, 14604, (716) 263-6480
New York—Fed. Office Bldg., 26 Fed. Plaza, Rm. 3718, Foley Sq., 10278, (212) 264-0634

NORTH CAROLINA
*Greensboro—324 W. Market St., P.O. Box 1950, 27402, (919) 333-5345

NORTH DAKOTA
Serviced by Omaha District Office

OHIO
*Cincinnati—9504 Fed. Office Bldg., 550 Main St., 45202, (513) 684-2944
Cleveland—Rm. 600, 668 Euclid Ave., 44114 (216) 522-4750

OKLAHOMA
Oklahoma City—5 Broadway Executive Park, Suite 200, 6601 Broadway Extension, 73116, (405) 231-5302
•Tulsa—440 S. Houston St., 74127, (918) 581-7650

OREGON
Portland—Suite 242, One World Trade Center, 121 S.W. Salmon St., 97204, (503) 326-3001

PENNSYLVANIA
Philadelphia—475 Allendale Road, Suite 202, King of Prussia, Pa., 19406, (215) 962-4980
Pittsburgh—2002 Fed. Bldg., 1000 Liberty Ave., 15222, (412) 644-2850

PUERTO RICO
San Juan (Hato Rey)—Rm. G-55 Fed. Bldg., 00918, (809) 766-5555

RHODE ISLAND
•Providence—(Boston, Massachusetts District) 7 Jackson Walkway, 02903, (401) 528-5104, ext. 22

SOUTH CAROLINA
Columbia—Strom Thurmond Fed. Bldg., Suite 172, 1835 Assembly St., 29201 (803) 765-5345
•Charleston—JC Long Bldg., Rm. 128, 9 Liberty St., 29424, (803) 724-4361

SOUTH DAKOTA
Serviced by Omaha District Office

TENNESSEE
Nashville—Suite 1114, Parkway Towers, 404 James Robertson Parkway, 37219-1505, (615) 736-5161
•Memphis—The Falls Building, Suite 200, 22 North Front St., 38103, (901) 544-4137

TEXAS
•Dallas—Rm. 7A5, 1100 Commerce St., 75242-0787, (214) 767-0542
•Austin—P.O. Box 12728, 816 Congress Ave., Suite 1200, 78711, (512) 482-5939
Houston—2625 Fed. Courthouse, 515 Rusk St., 77002, (713) 229-2578

UTAH
Salt Lake City—Suite 105, 324 South State St., 84111, (801) 524-5116

VERMONT
Serviced by Boston District Office

VIRGINIA
Richmond—8010 Fed. Bldg., 400 North 8th St., 23240, (804) 771-2246

WASHINGTON
Seattle—3131 Elliott Ave., Suite 290, 98121, (206) 442-5616
•Spokane—West 808 Spokane Falls Blvd., Suite 650, 99201, (509) 353-2922

WEST VIRGINIA
Charleston—3402 Fed. Bldg., 500 Quarrier St., 25301, (304) 347-5123

WISCONSIN
Milwaukee—Fed. Bldg., U.S. Courthouse, Rm. 606, 517 E. Wisc. Ave., 53202, (414) 291-3473

WYOMING
Serviced by Denver District Office

Appendix D

Sample Supply Agreements*

AGENCY AGREEMENT
(between foreign exporter and U.S. selling agent)

THIS AGREEMENT is made this _____ day of _____, 19___.

BETWEEN _____A CORP_____ incorporated in _____
with its registered office at:

_____

_____

_____

(hereinafter called "A Corp") of the one part

AND: _____B CORP_____ incorporated in _____
with its principal office at:

_____

_____

(hereinafter called "B Corp") on the other part

WHEREAS

(A) A Corp designs, develops, manufactures and sells widgets and ancillary equipment for use in the widget industry.

(B) In view of its previous experience in marketing widgets and ancillary equipment for the widget industry in the United States, its valuable contacts in that industry and its general marketing expertise and organization, B Corp wishes to undertake, and A Corp is willing to support, the marketing of widgets and ancillary

*Provided by Kaplan Russin Vecchi & Kirkwood, New York, N.Y.

equipment manufactured by A Corp in the United States under an agency from A Corp.

(C) The parties now wish formally to record the terms and conditions which shall govern their association for the purposes outlined in Recital (b) above.

NOW, THEREFORE, IT IS AGREED AND DECLARED AS FOLLOWS:

Clause 1. SCOPE

The parties agree that the terms and conditions set forth in this Agreement represent the entire agreement between the parties relating to the Agency of B Corp for A Corp and shall supersede any and all prior representations, agreements, statements and understandings relating thereto. The parties further agree that neither party places any reliance whatsoever on any such prior representations, agreements, statements and understandings except to the extent expressly set forth in this Agreement.

Clause 2. APPOINTMENT OF AGENT

A Corp hereby appoints B Corp to be its exclusive Agent in the United States during the currency of this Agreement for the sale of all widgets and ancillary equipment listed in Schedule 1. All such widgets and ancillary equipment are hereinafter collectively referred to as "The Products." A list of The Products which are standard as at the date of this Agreement is set forth in Schedule 1 to this Agreement and A Corp undertakes to give B Corp prompt written notice of any additions to or deletions from such list.

Clause 3. DUTIES OF THE AGENT

3.1 B Corp shall during the currency of this Agreement:
   3.1.1 Use its best endeavors to promote the sale of The Products to customers and potential customers throughout the United States and solicit orders for The Products to be placed with A Corp as per Clause 9 hereof. Without prejudice to the generality of the foregoing B Corp shall:
      3.1.1.1 maintain close marketing relationships with customers and potential customers so that their relevant equipment needs and future plans are ascertained.
      3.1.1.2 draw the attention of customers and potential customers to The Products suitable to their needs and

ascertain the equipment and technical commercial proposals being offered by A Corp's competitors.

    3.1.1.3 B Corp shall not, during the currency of this Agreement act as agent or distributor for any products directly competitive in price and specification to the products.

  3.1.2 Establish and maintain a product support service having the capacity of:

    3.1.2.1 dealing with routine service enquiries from customers either by telephone or telex advice or in the field.

    3.1.2.2 maintaining liaison with customers.

    3.1.2.3 asissting customers in the implementation of the A Corp Warranty for The Products.

  3.1.3 Promptly draw to the attention of A Corp any new or revised legislation, regulation or orders affecting the use or sale of The Products in the United States of America as and when such legislation, etc. come to its attention.

  3.1.4 Employ such technically competent sales, commercial and service staff as may be reasonably necessary.

  3.1.5 Receive within its B Corp's offices temporary visiting staff or A Corp and afford to such staff reasonable office, secretarial and communications services.

3.2 Recognizing its obligations to protect the reputation of A Corp, B Corp undertakes that it shall not undertake any obligations in respect of the performance of The Products in excess of the limits specified by A Corp in respect of The Products concerned and shall not offer any time for delivery earlier than that given by A Corp pursuant to the inquiry and order procedure provisions of this Agreement.

Clause 4. SUPPORT OBLIGATIONS OF A CORP

During the term of the Agreement, A Corp shall:

4.1 Continue to develop the Products to meet the requirements of the United States market.

4.2 Supply at its own cost B Corp with all reasonable requirements for technical data in reproducible form for us in catalogues, sales literature, instruction books, technical pamphlets and advertising material relating to The Products including developments of The Products as envisaged under Clause 4.1 above, and will pay the equivalent of _____% of the prior 12 months' gross billing, in every year, for the preparation of such material.

4.3 Make potential customers within the United States aware of the support available from B Corp as agent of A Corp and of A Corp's support of such agency.

Clause 5. DELIVERIES BY A CORP

5.1 Throughout the term of this Agreement A Corp shall assist the sales efforts of B Corp by holding a stock of certain of the Products in an authorized warehouse within 50 miles of B Corp's headquarters at a level not lower than that set forth in Schedule 2 annexed hereto, which schedule may be changed from time to time by the signature of both parties on the revised version thereof.

5.2 A Corp shall provide adequate and suitable storage accommodations for such stock at its authorized warehouse and all deliveries will be dealt with through that warehouse. The costs and charges of the warehouse company shall be billed directly to and settled by A Corp.

5.3 All stock belonging to and warehoused by A Corp as set forth is and shall at all times remain the exclusive property of A Corp, and neither title nor possession thereof or in part thereof, shall pass to B Corp or to any third party customer of B Corp save or until the precise terms and conditions of Clause 5.4 herein below have been completely and exclusively complied with.

5.4 B Corp shall have the authority to instruct A Corp's warehouse to release not more than 5 widgets on any given day. As to widgets released and shipped in accordance with the above authority, B Corp must receive payment in one of the following alternative ways: (a) By cash payment for the widget within 48 hours of such shipment; or (b) by delivery to Barclays Bank, N.Y., Jericho branch, within 48 hours of such shipment, of an irrevocable 45 day Letter of Credit, in the amount of the payment due.

Clause 6. PRICE

6.1 Customers solicited by B Corp shall pay the prices agreed or to be agreed from time to time and annexed as an Exhibit A hereto. Payment shall be made in accordance with paragraph 5.4 hereinabove. The parties hereto further agree that the said prices shall be reviewed every six months beginning on the date of this Agreement.

6.2 A Corp undertakes that it will give not less than three months' notice of any changes to its United States Dollar prices for the sale of The

Products. A Corp further undertakes that any non-standard Products and agreed modifications to The Products shall be priced on a basis consistent with its normal pricing arrangements under this Agreement.

Clause 7. COMMISSIONS EARNED

Upon delivery of, and payment for, each Product pursuant Clause 5 and 6, B Corp shall be entitled to a commission in the amount of _____ percent (_____%) of the list price of each of The Products as set forth in Exhibit _____ hereto less any discounts or other allowances made by B Corp in these prices to achieve the sale and any freight, packing, insurance, or other charges. Commissions shall be calculated at the end of each calendar month based upon deliveries during the preceding month. Payment shall be made within 10 days of the end of the calendar month to B Corp.

Clause 8. DIRECT SALES AND FOREIGN ORDERS

A Corp agrees not to solicit sales for use within the United States during the currency of this Agreement. However, nothing in this Agreement is intended to operate nor shall it be construed as operating to prevent A Corp from selling, should it receive direct orders from and to any customer within the United States or to any customer outside the United States which customer whether within the knowledge of A Corp or not, intends to resell or actually resells to a customer within the United States. In the event of a direct sale by A Corp to a customer within the United States then A Corp shall grant B Corp a commission upon such sale in an amount of _____ percent (_____%) of the sale price charged by A Corp to such customer provided always that thereafter The Product support obligations of B Corp pursuant to this Agreement shall apply in respect of the sale of The Product so made by A Corp to the said customer. A Corp shall notify B Corp of each and every such sale. Further and in addition, if B Corp obtains any order for A Corp's products for shipment outside the United States, A Corp shall grant B Corp the same said commission on such sale.

Clause 9. PROPRIETARY RIGHTS

9.1 The due and proper performance of its obligations and the exercise of its rights hereunder by B Corp shall not be deemed to be a breach of copyright or infringement of patent trademark or other proprietary right owned by A Corp.

9.2 B Corp shall not under any circumstances acquire any rights whatsoever in any copyright, patent, trademark or other proprietary
right of A Corp nor shall B Corp acquire any rights whatsoever in
relation to the design of The Products.

Clause 10. DELIVERY

10.1 A Corp reserves the right to specify and change delivery dates
and shall not be responsible for any delay in delivery or failure to
meet delivery schedules where such delay or failure arises due to
any cause outside the reasonable control of A Corp.

10.2 The parties hereto agree that, in the event that delivery of Products is delayed by an act or omission of a customer, B Corp shall
invoice such customers for the reasonable storage charges incurred
by A Corp as a result thereof, and will use reasonable efforts to
effect collection. Upon receipt of payment against such invoice, B
Corp shall remit such payment to A Corp after deduction of B
Corp's commission and costs of such collection.

Clause 11. WARRANTY

11.1 A Corp's warranty on all of The Products is limited to the following:
A Corp will repair or replace at its option any Product at its own
expense, save as to freight as to which it shall pay 50% of the round-
trip cost for all validated warranty claims, as to which Product any
defect in design, material or workmanship arises within a period of
one year from commencement of operation of such Product or
eighteen (18) months from the date of delivery of such Product,
whichever shall first occur.

11.2 The warranty contained in Clause 11.1 above is subject to:

11.2.1 The Product not being used for any purpose other than the
normal purpose for its specifications.

11.2.2 the observance by the user of all operating instructions
and recommendations issued by A Corp in relation thereto.

11.2.3 prompt written notice being given to A Corp within 30
days following discovery of such defect.

11.3 B Corp shall promptly issue a report to A Corp in respect of each
warranty claim brought to its attention.

Clause 12. PATENT INDEMNITY

12.1 In the event that any claim should be brought against B Corp that
The Products infringe letters patent or other protected proprietary
right, valid at the date of acceptance by A Corp of B Corp's order

for such Product, owned by any third party, not being an employee or officer or shareholder of B Corp and not being a subsidiary or associated company of B Corp, then A Corp shall indemnify B Corp against and hold B Corp harmless from any and all damages which may be awarded against B Corp by any Court of competent jurisdiction provided that:

12.1.1 B Corp notifies A Corp in writing within 30 days of learning of any such claim as aforesaid.

12.1.2 B Corp permits A Corp to conduct the defense to any such claim as aforesaid and the negotiation of any settlement thereof.

12.1.3 B Corp provides at the expense of A Corp such assistance as A Corp may require in the defense or settlement of such claim as aforesaid.

12.1.4 such indemnity and undertaking as aforesaid shall not apply if the infringement relates to any use other than a use authorized by A Corp.

12.1.5 such indemnity and undertaking as aforesaid shall not apply where the infringement relates to the combination of The Products with equipment not designed, manufactured or sold by A Corp, unless A Corp specifically was aware of and approved such combination in advance thereof.

12.2 A Corp reserves the right to settle any such claim as aforesaid on the basis of substituting non-infringing Products for the alleged infringing Products providing that such substituted Products are capable of performing substantially the same functions as The Products so replaced.

12.3 Such indemnity and undertaking as aforesaid shall not apply in the event the designs, the subject of such claim as aforesaid, were supplied by B Corp's customers. In that event B Corp shall request such customers to indemnify A Corp against any claims made against A Corp alleging the infringement of letters paten tor other protected proprietary rights arising out of the use of such designs or the manufacture or sale of Products utilizing such designs.

Clause 13. LIMITATION OF WARRANTY

13.1 The parties hereto agree that the express undertakings of A Corp pursuant to the provisions of the Warranty contained in Clause 11 constitute the only warranties of A Corp and the said undertakings of Clause 11 are in lieu of and in substitution for all other conditions and warranties express or implied INCLUDING WITHOUT

LIMITATION ANY WARRANTIES AS TO MERCHANTABILITY OR FITNESS FOR PURPOSE and all other obligations and liabilities whatsoever of A Corp whether in contract or in tort or otherwise, and B Corp shall so inform customers and potential customers. B Corp shall not offer or assume nor authorize anyone to offer or assume for or on behalf of A Corp any other Warranty or similar obligation in connection with The Products other than as authorized by Clause 11 and this Clause 13.

Clause 14. CAPACITY OF THE PARTIES

14.1 B Corp undertakes that it will at all times material to this Agreement make clear to customers and potential customers that it acts in the capacity of agent of A Corp. Except as specifically authorized under the terms of this Agreement, B Corp is not authorized to bind or commit or make representations on behalf of A Corp for any purpose whatsoever, and B Corp shall make this clear to customers and potential customers.

14.2 This Agreement is not intended nor shall it be construed as establishing any form of partnership between the parties.

Clause 15. ASSIGNMENT

The obligations and duties of B Corp hereunder are personal to B Corp and shall not be subcontracted to any third party without the prior written consent of A Corp nor shall B Corp assign this Agreement or any part thereof to any third party without the prior written consent of A Corp.

Clause 16. CONFIDENTIALITY

Any information which may during the currency of this Agreement be divulged by either party to the other on the express written basis that such information is confidential shall be so regarded and be protected whether in storage or in use. Furthermore, any such information shall not be used by the party receiving same otherwise than for the express purpose for which it is divulged and shall not further be divulged except to such of the said party's own servants and agents as may have a "need to know" for the purposes of this Agreement.

Clause 17. DURATION AND TERMINATION

17.1 This Agreement shall commence on the date of signature hereof and shall continue unless and until terminated by either party giving to the other not less than 30 days written notice to such effect.

17.2 Any termination in accordance with the provisions of Clause 17.1 above shall not affect the obligations of the parties to fulfill the terms of orders placed and accepted prior to the effective date of such termination.

17.3 If either party should enter into any liquidation, bankruptcy or receivership whether compulsorily or voluntarily or should enter into any Agreement with creditors compounding debts or should suffer the imposition of a receiver in respect of the whole or a material part of its assets or should otherwise become insolvent, then the other party may by notice in writing, forthwith terminate this Agreement.

17.4 Upon termination of this Agreement:

17.4.1 B Corp shall return at its own expense to A Corp any catalogues, sales literature, instruction books, technical pamphlets and advertising material relating to The Products which may have been supplied by A Corp.

17.4.2 B Corp shall immediately cease to trade as an agent of A Corp and shall cease to represent itself in such capacity.

17.4.3 Recognizing that the financial and other commitments to be made by the parties in order to operate this Agreement will be put at risk by a termination pursuant to Clause 17.1 above at any time, the parties agree that any termination by A Corp pursuant to the terms of Clause 17.1, other than a termination pursuant to the terms of Clause 17.3, and other than a termination for cause (which shall include but specifically not be limited to fraud, negligence, breach of the terms of this Agreement), shall entitle B Corp to receive, in addition to sums actually due pursuant to the terms of Clause 17.2 and 17.4.4 herein, an amount equal to the net commissions received by B Corp under this Agreement, during the twelve months immediately preceding the date of notification of such termination, such sum to be paid at the expiration of the 30 day notice period. In the event that termination is by reason of Clause 17.3 herein, or for cause as defined hereinabove, or if termination is at the request or by the notice of B Corp, B Corp shall be entitled only to the amount due to it pursuant to the terms of Clause 17.2 and 17.4.4 hereinabove. Since the exercise of such right to terminate would not constitute any breach of this Agreement such amount as shall be payable as aforesaid shall not be deemed a penalty.

17.4.4 A Corp shall continue to pay commissions on those orders obtained prior to the date of termination as invoices are paid and widgets delivered.

17.4.5 Subsequent to termination of this Agreement by either party in any manner and for any reason whatsoever, neither party shall be prevented or restricted from doing business with any person, corporation, partnership or other business entity within the United States or elsewhere, specifically including but not limited to persons, corporations, partnerships and business entities who have previously purchased A Corp's products, whether through B Corp or otherwise; except that if A Corp terminates this Agreement under circumstances which entitle B Corp to the payment of compensation pursuant to the terms of paragraph 17.4.3 hereinabove, then A Corp agrees that it will not solicit orders from any customers who received the products, or who requested a quotation therefor from B Corp during the currency of this Agreement, for a period of two years from the date of such termination.

Clause 18. NOTICES

Any notice required to be given hereunder shall be sufficiently given if forwarded by any of the following methods: registered mail, cable, telegraph or telex to the registered office of A Corp or the principal office of B Corp as the case may be and shall be deemed to have been received and given at the time when it is ordinary course of transmission it should have been delivered or received at the address to which it was sent.

Clause 19. WAIVER

Failure by either party at any time to enforce any of the provisions of this Agreement shall not constitute a waiver by such party of such provision nor in any way affect the validity of this Agreement.

Clause 20. AMENDMENT

This Agreement may not be amended except by an instrument in writing signed by both parties and made subsequent to the date of this Agreement and which is expressly stated to amend this Agreement.

Clause 21. HEADINGS

The clause headings of this Agreement are for reference purposes only and shall not be deemed to affect the interpretation of any of the provisions of this Agreement.

Clause 22. LAW

This Agreement shall be subject to and interpreted in accordance with the Laws of _____.

IN WITNESS WHEREOF, the parties have caused this Agreement to be signed on their behalf by the hand of a duly authorized officer.

FOR A CORP

_____ (Title)

FOR B CORP

_____ (Title)

DISTRIBUTORSHIP AGREEMENT
(between foreign exporter and U.S. importer/distributor)

AGREEMENT made this _____ day of _____, 1986, by and between A Corp, a company organized under the laws of C Country with its principal place of business located at _____ _____ (hereinafter called the "PRODUCER") and B Corp, located at S State (hereinafter called the "DISTRIBUTOR");

WITNESSETH:

WHEREAS, the PRODUCER is engaged in the design, manufacture and marketing of, among other things, widgets (the "Product"); under the brand name "Widgets."

WHEREAS, the DISTRIBUTOR maintains a marketing organization and markets widgets in the United States; and

WHEREAS, the PRODUCER and DISTRIBUTOR desire to cooperate for the purpose of marketing the product in the United States to civilians under the terms hereinafter set forth;

NOW THEREFORE, in consideration of the foregoing premises, the mutual covenants and agreements contained herein and other good and valuable consideration, the receipt, sufficiency and adequacy of which is hereby acknowledged, the parties hereto agree as follows:

SECTION I. APPOINTMENT

The PRODUCER hereby appoints the DISTRIBUTOR to be its exclusive Distributor of the Product to civilians in the Territories as defined below, and the DISTRIBUTOR hereby accepts that appointment and agrees to act as the exclusive Distributor for the PRODUCER. PRODUCER specifically reserves to itself the right to market the Product to all Local, State and Federal organizations and entities, and the term "civilian" shall not include any such organizations or entities.

A. As used herein, Territories shall mean the States of _____

_____

B. In addition to paragraph A, Section 1 above, Territories shall also mean all other states east of the Mississippi River at such time as the DISTRIBUTOR delivers to the PRODUCER a marketing plan acceptable to the PRODUCER. DISTRIBUTOR shall have _____ months from the date of this Agreement to deliver such plan.

C. In addition to paragraphs A and B of Section 1 above, the DISTRIBUTOR shall be given the first option to include all States west of the Mississipi River in the above defined Territories, at such time as the DISTRIBUTOR delivers to the PRODUCER a business and marketing plan acceptable to the PRODUCER for all States west of the Mississippi River. The option shall expire if such a plan is not delivered within _____ months from the date of this Agreement.

SECTION II. SALES AND PROMOTION

DISTRIBUTOR during the term of this Agreement shall:

A. Energetically and faithfully use its best efforts to promote the sale of the Product to civilian customers and potential civilian customers throughout the Territories;

B. Carry continuously and have readily available sufficient quantities of the Product to enable it to promptly meet current demands of all customers;

C. Agree to price the Product at competitive levels, at wholesale and at retail, to sell the Product in accordance with the customs in the trade and will abstain from using selling methods or practices which, in the PRODUCER'S opinion, are harmful to the reputation of the Product or the PRODUCER;

D. Employ such technically competent sales, commercial and service staff as may be reasonably necessary;

E. Vigorously advertise and promote the Product within the Territories and bear all expense therefrom, which shall not be less than US$_____ per year;

F. Attend and participate annually in all significant trade shows and exhibitions, which includes, at the minimum, having a booth for demonstrations, promotions and advertising to all attendees of such shows or exhibitions. The booths should be staffed with technically qualified people. Such trade shows and exhibitions shall include, but is not limited to the following shows: _____.

G. Not undertake any obligations or promote/advertise the performance of the Product in excess of the limits specified by the PRODUCER.

H. Be expressly permitted to make public announcements in the press of its appointment as the exclusive Distributor of the PRODUCER in the appropriate Territories.

I. Pay for and send the appropriate personnel of the DISTRIBUTOR to the PRODUCER's manufacturing plant for necessary technical update or general orientation should the PRODUCER find it necessary.

J. Not sell outside of the authorized Territories and if the Product is destined for outside the authorized Territories, the DISTRIBUTOR shall take all necessary and appropriate steps to stop such sales.

SECTION III. TERM

This Agreement shall be for a term of three years from the date first written above and shall continue from year to year thereafter until either of the parties shall give _____ months written notice to the other prior that this Agreement shall terminate. Should the DISTRIBUTOR not purchase the minimum quantities set forth below, the PRODUCER may, at anytime, terminate this Agreement upon _____ days written notice.

SECTION IV. MINIMUM QUANTITIES

Throughout the term of this Agreement, the PRODUCER shall sell and the DISTRIBUTOR shall purchase from the PRODUCER (and from no other source) such minimum quantities of the Product at the minimum prices hereafter set out:

A. In the first year of this Agreement, DISTRIBUTOR shall pruchase at least US$_____ of the Product from the PRODUCER;

B. In the first year of this Agreement, the DISTRIBUTOR shall purchase from the PRODUCER at least _____ pieces of the Product kits;

C. In the second year of this Agreement and every year thereafter, the PRODUCER shall have the option of increasing the above minimum requirements for price and quantities; however, in no event shall any increase by over US$_____ per year, or _____ pieces per year.

SECTION V. PAYMENT AND TERMS

A. Payment shall be made by the DISTRIBUTOR to the PRODUCER (unless otherwise directed by PRODUCER) by irrevocable Letter of Credit in US dollars.

B. The PRODUCER shall sell and the DISTRIBUTOR shall purchase the Products F.O.B. the manufacturing plant at the following prices for the first year:

After _____ months from the date of this Agreement, the PRODUCER shall have the option to raise or lower these prices by giving _____ days notice. However, in no event shall any price be raised by more than _____ percent (_____%) per year of the above prices.

C. Any duty, tax or other charge the PRODUCER may be required by any Federal, State, County, Municipal or other law, now in effect or hereafter enacted, to collect or pay with respect to the sale, delivery or use of the Product shall be added to the prices provided herein exclusive of Paragraph B above and be paid by the Distributor.

Distributor shall also maintain and pay for Product Liability Insurance of US_____ million dollars.

SECTION VI. LEGAL COMPLIANCE

A. The DISTRIBUTOR shall comply with all Local, State and Federal laws concerning the Product.

B. The DISTRIBUTOR shall promptly inform the PRODUCER of all aspects of any new or revised legislation, regulation or orders affecting the use, sale or promotion of the Product in the United States of America.

SECTION VII. TRADEMARKS, PATENTS, COPYRIGHT AND BRAND-NAMES

A. Any and all trademarks, patents, copyrights and brand-names now in effect, created, applied for or received in the future, of the Product shall always be and remain the property of the PRODUCER.

B. The DISTRIBUTOR shall not under any circumstances acquire any rights whatsoever in any trademark, patent, copyright, brand-name or other proprietary right of the PRODUCER.

SECTION VIII. NON-COMPETITION

A. The PRODUCER shall, at its discretion, repair or replace any Product at its own expense found by the DISTRIBUTOR to be defective, provided that:

(1) In the case of visible and apparent defects, immediate written notice is given by the DISTRIBUTOR to the PRODUCER of such defects and the defective Products are returned to the PRODUCER within _____ weeks of the date of their shipment by the PRODUCER;

(2) In the case of functioned or non-apparent defects, written notice is given by the DISTRIBUTOR to the PRODUCER of such defects and the defective Products are returned to the PRODUCER within _____ months of the date of their shipment by the PRODUCER;

B. The PRODUCER shall pay fifty percent (50%) of the round-trip cost for all validated warranty claims.

C. The above limited warranty is subject to:

(1) The Product not being used for any purpose other than the normal purpose that it was manufactured for;

(2) The observance by the user of all operating instructions and recommendations provided by the PRODUCER; and

(3) The DISTRIBUTOR'S cooperation in and with any investigation by the PRODUCER or its representative with respect to said defects, including but not limited to any reports of the circumstances surrounding the defect.

SECTION IX. CONFIDENTIALITY

A. The DISTRIBUTOR shall not, either directly or indirectly, in whole or in part, except as required in the marketing of the Product or by written consent of an authorized representative of the PRODUCER, use or disclose to any person, firm, corporation or other entity, any information of a proprietary nature ("trade secrets") owned by the

PRODUCER or any of its affiliated companies, including, but not limited to, records, customer lists, data, formulae, documents, drawings, specifications, inventions, processes, methods and intangible rights.

B. Any information regarding the Product which, during the term of this Agreement is divulged by either party to the other is confidential and shall be protected from disclosure.

C. The prohibited use or disclosure, as used herein, shall be for the term of the Agreement and at any time within five (5) years after the termination of this Agreement.

SECTION X. ASSIGNMENT

The obligations and duties of the DISTRIBUTOR hereunder are personal and shall not be subcontracted or assigned to any third party without the prior written consent of the PRODUCER.

SECTION XI. TERMINATION AND GOODWILL

A. In the event that the DISTRIBUTOR shall default in the performance of any of its obligations hereunder, or shall fail to comply with any provision of this Agreement on its part to be performed, and if such default or failure shall continue for _____ days after written notice hereof from the PRODUCER, the PRODUCER may terminate this Agreement and the rights granted to the DISTRIBUTOR hereunder upon written notice to the DISTRIBUTOR, and neither waivers by the PRODUCER nor limitations of time may be asserted as a defense by the DISTRIBUTOR for any such failure or default. Such right of termination shall be in addition to any other rights and remedies of the PRODUCER at law or in equity.

B. Upon expiration, termination or cancellation of this Agreement pursuant to the provisions of Section III, Section XI, or for any other reason, with or without cause, the PRODUCER will not be liable for, and the DISTRIBUTOR will not be entitled to, any compensation of any kind for goodwill or any other tangible or intangible elements of damages or costs, nor shall the PRODUCER be liable to the DISTRIBUTOR for any special or consequential damages of any kind or nature whatsoever.

C. Upon the expiration of the term of this Agreement or any renewal thereof, the Products in the DISTRIBUTOR'S inventory may be sold, with the PRODUCER'S trademarks or brandnames thereon, only for one year after such expiration, subject to all the terms covenants and conditions of this Agreement (other than the right of renewal), as though this Agreement had not expired. Any of the Products in the DISTRIBUTOR'S inventory upon the termination or cancellation of this Agreement for any reason other than the natural expiration of its term, as set forth in Section III hereof, shall remain the property of the DISTRIBUTOR and may be sold only upon the removal of the PRODUCER'S owned trademarks and brandnames from the Products.

SECTION XII. RELATIONSHIP OF PARTIES

Nothing in this Agreement shall constitute or be deemed to constitute a partnership between the parties hereto. It is understood and agreed that the DISTRIBUTOR is an independent contractor and is not, nor ever will be, an agent or an employee of the PRODUCER. The DISTRIB-UTOR shall not have the right, power or authority, express or implied, to bind, assume or create any obligation or liability on behalf of the PRODUCER.

SECTION XIII. CAPTIONS

The captions in this Agreement are inserted solely for ease of reference and are not deemed to form a part of, or in any way to modify, the text or meaning hereof.

SECTION XIV. NOTICE

Any notice required to be given shall be deemed to be validly served if sent by prepaid registered or certified airmail to the address(es) stated below or to such other address as may be designated by either party in writing. Said notice shall be effective when posted by either party to said address(es), postage prepaid.

A. PRODUCER: (address).

B. DISTRIBUTOR: (address).

SECTION XV. DIVISIBILITY

The provisions of this Agreement contain a number of separate and divisible covenants. Each such covenant shall be construed as a sepa-rate covenant and shall be separately enforceable. If a court of com-petent jurisdiction shall determine that any part of any paragraph or any part of any separate covenant herein contained, is so restrictive as to be deemed void, the remaining part or parts, or the other such separate covenants, shall be considered valid and enforceable, notwithstanding the voidance of such covenant or part of a separate covenant. If certain covenants of this Agreement hereof are so broad as to be unenforceable, it is the desire of the parties hereto that such provisions be read as narrowly as necessary in order to make such provisions enforceable.

SECTION XVI. GOVERNING LAW

This Agreement shall be deemed to have been made in, and the relationship between the parties hereto shall be governed by, the laws of the State of New York, United States of America.

SECTION XVII. PRIOR AGREEMENTS

This Agreement contains a complete statement of arrangements among and between the parties hereto with respect ot its subject matter, supersedes all existing agreements among them concerning the subject matter hereof and cannot be changed or terminated except in writing signed by all parties to this Agreement.

IN WITNESS WHEREOF, the parties hereto have executed this Agreement in duplicate by their duly authorized representatives and affixed their corporate seals (if any) the day and year first above written.

SEAL   PRODUCER:

                              By: _____
                              Title:

SEAL   DISTRIBUTOR:

                              By: _____
                              Title:

Index

273